A Plan of the English Commerce

Daniel Defoe

VERNON PRESS

First published in 1728 by C. Rivington.
This edition Copyright © 2013 by Vernon Art and Science Inc.
1000 N West Street, Suite 1200, Wilmington, Delaware 19801, United States

www.vernonpress.com
Vernon Press is an imprint of Vernon Art & Science Inc.

ISBN 978-1-62273-001-8

Printed in Spain.

Contents

Note about the new edition

The present volume has been typeset with modern techniques and for that reason the pagination differs from the original edition. To ease navigation, this New Edition contains a newly compiled *Index* of important topics. It has been painstakingly proofread to ensure that it is free from errors and that the content is faithful to the original, including unusually long chapter headings. In the interest of visual clarity and the minimization of redundancy, the New Edition drops the largely arbitrary italicization of words and applies a modern formatting style to the rudimentary tables found in the original.

Although the text was written in the early 18th century - with all that the fact implies for the vocabulary, spelling, grammar, syntax and idiosyncratic capitalization - the prose is generally accessible to modern readers. For some of the more challenging passages, the following guide to Early Modern English may be helpful:

Barber, Charles. (1997) *Early Modern English*, Second Edition, Edinburgh University Press.

The Publisher

Preface

In a Nation rais'd as we are by Trade, fam'd for carrying on the most extended Commerce in the World, and particularly prosperous in the greatest Undertakings, whether for Improvement at Home or Adventure Abroad, nothing is more wonderful, than to see how ignorant the Generality of our People are about it; how weakly they talk of it, and how little has been made publick for their better Information.

Every Man knows his own affairs, moves in his own Circle, pursues the Mechanism of his own particular Business; but take him out of his Road, he knows nothing of the Reason, or the End of what he is about: The Clothier sorts his Wool, dyes and mixes the Colours; the Comb, the Card, the Wheel, the Loom, are all set on Work by his Direction, and he is call'd a Master of his Art, and he is so; but ask him where his Cloths are sold, by whom bought, to what Part of the World they are shipt, and who are the last Consumers of them, he knows nothing of the Matter; he sends them up to London to the Factor that sells them, whether at Blackwell-Hall, or in his private Warehouse, and when sold, he draws Bills for the Money; there his Circle meets; the Money buys more Wool to be sorted, and comb'd, and spun; and so on, he ends just where he begins, and he begins just where he ended. To talk to him of Trade, Ships, Exportation, Markets Abroad, and Returns in Specie, or in Merchants Goods, tis as much out of his Way, as the Race and the Paddock is to a Carryer's Pack-horse.

The Merchant on the other Hand moves in another Sphere; and he being a Man of Correspondence, besides his own Adventure, receives Commissions from Abroad to buy such and such Goods, and good Remittances by Bills to pay for them, then he ships them according to Order, sends his Invoyces and Bills of Loading by the Post; and there's his Circle finish'd. As to the Wool which is the Principal of the Manufacture; as to the many Hands it goes thro'; how many Thousand Families are employed by it; how the Poor are subsisted, the Provisions consum'd, the landed Interest rais'd, the Nobility and Gentry enrich'd, and the whole Nation supported by the very Goods he buys; he neither knows or concerns himself about it.

The Captains, Masters, Owners, and Navigators of Ships, they move in another Orb, but still act in the same Round of Business; the Ship is built, and fitted out for a Voyage; Thousands of Tradesmen and Workmen subsist upon the petty Demands of the Captain or other Persons who direct the Voyage; the Timber, the Plank, the Iron-Work, the Masts, the Rigging, the Tar and Hemp, the Flax and Oyl, all pass thro' different and numberless Hands, till they center in the Builder s Yard; there the Frame of a Vessel is set on the Stocks. What Hands are then employ'd to creat the beautiful useful Form of a Ship! and what Art to perfect and launch her into the Water!

The Carpenters, Caulkers, Mastmakers, Joyners, Carvers, Painters, Smiths, &c. finish the Hull; the Tradesmen are employ'd to furnish and fit her out; the Sail-Makers, the Rope-Makers, Anchor-Smiths, Block-Makers, Gun-Founders, Coopers, and (for a Thousand small Things too trifling to mention, tho' absolutely needful) the Ship Chandler, and at last the Brewer, Butcher, Baker, &c. for Provision to victual her, all help on the Voyage.

All these supported by that glorious Head of Commerce, called the Merchant, are employed in the Outset of the Ship, but know nothing how to manage the Ship in the Ocean, how to cause her to find her Way on the wild and pathless Surface of the Water; they fit her out, and deliver all to the Commander, &c. But as to the sailing Part, that belongs to another Class of People, called the Sailers or Navigators; and when the Tradesmen have put the Ship into their Hands, their Work is done, till the Ship returns, and then they begin all again: So the Circle is continued, for ever the same.

Again, the Navigator or Commander, he puts up his Ship on the Exchange for such a Voyage, Lisbon, or Cadiz, or Hamburg, or Leghorn; he takes in the Merchants Goods, carries them safe to the delivering Port; he reloads there, and brings back his Cargoe; he knows no more; even his Bills of Loading are sign d, under a needful Profession of his Ignorance, naming the Bulk of what he receives on Board (so many Hogsheads, or Butts, or Bales) but adds the Contents unknown, &c.

When he brings home the Ship, he makes his Report at the Custom-house, and unlivers his Cargo, as they call it; then he receives his Freight, pays his Men, and lays the Ship up, and there's his Circle finish'd; his Sphere of Action, however important, reaches no farther; as to Trade or Commerce, whether general or particular, he knows no more of it than just lies before him.

I might run thro' almost all the Branches of Business, and all the Classes of the Men of Business, and give Examples of the like; but 'tis enough, the Conclusion is short: Hence then a general or universal Plan of Commerce is certainly much wanted in the World.

When we speak of some Men, who are the most acquainted in the World of Business, we say they are Men of a general Knowledge; and such a Man is an universal Merchant; I have indeed heard such Language talked among the trading Part of Mankind, but I cannot say that I ever saw the Man.

The Commerce of the World, especially as it is now carried on, is an unbounded Ocean of Business; Trackless and unknown, like the Seas it is managed upon; the Merchant is no more to be follow'd in his Adventures, than a Maze or Labyrinth is to be trac'd out without a Clue.

The Author of this Work is not quite so arrogant, after a Complaint of this Nature, as to tell you he shall present you with this universal Plan, for the whole Trade of the World: It is enough, if he is able to offer a Plan for the Trade of our own Country, in which it is but too true, there are many that talk of the general Commerce to one that understands it.

Nor even in this Plan of our Commerce, does he direct what the Trade of Europe, in general is with us; but what and how great our particular Commerce is; how it is arriv'd to its present Magnitude; how to be maintained and supported in its full Extent; (and which is, or ought to be, the true End of all such Attempts:) How it may yet be improv'd and enlarg'd.

We have loud Complaints among us of the Decay of our Trade, the declining of our Manufactures, and especially of our woollen Manufacture; the contrary of which is, I think, evidently prov'd in this Tract, and the Reasons given for it, will not be easily refuted. It is not any little Negative put upon our Manufactures, as to their Consumption in this or that petty Province or Country in Germany, or else where: Our Manufacture, like a flowing Tide, if 'tis bank't out in one Place, it spreads by other Channels at the same Time into so many different Parts of the World, and finds every Day so many new Outlets, that the Obstruction is not felt; but like the Land to the Sea, what it loses in one Place, it gains in another.

It is plain, the Manufacture cannot be declin'd, if the Quantity of Wool is wrought up, and the Goods are consum'd; on the other Hand 'tis evident, the Consumption of our Manufactures, both abroad and at home, is exceedingly encreas'd; the first by the Encrease of our Correspondencies, and the last by the Encrease of our People; and that to such a Degree, as infinitely out-weighs all that can be pretended of the Prohibitions of them in Germany, or the Imitations of them in France; nor are those things able to wound us so deep as our phlegmatick Complainers would insinuate.

But that a full Answer may be given to all they can say of what Loss we yet suffer, and to all they can suggest of what we may suffer hereafter; this Work is calculated, to shew how we may counteract it all at once: Namely, by improving and encreasing our Trade in other Places where those Prohibitions and Imitations cannot reach, and where, if half Europe should drop our Manufacture, which yet 'tis apparent can never happen, we shall raise an equivalent Vent for our Goods, and make Markets of our own; in which the whole World could not supplant us, unless they could subdue us.

This is the Substance of this Tract; 'tis the original Thought which gave Birth to the whole Work; if our Trade is he Envy of the World, and they are conspiring to break in upon it, either to anticipate it, or block it out, we are the more engaged to look out for its Support; and we have Room enough: The World is wide: There are new Countries, and new Nations, who may be so planted, so improv'd, and the People so manag'd, as to create a new Commerce; and Millions of People shall call for our Manufacture, who never call'd for it before.

Nothing is to me more evident, than that the civilizing the Nations where we and other Europeans are already settled; bringing the naked Savages to Clothe, and instructing barbarous Nations how to live, has had a visible Effect already, in this very Article. Those Nations call upon us every Year for more Goods, than they did the Tear before, as well woollen Manufactures, as others. The Portuguese Colonies in the Brazils, and on the East Coasts of Africa, are an unanswerable Proof of this. The European Manufactures now sent to those Colonies, are above five Times as many as were sent to the same Places, about 30 to 40 Years ago; and yet the European Inhabitants in those Colonies are not encreased in Proportion. We might give Instances of the like in other Places abroad, and that not a few.

New planting Colonies then, and farther improving those already settled, will effectually encrease this Improvement; for like Causes, will have like Effects; Clothing new Nations cannot fail of encreasing the Demand of Goods, because it encreases the Consumption, and that encreased Demand is the Prosperity of our Trade.

Here then is an undiscover'd Ocean of Commerce laid open to us, and some Specimens are offer d, which if entred upon, with the Authority, Power, and Vigor of the Publick, would open such new Channels of Trade among us, as it would be very hard for our Manufacturers to over flock the Market, and as no petty Prohibitions in Europe could flop the Current of.

It is surprizing that in a Nation where such Encouragements are given for planting and improving, where Colonies have been settled, and Plantations made with such Success; where we may truly be said to have filled the World with the Wonders of our growing Possessions, and where we have added not Provinces only, but Kingdoms to the British Dominion, and have launched out even to an Ocean of Commerce. That now, I say, We should, as it were, put a full Stop at once to all our great Designs; check the Humour of Encreasing, and from a kind of a mysterious unaccountable Stupidity turn indolent on a suddain. Not as if we found no more Room to launch out for the Contrary to that is apparent; but as if we had enough, and sought no more Worlds in Trade to conquer.

In all other Cases, and among all other Nations Success encourages Men to go on; encreasing, they endeavour to encrease, Crescit amor nummi, &c. - So in Trade, the growing and enlarging the Bounds of a Plantation, the swelling and thriving of Commerce, and the Advantages to the Merchant and Planter in all those Things, certainly encreases the Desire of planting, enlarges the Commerce and fires the Merchant with the Desires of enlarging his Adventures, searching out new Colonies, forming new Adventures, and pushing at new Discoveries for the Encrease of his Trading Advantages.

It is so in other Nations, and it seems wonderful it should not be so here; the Spaniards tho' an indolent Nation, whose Colonies were really so rich, so great, and so far extended, as were enough even to glut their utmost Avarice; yet gave not over, till, as it were, they sat still, because they had no more Worlds to look for; or till at least, there were no more Gold or Silver Mines to discover.

The Portuguese, tho' an effeminate, haughty, and as it were, a decay' d Nation in Trade; yet how do they go on Daily encreasing their Colonies in the Brazils, in Africa, as well on the East Side, as the West? And how do they encrease their Commerce in all those Countries, by reducing the numerous Nations in Melinda, in Zanguebar, in Congo, in Angola, in the Brazils, as well North as South, and every where else, to the Christian Oeconomy, and to the Government of Commerce! by which they subdue whole Nations of Savages to a regular Life, and by that Means bring them to be subservien to Trade as well as to Government.

But how little have we done of this kind? How little have we gain d upon the Natives of America in all our Colonies? How few of them are brought to live among us, how few to be subject to us! How little Progress of that kind can we boast of? All our Colonies seem to be carried on upon the meer Strength of our own People. Nor can we say we have any one considerable Nation reduced to entire Obedience and brought to live under the Regularity and Direction of a Civil Government, in all our Plantations; a few (very few) in New England only excepted.

As for new Colonies and Conquers, how do we seem entirely to give over, even the Thoughts of them, tho' the Scene is so large, tho' the Variety is so great, and the Advantages so many? On the Contrary, we seem to forget the glorious Improvements of our Ancestors, such as the great Drake, Cavendish, Smith, Greenfield, Somers, and above all, the yet greater Sir Walter Raleigh, upon the Foot of whose Genius almost all the English Discoveries were made, and all the Colonies and Plantations, which now form what they call the English Empire in America were settled and established. These I say we seem to sit down with, as if we had done our utmost, were fully satisfied with what we have, that the enterprising Genius was buried with the old Discoverers, and there was neither Room in the World or Inclination in our People to look any farther.

Whereas on the Contrary, the World presents us with large Scenes of Trade, new Platforms for Business, enough to prompt our Ambition, and even to glut our Avarice; yet we seem to have no Heart for the Adventure.

Nor is there any want of People among us; on the contrary, here are Thousands of Families who want Business, want Employment , want Encouragement, and many that want no Stocks to carry with them, and are ready to go abroad, were the adventuring Spirit reviv'd, and some Men fired with Warmth for the Undertaking, and but vigorous enough to make the Beginning.

This is the Way to raise new Worlds of Commerce, to enlarge and extend new Funds of Trade, to open Doors for an Encrease of Shipping and Manufacture; the Places are so many and the Advantages so great for the making such Attempts; that I say nothing is more wonderful of its kind, than to see how backward we are to push on our own Advantages, and to plant in the most agreeable Climates in the World, in a manner so advantageous as never to be supplanted, and such as should make the English Possessions abroad five Times as Great, as Opulent and as Profitable to Old England, as they have been yet.

The Description of these Places, so proper for Planting, so suited to Commerce, and so qualified to enrich and aggrandize the British Nation, is a Work not only too large for this Trad, but seems not suited to our present Tast; it must lye till the Trading Genius revives and the adventuring Temper is restored among us: Then it will appear, there will neither want Encouragement to such Undertakings or Undertakers to embrace the Encouragements which offer.

As these are Things of the utmost Importance to our Trade in general, and in that to the Prosperity of all his Majesty's Dominions in particular, the Author humbly hopes it shall not be thought assuming, that as we say in our Title, they are humbly referr'd to the Consideration of the King and Parliament; they are

Things worthy of a King, and worthy of a powerful Legislature to consider of; no Power less than that of King, Lords and Commons, can put these Wheels of Improvement into due Motion: And I conclude with an inexpressible Satisfaction, in saying, that as we know his Majesty has the Prosperity of all his Kingdoms at Heart; and will be always ready to listen to reasonable and practicable Proposals for that Purpose; and that the Parliament has always shewn their Readiness to concur in the same just Endeavour; and which is yet more, that the Proposals here offered, and others yet behind, are apparently practicable and rational; it cannot be doubted, but that the Time will come, and is near at Hand, when the Improvement of the British Commerce shall no more appear in Project and Theory, but shew it self in a due and daily Progression, till it compleats the Glory and Prosperity of the whole Nation.

Part I

Chapter 1

Of trade in general

TRADE, like Religion, is what every Body talks of, but few understand: The very Term is dubious, and in its ordinary Acceptation, not sufficiently explain'd. WHEN 'tis particular to a Place, 'tis Trade; when general, 'tis Commerce; when we speak of it as the Effect of Nature, 'tis Product or Produce; when as the Effect of Labour, 'tis Manufacture: In its Management 'tis the same, for when we speak of it in the gross, 'tis wholesale; when of the particulars, 'tis retale; when we speak of Nations, 'tis call'd Corresponding; when of foreign Import only, 'tis called Merchandizing; 'Tis the same also in the Manner, when we exchange Goods, 'tis call'd Barter; when we exchange Coin, 'tis call'd Banking, Negoce and Negotiating; Hence, our Money-Goldsmiths were formerly called Bankers, and our great national Treasury of Commerce is at this Day called the Bank.

THE general heads of Home-Trade are best contain'd in the two plain and homely Terms Labouring, and Dealing. ist. The labouring Part, this consists of Arts, Handicrafts, and all Kinds of Manufactures; and those who are employ'd in these Works, are properly called Mechanicks; they are employ'd, generally speaking, about the first Principles of Trade, (viz.) the Product of the Land or of the Sea, or of the Animals living on both: In a Word, the ordinary Produce of the vegetative and sensative Life; such as Metals, Minerals and Plants, the immediate Produce of Vegetation, or such as Flesh, Skins, Hair, Wool, Silk, &c. grown with, and produc'd by the Animals, as the Effect of sensitive Life.

2. The Dealing Part; this consists of handing about all the several Productions of Art and Labour, when finish'd by the Hand of the industrious Mechanick, and made useful to Mankind; conveying them from Place to Place, and from one Country to another, as the Necessity and the Convenience of the People call for them; and that upon such Terms and Conditions of Delivery, as they can best agree about among themselves, and this is Trade; whether it be carry'd on by the general Medium of all Exchangings call'd Coin, or by something substituted as Coin, and in the room of it, which we call Money.

(N. B. ANY Thing that is by the Authority of a Nation establish'd as the Medium of their Exchanges, is properly the MONEY of the Nation, tho' seldom any Thing but Gold, Silver, or other Metals is call'd COIN.)

THUS Dealing and Manufacturing comprehends all Trade; that is to say, in its meer natural and original Situation; and all the subsequent Divisions and Distinctions of Terms, by which we are taught to express the particular Parts of Trade, are but modern Names introduc'd by Custom, and legitimated by length of Time, and general Usage of the Men of Art, to distinguish Things, as accident and the Variety of the several Productions in Mechanism required.

So the Word GOODS is a general Term, comprehending all the several Kinds and Sorts, whether of Manufactures or Product, that the greatest Dealer in the World can be supposed to Trade in; it is a usual Thing to express it so to this Day, in the Language of Trade; for Example, in retailing, we say, such a Shop is well furnish'd with all Sorts of GOODS: In wholesale Trade, such a Dealer has his Warehouse well fill'd with GOODS: In Housekeeping, all the Furniture of a House are called the GOODS, or the Houshold-goods: In Merchandizing, such a Ship was Loaden with BALE GOODS; and in the East India Ships, after the bulky Goods, (so they call the Pepper, Salt-petre, Red-earth, Tea, and such like) are taken out, it is said the rest of the Loading was made up with PIECE GOODS.

As the Terms in Trade are various, so the People concern'd in Trade bear differing Titles, and are ordinarily known by different Denominations.

THOSE concern'd in the meaner and first Employments , are called in common, Working Men or Labourers, and the labouring Poor; such as the meer Husbandmen, Miners, Diggers, Fishers, and in short, all the Drudges and Labourers in the several Productions of Nature or of Art: Next to them, are those who, tho' labouring perhaps equally with the other, have yet some Art mingled with their Industry, and are to be particularly instructed and taught how to perform their Part, and those are called Workmen or Handicrafts.

SUPERIOR to these, are the Guides or Masters, in such Works or Employments, and these are call'd Artists, Mechanicks or Craftsmen; and in general, all are understood in this one Word Mechanicks; such are Clothiers, Weavers, &c. Handicrafts in Hardware, Brass, Iron, Steely Copper, &c .

SUPERIOR to these are the Dealers who only buy and sell, either by wholesale or retale as above: these are the Factor, the Pedlar, and the Merchant.

ALL these come under the general Denomination of Trading Men, and they are the principal Kinds or Professions which just now carry on the Trade of the World. HAVING thus, once for all, accounted for these several Distinctions, and for the trading People in their respective Denominations as above, we shall have no more Occasion to explain the Terms as we go along, or trouble the Reader with running out to enquire our Meaning, when we speak of the several Branches of Commerce in their proper and particular Distinctions or Terms of Art.

WE must also remove some Scandal out of the Way as we go on, and this is another Difficulty. This Scandal relates to the Dignity, Antiquity, and other Honours due to Trade, and claim'd in its Behalf; concerning which we meet with much weak headed Strife in the World; and which, as I take it, belongs properly to this Place, at least I shall discharge my self of it here, and by doing so, shall have no more Occasion to trouble you with it in the rest of our Debate, however, the impertinent Cavils of the Times may importune me upon that Head.

PRIDE, in Conjunction with abundance of Ignorance, is frequently in Arms against the peaceable trading World about Precedence, and in a Plea of Antiquity: They would divide the World into two Parts only, (viz.) the Gentry and the Commonalty; among the Gentry they rank the Nobility, the ancient Families of Gentlemen, (as they call them) Barons, &c, and those who were formerly called Barons; and with some Difficulty they admit the Men of Learning, and the Men of Arms, (viz.) the Soldiery and the Clergy, and all the Families, who by the Heraldry of their Houses claim to have been Gentlemen unmix'd with plebeian Blood for immemorial Ages.

THIS Family Jargon, for it is no more, they oppose to the trading Part of the whole World, whom they divest of all Dignity, as well as of Degree; and blend together under one general, or rather common Denomination of Mechanicks; tho' by the Accidents of Time, and Circumstances of Things, some of them are, and for many Ages have been true Members of the Gentry by collateral Branches; nay sometimes by the chief Lines of the best and most ancient Families in the Nation.

(N. B. OBSERVE, here I speak of our own Country chiefly, and of the Mistake, as it is particularly espoused in England, and nowhere else.)

FIRST, as to Antiquity; and even in this, I think the Tradesmen and the Gentry should never cap Pedigrees, since the most noble Descendants of Adam's Family, and in whom the Primogeniture remained, were really Mechanicks; for honest JUBAL and TUBAL were the first Fidle-makers and Tinkers in the World: The first invented and made musical Instruments, Fidles, &c. and the second was the first Hard-ware Manufacturer, that is in English, a Tinker, and no better; N. B. for long, (many long Ages) after them, the Sons and Grandsons of these Mechanicks were Kings and Princes, Dukes and Lords.

AFTER the second Peopling of the World, before there were any Distinctions of Nobility, or Mechanicks, they seem to have been all Labourers; as at the erecting that stupendous Work called Babel for Example; to be sure, the FREE-Masons and their Brother Bricklayers, who were the Master-Builders there, were some of the top of their Gentry at that Time.

As the World encreased, SIDON, Noah's Grandson, built a City, which remains in the same Place, and bears the same Name to this Day.

HERE Navigation began, and as Noah was the first Shipwright, or according to us, the first Ship-Carpenter, (a true Mechanick) his Posterity built the first Boats, and afterwards Ships at this Place; with these they traded to and with the neighbouring Nations upon the Coast, as Nature, Reason and Necessity guided them. In the Infancy of their navigating Skill, they Row'd along in these Boats, (for at first they had no Sails) from Place to Place Northward, to the Gulph of Alexandria now Scandaroon, and so on to the Coast of Cilicia where they built: Tarshish, the first grand Arsenal or Place for Ship-building in the World; whence great Ships were afterwards called Ships of Tarshish for many Ages, no Ships of Burthen being built any where else.

ALSO South they coasted to Joppa, now Jaffa, thence to Damiata and Egypt, where their great Grandfather CHAM reigned Emperor of all Africa for many Ages. See Sir Walter Rawleigh's History of the World.

ENCREASING thus in People, and in Wealth (by Trade) and growing too great for the Compass of one City, or the Commerce of one Port, they spread themselves by way of Colony, and settled first at Tyre, a convenient Situation also for Shiping and for Merchandizing. HERE they encreased again to such a Prodigy of Business, as I have good Reason to believe, was never equall'd. in the World, except just now, (viz.) by the great Trade carry'd on at this Time in England; of which in its Place.

AND here to prove to you beyond the Power of Cavil, that the Antients thought it not below their Quality to be Tradesmen; the Prophet Ezekiel says, Thy wise Men were the Pilots, and thy Merchants are Princes; or as read it, Thy Princes are Merchants, as it is expressly another Place, Ezekiel xxvii. 21. The Princes of were thy Merchants.

THUS much is sufficient for the Antiquity of and Navigation; as to the Antiquity of trading Families I say with a late low born Poet, but a Man of Wit,

Let Cæsar or Nassau go higher .

And why then are we to despise Commerce as a Mechanism, and the Trading World as mean, when the Wealth of the World is deem'd to rise from Trade? as the same Text said of Tyre, v.33. of the same Chapter, Thou didst enrich the Kings of the Earth with thy Merchandise.

BUT to bring this down to our selves; Are we a rich, a populous, a powerful Nation, and in some Respects the greatest in all those particulars in the World, and do we not boast of being so? 'Tis evident it was all deriv'd from Trade. Our Merchants are Princes, greater and richer, and more powerful than some sovereign Princes; and in a Word, as is said of Tyre, we have made the Kings of the Earth rich with our Merchandise, that is, with our Trade.

IF Usefulness gives an Addition to the Character, either of Men or Things, as without doubt it does; Trading-men will have the Preference in almost all the Disputes you can bring: There is not a Nation in the known World, but have tasted the Benefit, and owe their Prosperity to the useful Improvements of Commerce: Even the self-vain Gentry, that would decry Trade as a universal Mechanism, are they not every where depending upon it for their most necessary Supplies? If they do not all sell, they are all forc'd to buy, and so are a kind of Traders themselves, at least they recognize the Usefulness of Commerce, as what they are not able to live comfortably without.

NAY, in many Parts of Britain, they are really Traders, both Buyers and Sellers; for Example, where the Landlords are obliged to take their Rents in kind, as the Clergy do their Tithes; here they are (in a word) general Traders; they sell their Barley to the Malt-makers, their Wheat to the Millers and Bakers, their Oates to the Corn-factors, their Sheep and Bullocks are sold at the Markets to the Butchers, or at Fairs to the Graziers; they are Sheep-Shearers, and sell their Wool to the Stapler or Clothier; and when they kill a Bullock, or a Calf, or a Sheep, for their Family-Use, they are beholding to the Felmonger, and the Tanner, to buy the raw Hides and Skins; when they sell their Timber, they are oblig'd to turn Mechanicks , and sell the Bark to the Tanners, the Timber to the Ship-wright and the Carpenters, the Brushwood and Bavins to the Baker and the Brick-maker.

IN a Word, useful Trade supports the Gentleman; and without these Mechanicks he could not dispose the Produce of his Estate, or make any Rent of his Land; and rather than not dispose of it, such is his Necessity, that we see he will stoop to buy and sell for himself, and trade and deal like a meer Mechanick.

BUT this is not all, if they would look a little nearer, they would see themselves not by Practice only degenerated into Trading Men, but even their Fortunes, nay, their very Blood mingled with the Mechanicks, as they call them; the Necessity of their Circumstances frequently reconciles the best of the Nobility to these Mixtures; and then the same Necessity opens their Eyes to the Absurdity of the Distinctions which they had been so wedded to before.

IT is with the utmost Disgrace to their Understanding, that those People would distinguish themselves in the Manner they do, when they may certainly see every Day prosperous Circumstances advance those Mechanicks, as they will have them called, into the Arms, and into the Rank of the Gentry; and declining Fortunes reduce the best Families to a Level with the Mechanick.

THE rising Tradesman swells into the Gentry, and the declining Gentry sinks into Trade. A Merchant, or perhaps a Man of a meaner Employ thrives by his honest Industry, Frugality, and a long series of diligent Application to Business, and being grown immensely rich, he marries his Daughters to Gentlemen of the first Quality, perhaps a Coronet; then he leaves the Bulk of his Estate to his Heir, and he gets into the Rank of the Peerage; does the next Age make any Scruple of their Blood, being thus mix'd with the antient Race? Do we not just now see two Dukes descended by the Female Side, from the late Sir Josiah Child, and the immediate Heir a Peer of Ireland? Many Examples of the like Kind might be given.

ON the other Hand, the declining Gentry, in the Ebb of their Fortunes, frequently push their Sons into Trade, and they again, by their Application, often restore the Fortunes of their Families: Thus Tradesmen become Gentlemen, by Gentlemen becoming Tradesmen. I could give Examples of this too, but they are too recent for our naming.

THEY that learn thus to despise Trading People as such, must either be intirely ignorant of the World, or perfectly uncapable of the just Impressions of these Things; they must forget sure, that the Gentry are always willing to submit to the raising their Families, by what they call City Fortunes; and how useful Trade has always been, and still is in the World on that Account; while others who call themselves Gentlemen, by Way of Distinction, became unworthy, by the Scandal of their Morals, to match with the meanest Citizen, if she be a Woman of Modesty and Virtue.

BUT to go on in generals, which is proper to the Head I am talking of; Trade is the universal Fund of Wealth throughout the World; the Gold of Africa and Brazil, the Silver of Mexico and Peru had but for Trade remained undisturbed in the Mines, and in the Sands of the Rivers of Guinea and Chili: The Diamonds of Golconda, and of Borneo had been glittering in the Dirt, and remain'd unpolish'd to this Day, if Diligence had not found them out; if Navigation had not assisted the Discovery, and if Trade had not spread and dispers'd them over the whole Globe.

EVEN Solomon : had wanted Gold to adorn the Temple, unless he had been supply'd by Miracles; if he had not turn'd Merchant-Adventurer, and sent his

Fleets to fetch it from the East Indies, that is to say, from Achin, on the Island of Sumatra, which is supposed to be the Ophir which his Factors procur'd it at.

So effectually has Trade rais'd the Wealth of the World, that 'tis remarkable, and worth the most curious Observation, that throughout the known World, Nations, and Kingdoms, and Governments are rich or poor, as they have, or have not, a Share of the whole Commerce of the World, or more or less, some Concern in it.

THE Turks, who are Enemies to Trade, and who discourage Industry and Improvement, 'tis plain they dispeople the World, rather than improve and cultivate it: View their Condition; they are miserably poor! distressedly poor! they are idle, indolent and starving, their Governments have some Wealth, because they are tyrannical, and take what they please from the poor People, throughout a vast Extent of Dominion; so that if it be but a little in a Place, it amounts to a very great Sum in the whole, the People and Nations which are tributary to them, being so many; but those People and Nations are poor and wretched to the last Degree, and all for Want of Trade.

As to Trade, excepting what the Europeans and the Jews drive among them, it is so little, that it hardly deserves the Name of Commerce; they have neither Produce of the Land, or Labour of the People; neither Merchandise or Art, nothing is encouraged among them; Ignorance boasts indeed of the rich Return we bring from them, such as Drugs, Hair, Silk, &c. But we know it is not of Turky , or the Growth of Turky, but is either the Product of Armenia and Georgia, the Provinces of Guilan and Indostan, Part of Persia on the Shoar of the Caspian Sea, quite out of the Turk's Dominions, and even there they are the Product of the old Christians Labour, the original Inhabitants of those Provinces; the Mahometans, have little or no Hand in it; they abhor Business and Labour, and despise Industry, and they starve accordingly; or those Goods are the Produce of the Islands in the Levant and the Archipelague, where the Cotton-yarn, the Grogram or Goats-Hair Yarn, the white or Beladine Silks, &c. are the Manufacture of the poor Greeks Inhabitants of those Islands, and who by their Labour in Cultivation, cause the Earth to produce the Silk and the Wool, and by their Labours in Manufacturing, spin and make it up into Yarn, and into Form, as we have it from them. Now, see the Consequence; as the Mahometans I say have little Trade, so they have little Wealth, the Produce of their Lands yields little, and that little sells for such a little Value, that one would pity so vast a Body of People labouring, as it were, for nothing: All the fruitful rich Countries of Natolia and the Lesser Asia, from the Aegean to the Euxine Sea, once the most rich, populous, and fertile Provinces of the World, with all the Morea, the Achaia, (the Peloponnesus of the Antients) and the fruitful Plains of Thessaly, Macedonia, and Thrace, from the Ionian Sea, to the Banks of the Danube; what do they now produce? The great City of Constantinople is supplied with Corn indeed, but how? (N. B. This is the Reason of mentioning it) when produc'd, sold to the Merchant, shipt on Board the Vessels which carry it by Sea, the Freight paid, and all Charges of loading and unloading; yet their Barley has been bought in the Market at Constantinople for 3d. per Bushel.

IF this were some Ages ago, if it were not known to be so very frequently, and if there were not some Merchants now living in London, who are Persons of undoubted Credit, who assure me they have bought it so: I say if it were only, that it had been so some Ages ago, it had been nothing extraordinary, for all know it has been thus in England; but this has been so at Constantinople within these Ten or Twelve Years, and I doubt not it might be prov'd is often so still in the same Place, when plentiful Years of Corn happen; what the poor Husband-man must have for his plowing, sowing, harvesting, threshing, and carrying it out, is hard to imagine; or what the Landlord has for the Land: But I suppose the Grand-Seignior is general Landlord, and has his Tax from the whole Country, instead of Rent.

Now, whence is all this Poverty of a Country? 'tis evident 'tis Want of Trade, and nothing else: And we may go back for an Example of it to our own Country, when the Product of the Land, and the Labour of the People were as low here, when good Wheat was worth about 4 d. per Bushel, a fat Sheep about 3 s. 4 d. and a fat Ox about 18 to 24s. and when was this? But when we had no Trade, and because we had no Trade; neither is the present Difference owing to any Thing else, but to the Increase of Commerce, as well here as in other Parts of the World; and 'tis evident the Rate of Provisions, and the Value of Lands in all Parts of the World are high or low, great or small, as the People have or have not Trade to support it.

TRADE encourages Manufacture, prompts Invention, employs People, increases Labour, and pays Wages: As the People are employ'd, they are paid, and by that Pay are fed, cloathed, kept in Heart, and kept together; that is, kept at Home, kept from wandering into Foreign Countries to seek Business, for where the Employment is, the People will be.

THIS keeping the People together, is indeed the Sum of the whole Matter, for as they are kept together, they multiply together; and the Numbers, which by the Way is the Wealth and Strength of the Nation, increase. As the Numbers of People increase, the Consumption of Provisions increases; as the Consumption increases, the Rate or Value will rise at Market; and as the Rate of Provisions rises, the Rents of Land rise: So the Gentlemen are with the first to feel the Benefit of Trade, by the Addition to their Estates.

AND here it would not have been improper to have made a Transition to our English History, and to have enquir'd how punctually the Course of Things have obey'd the Laws of Nature : in this very particular; how as Trade has increased; so by equal Advances, Provisions have been consum'd, Lands cultivated, Rents raised, and the Estates of the Gentry and Nobility been improv'd: I mean as to Periods of Time, as well as to the Proportion of Value; which Enquiry would have been an unanswerable Proof of the Fact; but I am confin'd here to Generals, and must only lay it down as a Proposition.

As the Consumption of Provisions increase, more Lands are cultivated; waste Grounds are inclosed, Woods are grubb'd up, Forrests and common Lands are till'd, and improv'd; by this more Farmers are brought together, more Farm-houses and Cottages are built, and more Trades are called upon to supply the necessary Demands of Husbandry: In a Word, as Land is employ'd, the People increase of Course, and thus Trade sets all the Wheels of Improvement in Motion; for from the Original of Business to this Day it appears, that the Prosperity of a Nation rises and falls, just as Trade is supported or decay'd.

As Trade prospers, Manufactures increase; as the Demand is greater or smaller, so also is the Quantity made; and so the Wages: of the Poor, the Rate of Provisions, and the Rents and Value of the Lands rise or fall, as I said before.

AND here the very Power and Strength of the Nation is concern'd also, for as the Value of the Lands rises or falls, the Taxes rise and fall in Proportion; all our Taxes upon Land are a Kind of Pound Rate; and bring in more or less, as the stated Rents of the Land are more or less in Value; and let any one calculate, by the Rate of Lands in England, as they went in the Times of Edward IV. or even in King Henry VII. Time, when Trade began, as it were, just to live in England; and tell us how much they think a Land Tax would then have brought in: For example,

IF a Tax of Four Shillings in the Pound now brings in above Two Millions, I suppose it would have been thought very well then, if it had brought in Three hundred thousand Pound, all the rest is an Increase occasion'd by Trade, and by nothing else; Trade has increas'd the People, and People have increas'd Trade; for Multitudes of People, if they can be put in a Condition to maintain themselves, must increase Trade; they must have Food, that employs Land; they must have Clothes, that employs the Manufacture; they must have Houses, that employs Handicrafts; they must have Houshold Stuff, that employs a long Variety of Trades; so that in a Word Trade employs People, and People employ Trade.

I once saw a Calculation of Trade for the planting a new Town in the South Parts of England, where, for the Encouragement of People to come and settle, the Lords of the Manors, (for the Place lay in three Manors), agreed to give a certain Quantity of Lands to Fifty Farmers, who would undertake to bring each two hundred Pound Stock with them, and settle there.

To every such Farmer, they allotted two hundred Acres of good Land, Rent-free for Twenty Years; and if the Farmer brought three hundred Pound Stock, he had three hundred Acres; besides the Land, the said Lords agreed to find Timber, and all other Materials for the Building, to every Farmer a House, and out of their own Pockets to build to each House a Barn and Stables; and thus, with other Encouragements, Fifty Families of substantial Farmers were brought to live in a Kind of Circle within themselves, with every one a good Farm to manage, and sufficient Quantity of Land Rent-free; the Land was good in it self, tho' never cultivated before, so that being clear'd and inclos'd, and gradually plow'd or improv'd, it soon return'd them a profitable Increase.

THE Land was so laid out in a large Circle, that all the Farm-houses being built at the Extremities of the respective Farms, toward the Center, left a handsome large Square Piece of Land which the Lords reserv'd for the building a Town; and as the Farm-houses were so regularly plac'd, as to front all inwards, they left Ten Spaces like Streets before their Doors, of which Five of the Farm-houses, with their Out-Houses, made one Side, and the other remained to build into a Street as Occasion should present. AT the same Time they publish'd, That whoever would come and build on that vacant Ground, should have a certain proportion'd Measure of Land allow'd him, according to the Size of the House he would build, should have Timber given him gratis, out of the Woods belonging to the Estate, sufficient for his Building; and to every House, Land also added for a Garden and Orchard, no Rent to be paid for ten Years, and then a moderate Rent for twenty Years more; and then a certain Rent (not at last immoderate) for the Time to come.

WHEN the Farmers were settled, for there is the Substance and Reason of the Thing, and in this it is exactly to my Purpose; immediately comes a Butcher, and he runs up a little Shed for the present, till he could build a House, and sets up a Shop, to kill and sell Meat for the Farmers.

(N. B. As these Farmers had every one two Hundred Pounds Stock to begin, so they are supposed to be all Men of Families, that had Wives and Children, and every one had at least one or two, and some three Servants.)

NOR could one Butcher be sufficient to furnish Meat to fifty Families, but they were oblig'd to send to neighbouring Towns for Provision, till the first Butcher having Encouragement, two or three more came afterwards, and set up also.

AFTER the Example of the Butcher, in the next Place came a Baker, and he erects an Oven to supply them with Bread.

FIFTY Families of Farmers must necessarily find Work for a Smith or Farrier to Shoe their Horses, and at least two Wheelwrights to make and repair their Carts, Waggons, Plows, Harrows, &c. and these with the necessary Iron-work for so much Building, called in a couple of Black-smiths, whereof one being a Man of Substance, made himself a kind of Iron-monger, laying in a Stock of all Sorts of wrought Iron and Brass for Building and Furniture, which on such an Occasion they could not be without.

THIS Collection of Tradesmen naturally requir'd a Shoe-maker or two to set up, who soon found Trade enough to supply the growing Numbers of People with Shoes and Boots; and likewise a good honest Country Cobler or two could not fail of Employment to repair them; and (to add the other Trades working in Leather,) they could not be without a Collar-maker or two, for Harness, Pannels, Saddles, and all the necessary Things relating to a Team.

ADD to these a Turner, an Earthen-ware Seller, a Glover, a Rope-maker, three or four Barbers, (perhaps a Midwife) and several such Trades as the Nature of things required.

BUT to go back to the building Part, three Master Carpenters would be the least that could be employ'd in building Houses, and these would require at first five or six Pair of Sawyers at least, with Journeymen; that is to say, Workmen; two or three Bricklayers, with their Servants and Labourers, and perhaps hard by a Brick and Tile-maker.

To supply these, one of the Carpenters, a Man of Substance, builds himself a Windmil, and another builds a second, and they both find Work enough (as the Town encreased) to keep them constantly employ'd.

THE Town going thus forward, and standing in the great Post Road, comes an honest Victualler, and he sets up an Ale-house; and soon after, he is follow'd by five or six more; as the first encreasing in Stock, sees Room for it, he enlarges his Building, and makes his little Alehouse out into a good Inn, and a second follows him, and then a third, and in Process of Time, the Number of Public-Houses encrease to eleven or twelve in all; whereof as above, three are very handsome Inns, and perhaps sell Wine as well as strong Drink.

BY this Time the Lords of the Manors begin to think it proper to build their new Tenants a Church, for which they lay out a handsome Piece of Ground in the Center of the Town, and a large Burying-Ground added to it; and obtaining Licence from the Bishop, they consecrate the Building; and being joint Patrons, present in Turn, getting a Law: to erect it into a Parish, and to assertain the Tithe and Maintenance of the Incumbent, as in like Cases.

HITHERTO Nature acted it all, but this Part indeed, the Piety of the Patrons supplies; our Business is (in both) to observe the ordinary Course of Things, the Concourse of Tradesmen follow the Concourse of People, as naturally as Warmth attends the Approach of the Sun; the Settlement of the Farmers gives a Summons to the Tradesmen that supply them with Necessaries, and lets them know, that there they may find Business and Employment: The necessity of Meat and Drink, brings the Butcher, Baker and Victualler to settle with them, as naturally as Sutlers follow an Army.

BUT to proceed; Fame spreads the News of a Town newly erected, and a Number of Families brought together; A Grocer goes to see if there is no Room for him, and finding no Supplies of his Kind, he takes a Piece of Ground in one of the principal Streets, and marks himself out a Place for his House; but first, as before, runs up a Booth or Shed, stores it with Goods, and opens a Shop, and two or three Chandlers Shops do the same in remoter Parts, buying their Goods perhaps of him.

AN Apothecary does the like next Door to him, and a Mercer next to him; then a Haberdasher of Hats, a Draper and a Millener; and thus the Town is inhabited and furnish'd by Degrees with all Sorts of necessary People and Things; till after some Time, the Lords of the Manors, to carry on the Improvement, get a Patent for a Market once a Week, and a Fair perhaps twice a Year, or oftner, as there is Occasion.

IN these advanc'd. Circumstances, other Trades fall in; as 1st, more Ale-houses; 2d, a common Brewer; 3d, a Cooper for Casks of all Sorts; a Pewterer, two or three Lawyers (or Attorneys, rather) for drawing Writings, making Bonds, Bargains and Agreements between Man and Man, and one of these in Time gets himself made a Justice of Peace, and so there is an immediate Magistrate among them.

IN the mean Time other Trades fill up the Streets; a Malt-house, perhaps two or three are erected, that the Inhabitants may brew their own Beer if they please; a. Surgeon in Case of Disaster, for by this Time the Town begins to grow populous.

THE good Women : also being diligent, and good House-wives, they spin, and in Consequence of that, there must be a Linen Weaver, and a Woollen-weaver, a Flax and Hemp-dresser, and in a word, whatever depends upon their Thrift.

THUS far the Nature and Consequence of Things agree with what is advanced above: Thus Towns and Families, nay Nations and Countries are planted and peopled, and made flourishing and populous by their Commerce.

LET Us Now Cast Up The Account, And According To Antient Custom Number The People, The List By The Poll Will Stand Thus.

50 Farmers, With Their Wives And Two Children Each, One With Another, Which I Take To Be The Least That Can Be Supposed	200
Two Men Servants And One Maid To Each Farmer, No Farmer With 200 Acres Of Land Could Be Supposed To Make Shift With Less	150
THE Several Families Of Tradesmen Necessarily Brought Together On Such An Occasion, I Cast Up At 143 Families, At 5 To Each House	715
ADD To These Hired Servants Which Would Fall In From Other Countries; Nurses, Midwives, Hostlers, Apprentices, In All	335
	1400

HERE are fifty Farmers, who with their Servants make up but three hundred and fifty People in all; but necessarily draw one thousand one hundred People more to them. Thus People make Trade, Trade builds Towns and Cities, and produces every Thing that is good and great in a Nation; and wherever fifty Farmers were thus to settle, I insist, that at least one thousand People must of course throng to them, and live about them.

THERE are Numbers of Examples to be given of it, the Venetian Republick began thus; a despicable Croud of People flying from the Fury of the Barbarians which over-run the Roman Empire, took Shelter in a few inaccessible Islands of the Adriatic Gulph.

HERE they had Safety indeed, and Life; but nothing else. But falling into Trade, applying themselves to the Sea, to Navigation and Commerce; How soon did they raise themselves in the World, spreading themselves into the Archipelague, and into the Levant; conquering the great and rich Islands of Candia and Cyprus, Negropont and Scio, possess'd the Morea, Dalmatia and Epirus, and gradually rais'd their Dominion to such a Degree, as was superior to many Kingdoms.

THEIR City we see raised to a prodigious Splendour and Magnificence, and their rich Merchants rank'd among the ancient Nobility, and all this by Trade: Their Fleets of Men of War have oftentimes engag'd and beaten the Turkish Navy, driven them into Port, and dar'd them at the Mouth of the Dardanelli; and all this Power is rais'd by Trade.

I might from this Example lead you to the Hans, the great Confederacy of Commerce, the greatest in the World; who meerly by the acquir'd Greatness of their Trade, became so rich, and so powerful, that they were many Years the Terror of the North; whoever hired their Men of War, were sure to conquer their

Enemies at Sea, and several times they beat whole Fleets of the Danes, and at last brought the King of Denmark to make a dishonourable Peace with them; till the Kings of the neighbouring Countries grew justly jealous of them, and oblig'd all the Cities within their Jurisdiction to withdraw from their Alliance, and to renounce their Confederacy.

THE Dutch, I mean the States-General of the united Provinces, when they broke off from the Obedience of Spain, and as it may be rightly said, cast off the Spanish Yoke, were a poor, mean, frighted Generation, driven to the Refuge of the Water, by the terrible Power of King Philip, and reduc'd to such Distress, that, but for the Assistance of Queen Elizabeth, they had been ruin'd and destroy'd; yet pushing into Trade, and having Recourse to the Sea, they built themselves upon their Marine Power; and the Success of their Navigation rais'd them to that Pitch of Naval Greatness which we now see them at, in which they are superior to all the World, Great Britain excepted, of whom I shall speak by themselves.

As it has been with Nations, so it has been with Cities and Towns; such has been the Case of the Cities of Hamburgh, Dantzick, Lubec, Franckfort, Nuremberg, Rochelle, Marseilles, Genoa:, Leghorn, Geneva, and many other Cities that might be nam'd, who have been rais'd to a Pitch of Opulence and Wealth, equal to some Principalities, by their meer Situation for, and Success in their Commerce: I on the other hand might name several Cities, which being depriv'd of their Trade, have sunk again in Proportion, as their Trade has been taken away; such as the City of Antwerp, the Towns of Dunkirk, Southampton, Ipswich, and many more.

As their Trade has been cut off, their Merchants have removed, the Inhabitants decreased, and the Shells of the Towns remain without the Kernel, the Houses without the People, and the People without the Wealth.

WHEN the Dutch cut off the free Navigation of the Scheld from the City of Antwerp, how did it decline? the English Staple remov'd to Hamburgh, the Fishing Trade to Amsterdam, and the Merchants followed; and what is that City now compar'd to what it formerly was?

WHEN the King of France was oblig'd by the late War to demolish the Works, and ruin the Harbour of Dunkirk, so that the Navigation received a Blow; How did the Town sensibly decay? from eighteen thousand Families, which once inhabited that Place, 'tis said, not two Thirds remain; all the People depending upon the Naval Affairs, are gone with the royal Arsenal; all the Magazines of Naval-Stores, either for the King or the Merchant, employ'd and carried off; and the Trade that attended that Part sunk with it; few Ships now belong to it, few Merchants now reside in it, and in a few Years more, the empty Houses being unrepaired, may publish its Decay in a more visible Manner, and shew the Wounds receiv'd by the Loss of their Trade, as is the Case at Southampton, at Ipswich, &c. in a visible Manner.

I need not travel over the Globe, to give you Examples in remoter Places, where the great Emporiums, the greatest trading Cities in the World, have sunk into Ruin by the Stop of their Commerce, such as Tripoli, Sinope, and Trapezond in the Euxine or Black Sea, whose Trade is cut off, by the Turks stopping the Navigation of the Bosphorus, and cutting off the Trade they carried on with Europe; or such as Suez, and Alexandria, Ports antiently of prodigious Concourse, both of Ships and Merchants; but emptied of both, by the Europeans finding the Way to the East Indies by the Cape of Good-hope; or such as the famous Cities of Tyre and Corinth, who having been the Envy of the World for Wealth, and that Wealth obtain'd by their Commerce, were overturn'd; the first by the Grecians, the last by the Romans, purely for the avaritious Part; and who, their Merchants being destroy'd, and the Trade overthrown, never recover'd their Figure any more than their Fortunes in the World.

IN a Word, it appears by innumerable Examples, that Trade is the Life of the World's Prosperity, and all the Wealth that has been extraordinary, whether of Nations or Cities, has been raised by it.

THE Nature of the Thing indeed implies it; as the Industry of Mankind is set on Work, their Hopes and Views are rais'd, and their Ambition fir'd: The View and Prospect of Gain inspires the World with the keenest Vigor, puts new Life into their Souls; and when they see the Success and Prosperity of trading Nations, it rouzes them up to the like Application.

LET us view the differing Face of the Nations, (and of the People who inhabit them) where they have no Trade; how miserable is the Scene of Life? The Countries look desolate, the People sad and dejected, poor and disconsolate, heavy and indolent; not for Want of Will to labour, but for Want of something to labour profitably at; the Rich are slothful, because they are rich and proud, the Poor, because they are poor and despair; for it will ever be true

That Poverty makes Sloth, and Sloth makes Poor.

We say of some Nations, the People are lazy, but we should say only, they are poor; Poverty is the Fountain of all Manner of Idleness; they have in short nothing to do, no Employment in which they can get their Bread by their Labour; their Work gets no Wages: for Want of Trade, and their Trade no Increase for Want of Labour; Diligence promotes Trade, and Trade encourages Diligence; Labour feeds Trade, and Trade feeds the Labourer.

THERE is hardly that Country to be nam'd in the World, where there is no Room for Improvement by Industry and Application; nay, we find an industrious People often thriving and wealthy, under the weighty Discouragements of a barren Soil, an inhospitable Climate, a tempestuous Sea, a remote Situation, having yet something or other for Trade to work upon.

THE People of Norway and Russia having nothing but Mountains and Woods, and the most barren inclement Air and Soil in the World; yet, rather than not trade, and rather than not labour, they cut down their Trees, and send them abroad to build Cities, and build Navies in other Countries, and have hardly any of their own.

IF their Woods grow remote from the Sea or Water Carriage, Industry dictates to them to cut them down and burn them; and to trade, if it be but with the very

Sap and Juices of the Trees: Hence they send us Tar, Pitch, Rozin, Turpentine; and we see as it were a whole Wood brought away in Cask; Ten, Twenty Thousand Last of Tar brought from Russia at a Time, every Last being Ten or Twelve Barrels.

IF Greenland and Spitsbergen are unsufferably cold; if Nature, not being able to support the Violence of it, leaves those Places uninhabited; the diligent Trader not being to be discouraged by Difficulties, flies directly thither; there among a Thousand Dangers, surrounded with Mountains of Ice, terrible, and Horrors enough to chill the very Soul to describe them, Hunts the great Leviathan of the Seas, and loads his Ships with the fat (BLUBBER) of a Thousand Whales.

I might instance in the Severities of the torrid, as well as frigid Zone, and shew the Hardships undergone in Places scorch'd with the Violence of the Heat; and which are every Way as terrible in their Kind, as those of excessive Cold; such are the Diseases and Terrors of the long Calms, where the Sea stagnates and corrupts for Want of Motion; and by the Strength of the Scorching Sun stinks and poisons the distrest Mariners, who are rendered unactive, and disabled by Scurvies, raging and mad with Calentures and Fevers, and drop into Death in such a Manner, that at last the Living are lost, for Want of the Dead, that is, for want of Hands to work the Ship.

YET nothing discourages the diligent Seaman, or the adventrous Merchant in Pursuit of Trade, and pushing on Discoveries, planting Colonies, and settling Commerce, even to all Parts of the World.

Now as I said before, that the Nations who want Trade look dejected and sad, so on the contrary, let the curious Traveller observe, as he passes thro' the World, the trading manufacturing Nations have a quite different Aspect; their Labour, however hard and heavy, is perform'd chearfully; a general Sprightliness and Vigour appear among them; their Countenances are blith, and they are merrier at their Labour, than others are at their Play; their Hearts are warm, as their Hands are quick; they are all Spirit and Life, and it may be seen in their Faces; or which is more, it is seen in their Labour; as they live better than the Poor of the same Class in other Countries, so they work harder: And here the same Antithesis is observable as before, tho' in its contrary Extreme; for as I said there, that Poverty makes Sloth, and Sloth makes Poor: So here,

Labour makes Gain, and Gain gives Strength to Labour.

As they labour harder, so they get more for their Work than other Nations, and this gives them Spirit for their Labour. And this is the immediate Effect of Trade, for the Poor of the trading and manufacturing Countries are employ'd on better Terms, and have better Wages for their Work, than the Poor of those Countries where there is less Trade.

WE are told, that in Russia and Muscovy, when for want of Commerce, Labour was not assisted by Art; they had no other Way to cut out a large Plank, but by felling a great Tree, and then with a multitude of Hands and Axes hew away all the Sides of the Timber, till they reduc'd the middle to one large Plank; and that yet, when it was done, they would sell this Plank as cheap, as the Swedes or Prussians did the like, who cut three or four, or more Planks of the like Size from one Tree by the Help of Saws and Saw-Mills: The Consequence must be, that the miserable Russian labour'd ten times as much as the other did, for the same Money.

WE are told frequently, when such and such great Works or Buildings were finished, Men work'd for a Penny a Day here in England; and perhaps they did so; but as I said before, speaking of the Cheapness of Provisions, that it was before we had any Trade among us; so it must be as to Wages, for as Trade raises Wages, so Wages raise Provisions; and this is the Reason, why, as all Foreigners grant that our Poor in England work harder than they do in any other Nation; so it must be own'd, they eat and drink better in Proportion; and this is, because they have better Wages:.

I might examine this Article of Wages, and carry it thro' almost every Branch of Business in England; and it would appear, that the English Poor : earn more Money than the same Class of Men or Women can do at the same kind of Work, in any other Nation.

NOR will it be deny'd, but that they do more Work also: So then, if they do more Work, and have better Wages too, they must needs live better, and fare better; and it is true also, that they cannot support their Labour without it.

AND here I may grant, that a French Man shall do more Work than an English Man, if they shall be oblig'd to live on the same Diet; that is to say, the Foreigner shall starve with the English Man for a Wager, and will be sure to win: He will live and work, when the English Man shall sink and dye; but let them live both the same Way, the English Man shall beggar the French Man, for tho' the French Man were to spend all his Wages, the English Man will out-work him.

IT is true again, the French Man's Diligence is the greatest, he shall work more Hours than the English Man; but the English Man shall do as much Business in the fewer Hours, as the Foreigner who sits longer at it.

To conclude this Head, I would not seem to be partial in Favour of our own Country; but in must be added, that their Work is better perform'd also; and I appeal for the Truth of it, to their several Performances, of which I could give Examples, and which all the Markets in the World are at this Time Witnesses to; but this begins to be particular, I shall speak at large to the several Examples of it in their proper Places.

IT is sufficient to the Purpose here to observe as above, that the diligent trading manufacturing World work chearfully, live comfortably; they sing at their Labour, work by their Choice, eat and drink well, and their Work goes on pleasantly, and with Success: Whereas the unemploy'd World groan out their Souls in Anguish and Sorrow, not by their Work, but for want of it; and sink, as I may justly say, under the Weight of their Idleness and Sloth; what little Work they do, is done with Reluctance and Grief, because the small Wages they have for it, gives them no Comfort when it is done.

TRAVELLING in the North Part of Britain, I observed, that, in the Time of their Harvest, they had always an Overseer to keep the Reapers to their Work, and a Bagpipe to encourage them while they were at Work: And one of our Company observing that we had no such merry Doings at our Harvests in England; another answer'd him, 'twas true, nor was there any need of it, for that the English work'd merrily enough without Musick; adding, our Workmen have good Victuals and good Drink: Let's enquire how these poor People feed, said he; and so we did, when we found that the best of their Provision was a Cake of Oat Bread, which they call a Bannock, and a Draught of Water only; and twice in the Day, the Farmer or Steward gave them every one a Dram of Glasgow Brandy, as they call'd it; that is to say, good Malt Spirits.

UPON the whole, it was evident, the poor Men had need enough of Music to encourage them at their Labour; nor would the Music do neither, without the Overseer or Steward being in the Field too, to see that they stood to their Work.

IN England we see the Farmers in Harvest Time, providing good Beef and Mutton, Pyes, Puddings, and other Provisions to a strange Profusion, feasting their Workmen, rather than feeding them; and giving them good Wages : besides: But let any Man see the difference of the Work, these need no Music, the Feast: is better than the Fiddle, and the Pudding does more than the Bag-Pipe; in short, they work with a Vigor and Spirit, not to be seen in other Countries.

I could give like Examples among the Manufacturers; the Spirit and Courage of the Workmen, is seen in the Goodness and Substance of their Manufacture; of which, this must be said, our Manufacture may not be so cheap as the same Kinds made in other Countries; but bring them to the Scale and try their Substance, you will find the English Man's Work, according to his Wages, out-weigh the other; as his Beer is strong, so is his Work; and as he gives more Strength of Sinews to his Strokes in the Loom, his Work is firmer and faster, and carries a greater Substance with it, than the same Kinds of Goods, and of the same Denomination made in foreign Parts.

I remember in our former Contests about Commerce, great Noise was made of the French imitating our woollen Manufacture, and making them to such Perfection, as to out-do us in foreign Markets; from whence it was inferr'd, that they would in Time supplant our Trade, and carry away the Business from us: The Reason that was given, was, that their Poor could work so much cheaper than ours, that their Goods would be sold cheaper than the English, and consequently they would have the first and best of the Market always from us; and had this been fully and fairly made out; had they brought sufficient Evidence of the Facts suggested, the Inference had been good. Now to prove how finely the French perform'd, and how good their Cloths were; Patterns were shew'd here of their several Cloths, as finish'd for the Turky Trade, by the great Manufactory, as they call it, in Languedoc; for it was this Part that was brought for the Support of the Argument; and it is true, that the Patterns were extraordinary, the Cloth well dress'd, the Colours well dy'd; nay to Perfection; and to a superficial Eye, they rather went beyond the English, than come short of them.

BUT when they came to be look'd well into by Clothiers and Workmen who understood it, and whose Business it was; the Deficiency soon discover'd it self; their Cloths appear'd to be slight, thin, without Substance and Proportion, and unfit to do Service in wearing; in a word, they were no Way equal in Goodness to the English Manufacture of the same Kind. This was farther prov'd by the Armenian Merchants at Aleppo, at Smyrna, and other Places in Turky, where the said Goods were usually sold; where upon bringing the English and French Cloths to the Scale, there was no Comparison between them; but the English always outweigh'd them forty to fifty Pounds per Bale, and sometimes much more; the Consequence of which was,

1. THAT those Armenian Merchants would very seldom buy the French Cloths, so long as there were any of the English Cloths left at the Market.

2. THAT when they did buy them, they always had them at a much cheaper Rate.

THIS is an evident Proof of the English manner of performing; and it will hold in many other Cases, perhaps in all Manufacturing Cases: The strong Labour of the English Workmen in all their manual Operations is very remarkable in the Works themselves: And I say, it is evident in many other Manufactures, besides that of Broad Cloths; in a word, our Workmen, by the meer Vigour and Strength of their Spirits, supported by their strong Feeding, and by their better Wages than in any other Nation, are not used to work slight and superficially, but strong and substantial in every Thing they do; and as they have better Wages: for it than other Nations give, and perform their Work accordingly, so their Goods make it evident, for that they fetch a better Price at Market, than any Goods of the same Species, made in any other Country.

IT is the same Thing in their several Manufactures of Brass and Iron, and other Hard-ware Works; but especially, in their building of Ships, in which it is evident, the Dutch and French, Swedes and Danes, build cheaper; but the English build stronger and firmer; and an English Ship will always endure more severity, load heavier, and reign (as the Seamen call it) longer, than any foreign built Ship whatever; the Examples are seen every Year, particularly in the Coal Trade, the Loading of which is very heavy, and the Ships swim deep in the Water, by the Eagerness of the Masters, to carry large Burthens; and yet it is frequently known, that a Newcastle or Ipswich built Colier, shall reign, (as I say the Seamen call it) forty to fifty Years, and come to a good End at last; that is, be broken up; not founder at Sea, or break her Back upon the Sands, as Ships weaker built, often, nay generally do.

THE firm Building, as well as beautiful Moulds of our Men of War confirm this also, in which they out-last, as well as outshine, the strongest and finest built Ships of most other Nations, if not of all Nations in Europey except only those Castle-built clumsy Things called Galeons, which are built so strong, that is, so thick, that they are scarce fit for any thing.

THE Comparison is still to my Purpose in every Part, (viz.) that Trade invigorates the World, gives Employment to the People, raises Pay for their Labour, and encreases that Pay as their Labour encreases, and as their Performance excels;

and it appears that what is said of England is no Compliment to our own Country, but a real, historical Truth; for that 'tis undeniable, that the Labour of the Poor is no where rated so high as in England: There is no Nation in the World where the Poor have equal Wages for their Work as in England, in Proportion to the Rate of Money, and to the Rate of Provisions.

BY this Means the labouring Poor are kept in Heart, kept strong, and made able for the Business they are employ'd in; and the contrary, is the Reason why the French, the Italians, and most other Nations, rather make their Manufacture (of any Kind) gay than good, fine than strong. I allow them to be as exquisite in Art, nay I may allow them to be more apt to invent and contrive, and perhaps finish some Things with more Ornament: But for Strength of Hand in their Works, where Strength is essential to the Value of the Work, there our People out-do them all.

I could carry this on thro' many Particulars, and it would lead me into some very useful Speculations, but they would be remote from my Purpose; I bring it back therefore to the single Point which I am upon; namely, the great Advantage of Commerce to the World, and to particular Nations.

WHEN we had no Trade, we had no Ships, no popud lous Cities, no Numbers of People, no Wealth compar'd to what we see now; Provisions bore no Price, Lands yielded no Rent; and why? The Reason is plain and short; 'tis sum'd up in a Word, Labour brought in no Wages.

(N. B. OBSERVE by the Word, no, or none, is not meant litterally and strictly none at all; but comparatively none compar'd to what is seen now.)

THE People were divided into Master and Servant; not Landlord and Tenant, but the Lord and the Vassal; the Tenant paid no Rent, but held his Lands in Vassalage; that is, for Services to be performed; such and such Tenants plow'd his Land; such and such fenc'd his Park; such and such Lands were let out to furnish the Lord's Kitchen with Poultry, such with Eggs, some with one Thing, some with another; and thus one Lord liv'd, as the Scots call it, in the middle of his Geer.

THE under People to these Tenants held by Villenage; that is, the Labourers, those we now call Husbandmen and Cottagers, these did the Drudgery, were Grooms to look after his Horses, drive his Teams, fell his Woods, Fence, Hedge, Ditch, Thresh, and in a Word, do all servile Labours; and for this they had their Bread; that is, they had a poor Cottage, scarce so good as a tolerable modern Hogstye to live in, they drank at the Pump, and eat at the Kitchen Door, Beggarlike: As for the rest, the Lord of the Manor was their King; nay, if I had said their God, I had not err'd, so much as some may think; for they worship'd him with such a blind Subjection, that at his Command they would rebel against their King, and take up the Bow and Arrow against whomsoever he commanded them.

THIS was the Case, even in this flourishing Nation of England, till Trade came in to make the Difference; and give me leave to assume so much, I insist upon it, that Trade alone made the Difference; and the Climax is very remarkable.

BEFORE the People fell into Trade, what was the Case as to Wealth? You see how it stood with the People; but what was the Case of the Trade.

1. WE had no Manufacture; we had Wool indeed, and Tin, and Lead, those were Funds, and brought in some Substance; but who had it? Truly, the Church and the Gentry; the religious Houses and the Barons had the Lands and the Sheep, and consequently the Wool; And we find that in King Edward III's Time, the Clergy and the religious Houses gave the King a fifth Part of all their Wool for carrying on his Wars against France: This Wool was sent abroad to the Flemings, and this Money was the Wealth of the Nation.

2. THIS Money went all abroad again generally speaking, for those ruinous Wars, which for many Ages the Kings of England carried on, sometimes in France, sometimes in the Holy Land, sometimes in Flanders, sometimes in Brittany, and the like in other Places; so that still the People were impoverish'd, I mean the Gentry and Clergy; for this Wealth was theirs, and they paid all the Taxes: As for the labouring Poor, they scarcely knew what Money was.

3. As to Trade, it was carry'd on by the Esterlings; that is to say, the Hans Towns, and by the Flemings; and they carry'd away your Wool, Lead, Tin, and whatever else you had, and supply'd you again with Cloths, Spice, (Wine there was none, or but little to be had) and in a word, with Hemp, Flax, Pitch, Tar, Iron, and whatever else was to be had from Abroad; and these run away with all the little Wealth which the King and the Wars left among you; they brought you Ships, they coin'd your Money, and they in short grew rich by you, and you look'd on and starv'd.

AT last, by the Prudence of King Henry VII. you fell to Trade among yourselves; and gradually getting Ground of the World, you made yourselves Masters of your own Manufactures, about the middle of Queen Elizabeth's Reign; and what she did to encourage it, I shall shew in its Place. And now what follow'd? The Consequences were most gloriously seen in a few Years, as follows.

1. YOUR People turn'd Merchants abroad, as well as Manufacturers at home: They tasted the Sweets of Commerce, and being encourag'd by the Gain, soon supplanted their Supplanters, built their own Ships, sent out their own Goods, brought Home their own Returns, cashier'd the Esterlings, forbid the Wool going Abroad, and thereby ruin'd the Flemings; and thus they set up for themselves.

2. As to the Country, the Revolution of Trade, brought a Revolution in the very Nature of Things; the Poor began to work, not for Cottages and Liveries, but for Money, and to live, as we say, at their own Hands: The Women: and Children learnt to spin and get Money for it, a Thing entirely new to them, and what they had never seen before. The Men left the Hedge and the Ditch, and were set at Work by the Manufacturers to be Wool-Combers, Weavers, Fullers, Clothworkers, Carriers, and innumerable happy Labours they perform'd, which they knew nothing of before; nay the Flemings came over (for Money) and taught them how to perform those Things at first, I say at firtt, for the People soon became able to send Home their Masters, and teach one another; then the Villains and Vassals were taken Apprentices to the Manufacturers, till coming to be Masters, the Name, nay the very Things themselves call'd Vassalage and Villanage grew out of Use. The Vassals got Money by Trade, and the Villains by Labour; and the

Lords found the Sweets of it too, for they soon buy off the Services, and bring the Lords to take Money. Thus the Cottagers growing rich, bought their little Cotts with right of Commonage for their Lives, renewable so and so, as they could agree, and this was called Coppyhold. On the other hand, the Vassals and Feuholders, as they are call'd to this Day in the North, growing rich, lump'd it with the Lords, and for a Sum of Money bought off their slavish Tenures, and got their Leases turn'd into Free-holds; and to finish the great Fabrick, the Farmers of Lands were now enabled to take them at a Rent certain, and the Gentry got a Revenue in Money, which they understood nothing of before.

I might enlarge here upon the differing Effects of Luxury and Frugality, which became more than ordinarily visible upon this Change of Affairs; namely, that as the frugal Manufacturers, encourag'd by their Success, doubled their Industry and good Husbandry, they lay'd up Money, and grew rich; and the luxurious and Purse proud Gentry, tickl'd with the happy Encrease of their Revenues, and the rising Value of their Rents, grew vain, gay, luxurious and expensive: So the first encreas'd daily, and the latter, with all their new encreas'd and advanc'd Reve-nues, yet grew poor and necessitous, till the former began to buy them out; and have so bought them out, that whereas in those Days, the Lands were all in the Hands of the Barons; that is to say, the Nobility, and even the Knights and Es-quires who had Lands, and were call'd the Gentry, held them by servile Tenures, as above: Now we see the Nobility and the ancient Gentry have almost every where sold their Estates, and the Commonalty and Tradesmen have bought them: So that now the Gentry are richer than the Nobility, and the Tradesmen are richer than them all.

I have given this Sketch of the growing Wealth of the World by Trade, as in Eng-land; that is, I have placed the Scene as in England, because being talking to the English Nation, it will be understood with the more ease. But the Subject is gen-eral, and the Thing is not of private Interpretation: It will hold in its Degree, in all the trading Nations of Europe, as well as here; tho' perhaps in none more emi-nently, the Trade here having made so visible a Change in the Face of the Nation, and in the Circumstances of the People, that the like is not to be shewn of any other Nation, in so very remarkable a Degree; so that if I had been Writing in any other Country or Language, I should certainly have singled, out England for an Example.

I may, however, refer to other Nations for Evidence in their Proportion, for in all the Manufacturing Countries in Europe the Case is the same in Degree; as Trade has encreas'd, the Miseries of the People have abated, the Poor being employ'd by Manufacture, by Navigation, and the ordinary Labours which Trade furnishes for their Hands; they have accordingly liv'd better, their Poverty has been less, and they have been able to feed, who before might be said only to starve; and in those Countries 'tis observable, that where Trade is most effectually extended, and has the greatest Influence, there the Poor live best, their Wages: are highest; and where Wages are highest, the Consumption of Provisions encreases most; where the Consumption of Provision is most encreas'd, the Rate of Provision is highest; and where Provisions are dearest, ihe Rents of Lands are advanc'd most.

AGAIN, for the Climax does not end her; where the Rents of Lands are advanc'd, the Taxes and Payments to the Governour are the larger; and where the larger Taxes are levy'd, the Revenue being encreased, that Prince or Governour is the richer; and where Nations grow richer, they in Proportion grow more powerful.

THUS Trade is the Foundation of Wealth, and Wealth of Power; In former Days the Poverty of the northern Nations added to their Multitude, made them formidable; as the People encreas'd, the Country not being able to maintain them, the old ones drove the young ones out, as Bees cast their Swarms, to seek Place to dwell in, and by the force of their Arms, to make Room for themselves in warmer Climates, and move in a more fruitful Soil. Thus the Alani, the Gauls, the Hunns, invaded Italy; the Goths overrun Spain; the Vandals, Spain and the Northern Parts of Africa; the Thracians, Natolia and Macedonia, and the like.

BUT in our Times, the Case alters universally, the Art of War is so well study'd, and so equally known in all Places, that 'tis the longest Purse that conquers now, not the longest Sword. If there is any Country whose People are less martial, less enterprising, and less able for the Field; yet, if they have but more Money than their Neighbours, they shall soon be superior to them in Strength, for Money is Power, and they that have the Gelt, (as the Dutch call it) may have Armies of the best Troops in Europe, and Generals of the greatest Experience to fight for them at the shortest Warning imaginable; thus upon sudden Quarrels, Princes and States do not now go Home and raise Armies, and list Men, but they go Home and raise Money; and that being done, they look abroad to hire Armies, and hire Men, and even to entertain Generals; so that they need never bring any new raised Troops into the Field, but old Veteran experience Soldiers, such as Swiss, Germans, &c. well Officer'd, and led on by the greatest Generals in the World; so that War is made in a trice, and decisive Battles are fought now in shorter Time than Troops in former Times could be brought into the Field.

THUS the Venetians have had their Generals Shuylenbergh, Coningsmark, Baden, &c. to lead their Troops; the Spaniards had their Marquis de Lede; the Muscovites their Duke of Croy, their Generals Gordon, Konningseck, &c. and Armies of Danes, Prussians, Lunenbergers, Saxons, Hessians, and Bavarians, and other Germans, besides Swiss and Grisons, are to be hired for Money, alternately to fight, for now one Side, then another; I say, alternately, as the Persons direct them whose Money they take; without Regard to Parties or Interests, either of Politicks or Religion, tho' whether for or against the Party or Religion they profess; to Day for Papist, to Morrow for Protestant; be it for God or for Baal, as they're hired, they go

And always fight according as they're paid.

THUS Money raises Armies, and Trade raises Money; and so it may be truly said of Trade, that it makes Princes powerful. Nations valiant, and the most effeminate People that can't fight for themselves, if they have but Money, and can hire other People to fight for them, they become as formidable as any of their Neighbours.

SEEING Trade then is the Fund of Wealth and Power, we cannot wonder that we see the wisest Princes and States anxious and concerned for the Encrease of the Commerce and Trade of their Subj ects, and of the Growth of the Country; anxious to propagate the Sale of such Goods as are the Manufacture of their own Subjects, and that employs their own People; especially, of such as keep the Money of their Dominions at Home, and on the contrary, for prohibiting the Importation from Abroad, of such Things as are the Product of other Countries, and of the Labour of other People, as which carry Money back in return, and not Merchandize in Exchange.

NOR can we wonder that we see such Princes and States endeavouring to set up such Manufactures in their own Countries, which they see are successfully and profitably carried on by their Neighbours, and to endeavour to procure the Materials proper for setting-up those Manufactures by all just and possible Methods from other Countries.

HENCE we cannot blame the French or Germans for endeavouring to get over the British Wool into their Hands, by the help of which they may bring their People to imitate our Manufactures, which are so esteem'd in the World, as well as so gainfull at Home.

NOR can we blame any foreign Nation for prohibiting the Use and Wearing of our Manufacture, if they can either make them at Home, or make any which they can shift with in their stead.

THE Reason is plain; 'tis the Interest of every Nation to encourage their own Trade, to encourage those Manufactures that will employ their own Subjects, consume their own Growth of Provisions, as well as Materials of Commerce, and such as will keep their Money or Species at Home.

'Tis from this just Principle, that the French prohibit the English Woollen Manufacture, and the English again prohibit or impose a Tax equal to a Prohibition, on the French Silks, Paper, Linen, and several others of their Manufactures. 'Tis from the same just Reason in Trade, that we prohibit the wearing of East India wrought Silks, painted Callicoes, &c. that we prohibit the Importation of French Brandy, Brasil Sugars, and Spanish Tobacco; and so of several other Things.

I remember a Story told me by a Gentleman who liv'd many Years in Muscovy, where as weak and sordid a Nation as the Russians were, and how gross soever in their Politicks; yet this Principle prevailed with them, as the Result of meer Nature in Trade: The Case was thus;

AN English Man who had lived long in the City of Casan upon the Wolga, and was it seems concern'd in the great Salt Mines there, had observ'd with Regret, the great vast Luggage Boats, as we might call them, and which he call'd Balla-toons, carrying Goods by the River from Astracan, and from the Caspian Sea, and perhaps from Persia to Moscow; these Boats as the Relater told me, carry'd a prodigious Burthen, from 100 Ton, to near twice as much; but were unwieldy, heavy, ungovern'd Things, and requir'd as they might well do, a great many Hands to guide, and perhaps to tow them up against the Stream of that mighty

River, and the Distance being above 1800 Miles too, they were in Proportion a long Time on the Voyage.

THE English Man fancy'd with himself, that he could contrive a kind of Vessel, that tho' it should not carry quite so much Burthen, should yet carry near 100 Ton, and should, by the help of Sails and good Management, perform the Voyage in much shorter Time, and with much fewer People.

(N. B. THOSE Ballatoons it seems had each 100 to 110 or 120 Men employ'd in them to drag them along; and the English Man proposed to do the same Work with 18 or 20 Men, and perform the Voyage in about one third of the Time.)

BIG with this Project, and expecting to be very well accepted at Court, and rewarded too, away goes the English Man to Moscow, where after some Attendance, and making known to some of the Boyars and great Men, that he had a Proposal to make to the Great Duke, that would be very much to the Advantage of their Country, and for the Advantage of the capital City, and the like, he obtain'd Audience, and lay'd the whole Scheme before his Majesty.

THE Grand Duke, for they did not then call him Emperor, took the Thing very readily, and at the second and third Audience, called him to him, and began to question him about several Particulars, but chiefly this: How many Men were employed in these Boats before? And the English Man answer'd, 120.

AND how many will you perform it with, says the Grand Duke.

EIGHTEEN or twenty Men at most, says the Projector.

AND how long Time are my Subjects performing the Voyage now? Says his Russian Majesty.

ABOUT four or five Months, says the English Man.

AND how long will you perform it in? Says his Majesty.

IN about two Months, says the English Man.

UPON this the Great Duke stop'd, and look'd angrily; but seem'd to be musing, as if he was calculating the Thing; after some Pause, he turns to the English Man, And what Country Man are you? Says his Ducal Majesty.

An English Man, says the Projector.

VERY well says his Majesty, 'tis well for you, that you are not one of my Subjects; do you come hither to set up Projects, to starve my People? Get you gone forthwith, and with the utmost Expedition out of my Dominions upon pain of Death: You perform that Work with eighteen Men, which now one hundred and twenty Men are employ'd, and get their Bread by! What must the hundred and two Men do, that are to be turn'd out of their Business! Must they perish and be starv'd for want of Employment! Get you gone, adds his Majesty, and see my Court no more; and immediately gave Orders for having him carry'd away directly to Novogorod, on the Frontiers of Muscovy, towards Livonia and the Swedish Dominions, lest he should propagate such dangerous Inventions, as should lessen the Employment and Labour of his Subjects.

THE Folly of this Conduct makes a kind of Jest upon the People of Moscow; but the Moral of the Fable, be it so or not, is good; 'tis certainly the Wealth and

Felicity of a Nation, to have the People fully employ'd for Wages, let that Wages be what it will.

BY the same Rule, those Nations are the richest and wealthiest, as well in general as in particular, where the Labour of the People, without Injury to the Government, brings the most Money for their Work.

IT is certainly a wrong Maxim which some People dogmatize so very much upon, viz. that it is the general Interest of this Nation to reduce the Price of their Manufacture.

IT is true, there are some old Notions which chime in with the Piece of trading Policy, viz. that Cheapness causes Consumption; and that by underselling other Nations, we shall carry away the Trade from them; and there is something popular in the Notion too: But it will not hold in all Cases, and particularly not in our Manufacture.

FIRST, I insist, that if you would reduce the Price of our Manufacture, by reducing the Wages of the Poor, who are the Workers or Manufacturers, it is not possible but that you will reduce the Value and Goodness of the Manufacture.

IF you expect the Poor should work cheaper, and not perform their Work slighter and more overly, as we call it, and superficially, you expect what is not in the Nature of the Thing.

AGAIN, if you lower the Wages of the Poor, you must of Course sink the Rate of Provisions, and that of Course will sink the Value of Lands, and so you wound the Capital at once; for the Poor cannot earn little and spend much, the End of that is, starving and misery; the Rate of Provisions will follow the Rate of Wages, there is no possibility of its being otherwise; it has ever been so, and ever will be so, the Nature of the Thing requires it.

THIS therefore is beginning at the wrong End of Trade; but the true Way is, keep up the Goodness of your Manufacture, so as to make it excel in Quality, and its exceeding in Price will be no Deficiency in Trade.

THINGS are not dear or cheap, according as they sell for more or less; but according as the Price they sell for, bears a Proportion to the goodness or meanness of the Goods sold. A high priz'd Manufacture may be as cheap, as a low priz'd Manufacture of the same Kind, according to the well or ill performing and finishing the Work; as a fine Piece of Painting may be cheaper than a coarser Piece of the same Dimensions, in Proportion to the Goodness of its Workmanship; tho' one should be sold for one hundred Guineas, and the other for one hundred Shillings.

LET your Manufacture gain the Credit of the best in the World of its Kind, it shall accordingly bear the best Price of any in the World, and yet be cheap too; that is, it shall be cheap of the Price, tho' not under Price. I shall speak more of this in its Place; 'tis only hinted superficially here, to argue the great Advantage to a Nation, of having such an Employment for their Poor, as may make them not live only, but live comfortably. The poor Muscovite Wretches who mann'd the Ballatoon with one hundred and twenty Men, liv'd on that Employ; that is to say, they did not immediately perish; but the Truth is, they might be said to starve at it, not live at it.

BUT our labouring Poor really live, keep Families, pay Taxes, Scot and Lot, as we call it, wear good Cloths, eat the Fat, and drink the Sweet; and yet, labour hard too. And this is not only the Glory of Trade in general, but of our Manufacture in particular; nay, and is the Support of the Manufacture too; for by this means, the Manufacture is kept up to its Price at Market; the Goodness being kept up at Home, the Credit of it is kept up Abroad, and one reciprocally is the Life of the other; the Wages support the Manufacture, and the Manufacture supports the Wages; by the good Pay, the Weaver and all his Dependent Tradesmen are encourag'd to make the Wares good, by the Goodness their Credit Abroad is kept up, by the Credit the Price, and by that Price the Wages; one Hand washes t'other Hand, and both the Hands the Face.

HENCE I insist also, that our Manufacture is the cheapest in the World, because it is the best; and our Poor work as cheap as any Poor in Europe, because their Work is best perform'd: And this I shall prove more particularly as I go on.

LET us therefore cease those narrow Notions in Commerce, or at least lay less Stress upon them; that Cheapness causes Consumption, may be allow'd in many Things; but 'tis not a Rule without Exception, nor a Foundation to build upon in every Case; it is true, in the Consumption of Trash, and in the Consumption of Eatables and Drinkables: If good Wine was to be sold at six Pence a Quart, instead of two Shillings, or at three Pence a Pot, as strong Beer, there would be much more Wine drank than is now; but in Things of Substance, weighty and durable, the Case many times alters, and it is a true old Proverb, the best is best cheap.

NEITHER is it true in every Article, that the Consumption of Quantity is the Prosperity of Trade, unless it be also true, that some Gain is made by the Trade: For Example, when our Gold Coin in England, was with the greatest Infatuation imaginable, advanc'd from twenty one Shillings and six Pence, to thirty Shillings each Guinea, the same Price being not in Proportion raised in foreign Countries, the Dutch, Germans, French, and Portugueze, hurry'd over their Gold hither, coin'd it at forty per Cent. Profit, and immediately vested it in our Produce and Manufacture. Had they gone on thus, and bought all the Woollen Goods, Corn, Tin, Lead, wrought Iron and Brass, Sugar and Tobacco in England, as they would soon ha' done with Gold at six Pound an Ounce, that Consumption of Quantity would ha' ruin'd the whole Commerce; for they would have stagnated all our Markets Abroad, being able to sell twenty or thirty per Cent. cheaper than the English Merchants, they would in short have carried away all our Quantity, and left us full of Gold, at a third of Price more than it was worth.

BUT this is not all; neither may the carrying off the Quantity of our Goods be always a Benefit, if the Price should be reduc'd below the Standard of our Trade: By the Standard of our Trade, I mean, the stated ordinary Rate of the Poors Labour. What Benefit is a great Consumption of your Goods, at a Rate with which the Merchant cannot gain, and the Maker cannot live? There is no Question, but you may sell all the woollen Manufacture at this Time in the Nation, in three

Months Time, if you will give them at an Abatement of twenty to thirty per Cent. upon the Value; and so the Cheapness will certainly cause the Consumption.

BUT what Gain would this be to the Commerce, and what Advantage to the Trade in general? Since you cannot replace the Quantity at that Price, and you cannot hold the Trade upon that Foot without falling into Circumstances as ruinous to Trade, as want of a Market; namely, the sinking Wages, sinking Provisions, and sinking Land; which, in a word, is a sinking Fund in the literal Sense.

A much better Way to support Trade, is to sink your Quantity at Home, proportioning the Quantity to the Consumption, if you cannot proportion the Consumption to the Quantity; and you had much better have some of your People want Work, and seek Employment some other way, than to have all Hands at Work to no Profit: Of which also I shall speak fully and at large in its Order.

UPON the whole, I insist, and doubt not to make it appear, (without any Impeachment of the old popular Notion, of Cheapness causing Consumption;) That it is the true Interest of any Trading People to keep up the Value, I mean the intrinsic Goodness of their Manufactures, to their just Standard; and make them cheap by their real Worth, rather than by meer lowering the Price at the Expence of their Credit, and meerly to bring them to a low Rate at the Market.

I insist, that this keeping up the Credit of a Manufacture, by its intrinsic Worth, is the only Prosperity of a national Production, by which the People that make it are enrich'd, and the Nation they live in made prosperous and powerful.

IT is apparent in the manufactures of China, India and other Eastern Countries, they have, it is true, the most extended Manufacture, and the greatest Variety in the World; and their Manufactures push themselves upon the World, by the meer Stress of their Cheapness, which according to the Principle mentioned above, causes their Consumption.

BUT then look back to the Country or Countries from whence they come, and there you see the Consequence most evident; the People who make all these fine Works are to the last Degree miserable, their Labour of no Value, their Wages would fright us to talk of it, and their way of Living raise a Horror in us to think of it: Their Women: draw the Plough instead of Horses; their Men perish and sink under the Weight of their heavier Labour, because the Food they eat is not of sufficient Nourishment to support them, and the Wages they get cannot provide better Food for them; and yet their rigorous Task-masters lash them forward as we (cruelly too) sometimes do our Horses.

MONS. Niuenhoff in his Description of China gives such an Account of the Misery of the poor People dragging, or as we call it, towing the Boats up the Stream of the royal Canal there, the greatest in the World; and how their Drivers, like our Carters, whip them on till the poor exhausted Creatures drop down and die under the Labour of it: I say, he gives such an Account as would make the Heart of a merciful Man bleed to think of it; and the utmost of their Wages for all this Labour does not, as I can calculate it, amount to so much as 2 d. a Day Sterling in England; and the like no doubt is the Case in their Manufacture in Proportion.

IF then these Gentlemen, who are for forcing the Consumption of our Manufacture in England, (or in any of those Countries in Europe where they work cheapest,) by their meer Cheapness, are content to reduce the Wages of the People that make them, to the Rate of those in China or in India,, there is no doubt they might encrease the Consumption, and sell off the Quantity; but what would be the Advantage? They would sell their Goods and ruin their People; the Benefit of which in the Gross, I confess I do not understand.

I shall speak of all this again, as it more particularly relates to our Commerce in England; and therefore I only mention it here, as this Notion of reducing the Price of the Manufacture is received, for a general Principle in Commerce, and apply'd by Mistake to particular Cases.

THERE is an Exception in the Article of Wages, which may be brought here against what I have advanc'd above as to England, viz. that we give the highest Wages to our Poor, of any Nation in the World; and it may be thought I have either forgot, or am ignorant of the high Wages given in the European Colonies in America, as well English, as French, Spanish, where a Piece of Eight, or rather five Shillings, and in Jamaica, six to seven Shillings per Day, is given to Handicrafts, and labouring People for their Work; and where the Price of Slaves: is risen within these few Years, from twenty Pound a Head, to thirty and forty Pound, on the meer Account of the Dearness of: Wages.

BUT this is explain'd, and fully answered in few Words; namely, that the Dearness of Wages there, is occasioned by two things viz. the Dearness of Provisions, and the want of People; the Dearness of Provisions in the Islands, and the want of People in the Colonies on the Continent; and let any Man of Experience calculate the Proportion of those Things, and he will find that in a due Equality or Proportion to the Dearness of Living, the Wages are as cheap there as here, and in some Articles rather cheaper; the particular Examination of it, I refer to its proper Place.

UPON the whole, to sum it up in a few Words, Trade is the Wealth of the World; Trade makes the Difference as to Rich or Poor, between one Nation and another; Trade nourishes Industry, and Industry begets Trade; Trade disperses the natural Wealth of the World, and Trade raises new Species of Wealth, which Nature knew nothing of: Trade has two Daughters, whose fruitful Progeny in Arts may be said to employ Mankind; namely,

MANUFACTURE

And

NAVIGATION.

SEE how they unite their Powers to do good to the World, and to teach Men how to live happy and comfortably; let us see, I say, how these two join, and that in the only Means of living comfortably, I mean Diligence, for a Life of Sloth and Idleness, is not Happiness or Comfort; Employment is Life, Sloth and Indolence is Death; to be busy, is to be chearful, to be pleasant; to have nothing to do, is all

Dejection, dispiriting, and in a word, to be fit for nothing but Mischief and the Devil.

MANUFACTURE supplies Merchandize.

NAVIGATION supplies Shipping.

MANUFACTURE is the Hospital which feeds the Poor.

NAVIGATION is the Nursery which raises Seamen.

MANUFACTURE commands Money from Abroad.

NAVIGATION brings it Home.

MANUFACTURE loads the Ships out.

NAVIGATION loads them in.

MANUFACTURE is Wealth.

NAVIGATION is Strength.

To conclude, Manufacture for Employment at Home, and Navigation for Employment Abroad, both together, seem to set all the busy World at Work; they seem to joyn Hands to encourage the industrious Nations, and if well managed, infallibly make the World rich.

Chapter 2

Of the trade of England in particular

WHEN I speak of the Trade of England in particular, as in the Title of this Chapter, I claim to be understood, not in too narrow and confin'd a Sense, as if I meant it meerly of England abstracted; limited to its geographical Dimensions, and that little Spot within the Lines of its Situation, as it appears on the Surface of the Globe, which is little indeed.

BUT I am to be understood in the Language of Trade; and so the Trade of England is the Trade of all the Places within the Dominions of England; or, as it is usually express'd, the Countries subject to the English Government.

I am not at all fond of that modern assum'd Stile, by which some Authors think they do us an Honour, when they call the extended scattered Colonies and Dominions of the English or British Nation, the English Empire: I don't think they do His Majesty or the English Nation any Honour at all by it; 'tis enough the King of Great Britain has the Opulence of an Emperor, without affecting or at all valuing the Title.

NOT but that as the Humour of the World goes, I believe in a few Ages more all Degrees of Men, or at least many of them, will advance their Plumes, and cock their Feathers, in proportion as their Pride increases, in all the Nations about us, and that as the Counts and Princes are increased in several Nations already, even to a Scandal: so they will go on.

THUS in Time the Counts may be Dukes, the Dukes Princes, the Princes be Kings, and the Kings Emperors; in a Word, 'tis not improper, as we are talking of Trade, to observe how Honour is become a Merchandize, Nobility grows cheap, and Dignities come to Market upon easy Terms in the World; and what with the Church Politicks on one Hand, and State Politicks on the other, the World may in a few Years be overrun, not with real Honours, but with Titles. Honour blooms and runs to Seed; (I mean Abroad, not in England) and Titles without Merit are the Scandal of the World. But of this hereafter.

BUT I return, The Trade of England, I say, is the Trade of the English Dominions, the Commerce of the Countries subject to the English Government, particularly, 1st, The Trade of Great Britain and Ireland. And, 2 dly, The Trade of the English Colonies and Factories in America, Asia, and Africa; These all put together, make the Trade of England.

WHEN I come to speak of the general Commerce of the Subjects of England, in other Countries, where they are said to trade as Merchants, not to be possest of the Country in Sovereignty; that is quite another Thing, and will be discoursed of in another Manner, for we must always distinguish between the Trade of a Country, and the Dealings of the People, by Correspondence in other Countries; and I shall take Care to preserve that Distinction, as Justice requires, on all Occasions as we go on.

THE Trade of England is one Thing, the Trade of the English People is another; the first is confin'd to the Place, the second is carried on by the Persons; however, and wherever they may be scattered, removed, and by Indus ENGLISH COMMERCE try settled, as Occasion directs, in any or every Part and Country of the known World.

IT is true the Greatness and Opulence of the English, as a trading Nation, is very conspicuous on this very Account, viz. that not only the Merchandize, but the Merchants also of our Nation, are found in all the trading Parts and Ports of the known World; and which is still more, they are placed there, and supported by the Strength of their own Stocks, and the Value of the Merchandizes they carry thither, more than of the Goods they buy there.

IN some parts of the World, indeed, they seem to be settled and employed rather to buy, than to sell; as in the several Factories and trading Ports of India, at Mocha, at Suratte, the Bay of Bengale, and all the Coasts of India and China; but in most of the other Parts of the World, we rather sell than buy; at least we trade equally both Ways, to the great Advantage of the English Commerce in general, and of the Merchants in particular; as in Turky, Italy, Spain, the Coast of Barbary, and the Kingdom of Portugal; the Dutch, the German, and the Danish Coasts, the Baltick, and Northern Seas, &c.

IN all these Countries, the Growth and Product of our Lands and Seas, as mentioned already, and the Labour and Manufacture of our People are the principal Subject of our Merchants Business; and what they buy in those Countries is the Return only, or rather in Part of the Return for those Goods, which to our great Advantage they first carried thither, and sold in those Markets; the Overplus or Ballance being made good, according to the Nature of Things, and of the Country, several Ways; some by Exchanges, some in Specie, some directly, some from one Country to another, as we shall see in its Place.

BUT the Trade of England in particular, as distinguish'd above, and as we are to speak of it under the Title of the English Commerce, is contain'd in these Generals.

1. THE Product and Manufacture of the Country, for Exportation into foreign Parts only.

2. THE Shipping and Navigation.

3. THE Home Consumption of our own Goods, and foreign Importations.

4. THE Employment of the People in Consequence of all these, and in the particular Works for the Management of them.

UNDER these four Heads, what an immense Weight of Business is carried on, or, as it is ordinarily express'd, is managed in this Kingdom? How many Millions of People are kept in constant Motion, Men, Women, and Children employ'd, Infants (so they may properly be called) of five, six and seven Years of Age, made capable of getting their own Bread, and subsisting by the Labour of their own Hands, and a prodigious Wealth, accumulated among the common People? insomuch, that if it were cast up together, the Poor, that is to say, such as were formerly counted among the Poor, I mean the Tradesmen, the Shopkeeping, trading and labouring Part of the People, have more real movable Wealth among them, than all the Gentry and Nobility in the whole Kingdom, not reckoning the real Estates in Lands, Tenements, &c. of which they possess a surprizing Share also.

AND here it is worth our making a Stop, and reflecting a little on a most considerable Incident, in the English Trade, and which is to be parallel'd in no Place that I know of in the World; namely that the Fund of our Trade in England is raised wholly within it self; it is a Kind of Peculiar to us, that all our Commerce is deriv'd from our selves: It is not so in other Nations; the Trade of the Hollanders is all exotick; it consists in meer Buying and Selling, Fetching and Carrying, and they export little or nothing, but what they first import; even the Linnen which they are said to make, they import most of the Yarn (for it) from Silesia and Saxony, and the Flax for the rest from Russia and Poland.

THE Dutch buy to sell, the English plant, dig, sheer, and weave to sell; not only our Manufactures are our own, but almost all the Materials of them are our own: I say almost, because there are some Exceptions, but they are not many.

IN our Manufacture of Wool, all the Materials are our own, but the Oyl, and some dye Stuffs, such as the Galls, the Indigo, the Cocheneal, and a few others; as to Spanish Wool, it is an Extra, 'tis a Step out of the ordinary Way; most of our Manufactures are, and might be, made without it.

IN our Manufacture of Hard Ware, the Tin, the Lead, is our own; the Copper, and Iron are our own, except a part of the Iron from Sweden and Spain, and but a part: For in the Gross, and in all our Foundaries of Iron, the Metal is our own.

IN our Manufacture of Silk, it is true, the grand and fundamental Materials are foreign. But then, 1. The Silk Manufactures are but of late called our own; it is an Improvement, and it is within the Reach of our Memory, that we bought all our wrought Silks, a few Ribbands excepted, from Abroad, to the Value of near two Millions a Year; and it may not be long before an improving Nation, as we are, may raise the Silk at Home too, or at least in our Colonies, as well as other Countries have done, which had none before, viz. France, Italy and Spain: For 'tis well known, that Italy at first, and France but lately, had no Silk of their own, but brought it all from Turky and India: As to our Product for Exportation, 'tis all our own, or of our Colonies, which is the same thing, such as,

(Corn, Lead, Alloms, Cotton, Coal, Fish, Sugar, Melasses, Salt, Drugs, Tobacco, Ginger, Malt, Copperas, Peltry (Furs), Indigo, Tin, Rice, Flesh &c.)

THESE as Exportations, being all our own, and being in themselves so vastly great, are the Fund of our Wealth, and the Encrease of our Numbers. A People numerous and rich, necessarily make a great Home Consumption, as well of their own Growth, as of foreign Importations: And this is the Sum of the English Trade.

IT is no Boast, much less is it assuming to say, that we consume at Home the greatest Quantity of Foreign Product, but the least of Foreign Manufacture of any trading Nation in the World; the only foreign Manufactures we may be said to import wholly, is Linen and Paper, and Tin Plates; and yet those not wholly neither, tho' 'tis acknowledged they are chiefly imported.

Spain imports the Manufactures of other Countries more than we, but very little of their Growth and Produce, except Fish; the like is said of France, tho' they have now so great a Share of Manufacture of their own.

WE import Gold, Silver, Wine, Brandy, Hemp, Pitch, Tar, Flax, Wax, Oyl, Iron, Steel, Fruit, Wool, Silk, Hair, Drugs, Dye Stuffs, Salt-Peter, Tea, Coffee, Timber, Spice: All these and many more. But these are all the Growth and Produce of the Lands, not the Manufacture and Workmanship of foreign Countries: And all these we consume at Home in such Quantities, as are not to be equalled in any other Country.

But of the Manufacture of other Countries, we import very little, Linen excepted, Paper and Tin-Plates; and of all these, except Tin Plates we make now great Quantities at Home also: The Consumption of Wine and Linen in England is prodigious, and we import more than any single Nation in the World, notwithstanding a very great Quantity of the first made at Home especially in Scotland and Ireland; as for East India Manufactures, the Quantity now consum'd in England is small, and those that are, (viz.) the Callicoes may be esteem'd as Linen, being of the same Species as to their Use.

BUT to bring it back to the first Head as a Trade, the Trade of England consists then in short,

Of the greatest Inland Production Exported, and the greatest foreign Production imported of any Nation in Europe.

THE Exportation lays in a Stock of Wealth from Abroad, multiplies and enriches our People, and our People in general being in good Circumstances, I mean the middling, trading, and industrious People, living tolerably well, their well-faring gives Occasion to the vast Consumption of the foreign, as well as home Produce, the like of which is not to be equalled by any Nation in the World; the Particulars we shall enquire into in their Order.

How far the Multitudes of our People are encreased by these very Articles, and that to such a Degree as is scarce conceivable, is worth our Enquiry, were it not too tedious for this Place. What populous Towns are rais'd by our Manufactures, from within few Years! How are our Towns built into Cities, and small Villages (hardly known in ancient Times) grown up into populous Towns! Let any one that is curious in such Observations, take notice of the manufacturing Counties and Towns, the Sea Ports, and the Coast Counties, and compare them with the Counties where there are no Manufactures carried on, and where there being no part of the Land bordering on the Sea, the Encrease of Trade could not have that immediate Influence on them; and let them but observe the Difference between these in the Numbers of great and populous Towns, the Throngs and Multitudes of People, and the still encreasing Greatness of the Towns that were larger before.

LET them see how the People gather about the Manufacture, how they crowd into the clothing Countries, however barren and remote: And on the contrary, how thin of Inhabitants, compared to those populous Parts, tho' otherwise populous, too, are the other Parts of the Country; some of which are much more fruitful and fertile, the Soil richer, the Situation more agreeable, and the Air milder and wholsomer than those that are so populous? But where the Trade is, there are the People, there the Wealth, there the great Markets, and the large Towns; and in a Word, there the ready Money: For it is the Trade that has made the common People rich, as Pride has made the Gentry poor.

WELL might I say, as in the foregoing Chapter, That it is a Scandal upon the Understanding of the Gentry, to think contemptibly of the trading part of the Nation; seeing however the Gentlemen may value themselves upon their Birth and Blood, the Case begins to turn against them so evidently, as to Fortune and Estate, that tho' they say, the Tradesmen cannot be made Gentlemen; yet the Tradesmen are, at this Time, able to buy the Gentlemen almost in every part of the Kingdom.

AND let me add, were it not for two Articles, by which the Numbers of the Families of Gentlemen are recruited when lessened by Fate and Folly, and restored when sunk and decayed, and both by Trade, this Nation would, in a few Years, have very few Families of Gentlemen left; or, at least, very few that had Estates to support them.

1. THE ancient Families, who having wasted and exhausted their Estates, and being declin'd and decay'd in Fortune by Luxury and high Living, have restor'd and rais'd themselves again, by mixing Blood with the despis'd Tradesmen, marrying the Daughters of such Tradesmen, as being overgrown in Wealth, have been oblig'd, for want of Sons, to leave their Estates to their Female Issue; we find innumerable Families not of Gentlemen only, but even of the Nobility of the highest Rank, have restor'd their Fortunes by such Heiresses, and by such Matches, to the Degree of 50, to 100 and 150 Thousand Pounds at a Time.

2. As thus the decay'd Estates of the Nobility and Gentry have been restored, and their Family Wounds heal'd by the Daughters of the richer Tradesmen; so on the other Hand, by the Tradesmen themselves, or by their Sons, the Numbers of the Families of the Gentry have been recruited, when sunk quite out of Rank, and lost in Poverty and Distress:

FAMILIES are as effectually extinct, and lost, and as much forgotten, when the Heirs are left in Misery and Poverty, and the Estate sold from them, as if they were sunk into the Grave. I could instance at this Time, in a Family, who once flourish'd within a few Miles of this City, the eldest Son a Baronet without Bread, wears a red Coat without a Commission, and goes in a disguised Name, that he may not have a SIR tack'd upon his Rags, and have his Honour be an Addition to his Misery: The Children that are young, are kept upon Charity, and the grown Daughters go to Service, from a Coach and four Horses.

THE Estate (of one thousand eight hundred Pound per Annum) is purchased by a Citizen, who having got the Money by honest Industry, and persuing a prosperous Trade, has left his Books: and his Warehouses to his two younger Sons, is retir'd from the World, lives upon the Estate, is a Justice of Peace, and makes a compleat Gentleman: His eldest Son bred at the University, and thoroughly accomplish'd, is as well receiv'd among the Gentry in the County, and upon the valuable Fund of his true Merit, as if he had been a Gentleman by Blood for a hundred Generations before the Conquest.

I might add here, that it would be worth the while for those Gentlemen, who talk so much of their antient Family Merit, and look so little at preserving the Stock, by encreasing their own: I say, it would be worth their while to look into the Roll of our Gentry, and enquire what is become of the Estates of those prodigious Numbers of lost and extinct Families, which now even the Heralds themselves can hardly find; let them tell us if those Estates are not now purchased by Tradesmen and Citizens, or the Posterity of such; and whether those Tradesmens Posterity do not now fill up the Vacancies, the Gaps, and Chasmes in the great Roll or List of Families, as well of the Gentry, as of the Nobility themselves; and whether there are many Families left, who have not been either restored as in our first Head, or supply'd, as in the second, by a Succession of Wealth, and new Branches from the growing Greatness of Trade.

TRADE, in a word, raises antient Families when sunk and decay'd: And plants new Families, where the old ones are lost and extinct.

I dare oblige my self to name five hundred great Estates, within one hundred Miles of London, which within eighty Years past, were the Possessions of the antient English Gentry, which are now bought up, and in the Possession of Citizens and Tradesmen, purchased fairly by Money raised in Trade; some by Merchandizing, some by Shop-keeping, and some by meer Manufacturing; such as Clothing in particular, of which Sort, notwithstanding all that is, or has been said of the Decay of our Manufacture, it is not difficult to find in the clothing and manufacturing Countries of Wiltshire and Gloucestershire, many, (very many) Clothiers, worth forty to fifty thousand Pounds a Man, and some of them worth from five hundred to one thousand Pound per Annum, Estates in Land, besides their Stock in Business; whose Posterity will never be reproach'd with their being upstart Gentlemen, or be thought Mechanick, for being of the Blood of a Clothier.

BUT to return to the populous Towns rais'd by these Manufactures, let the curious examine the great Towns of Manchester, Leeds, Froom, Warrington, Wakefield, Taunton, Macclesfield, Sheffield, Tiverton, Hallifax, Birmingham, and many others.

SOME of these are meer Villages; the highest Magistrate in them is a Constable, and few or no Families of Gentry among them; yet they are full of Wealth, and full of People, and daily encreasing in both; all which is occasion'd by the meer Strength of Trade, and the growing Manufactures establish'd in them; and of every one of them it may be said, they have severally more People in them, than the City of York; besides that, (as I have said above) they are all visibly and daily encreasing, which York is not.

FROM these which are all Inland Towns, let the same curious Enquirer cast his Eye upon some of our SeaPort Towns, where Trade flourishes, as well foreign Trade, as home Trade, and where Navigation, Manufacturing, and Merchandize seem to assist one another, and go Hand in Hand to encrease both the Wealth and the People: Few Cities in England, London and Bristol excepted, can equal them; and in Time, some of them bid fair to be superior to even Bristol it self; such as (Yarmouth, Hull, Plymouth, Liverpool, Newcastle, Whitehaven, Colchester, Lyn, Biddeford, Deal,) and several others.

How are all these Towns raised by Trade, and the Numbers of their Inhabitants drawn to them by the Employment, and consequently the Money which Trade spreads and diffuses so liberally among the People.

BUT this is not all; let the curious Enquirer travel a little farther, and look into the Countries adjacent to these Towns, and there they will see a manifest Difference in the very Face of Things, where the Manufactures are settled and carry'd on; they shall see the Villages stand thick, the Market Towns not only more in Number, but larger, and fuller of Inhabitants; and in short, the whole Country full of little End-ships or Hamlets, and scattered Houses, that it looks all like a planted Colony, every where full of People, and the People every where full of Business.

LET them view the County of Devon, and for 20 Miles every Way round the City of Excester, where the Trade of Serges is carry'd on.

THE County of Norfolk, and for as many Miles every Way about the City of Norwich, where the Stuff-weaving is carry'd on.

THE County of Essex, for near 40 Miles every Way, where the Bay-making Trade is carry'd on.

THE County of Wilts, thro' that whole flourishing Vale, from Warminster South, to Malmsbury North inclusive, and all the great Towns of Bradford, Troubridge, Westbury, Tedbury, Froom, and the Devizes, &c. where the Manufacture of fine Spanish, and Medley-Clothing, and Drugget-making is carry'd on.

THE Counties of Gloucester and Worcester, from Cirencesterand Stroudwater, to the City of Worcester, where the White-Clothing Trade, for the Turkey Merchants is carry'd on.

THE Counties of Warwick and Stafford, every Way round the Town of Birmingham, where the Hard-Ware Manufacture and Cuttlery Trade is carry'd on; as also about Coventry.

THE Counties of Yorkshire and Lancashire, round about, and every Way adjacent to the great Manufacturing Towns of Manchester, Sheffield, Leeds and Hallifax, where the known Manufactures of Cotton-ware, Ironware, Yorkshire-Cloths, Kersies:, &c. are carry'd on.

IN all these, and many others which might be mention'd, how infinitely populous is the Country? not to say how rich; how thick the Towns, how full the Markets, how stor'd with People are the Villages, and even the open Country! in so much, that in the Parish or Vicaridge of Hallifax alone, they reckon up sixteen Chapels of Ease, and an hundred thousand Communicants, besides fourteen or fifteen Meeting-houses, the People of all which live at large, scatter'd and spread over Hill and Dale, (for 'tis a mountainous Country) as the Convenience of Water, Coal, and other Things proper to their Manufacture obliges them; so that the whole Parish, which is a Circle of twelve Miles diameter, is, as before, like aplanted Garden, or a Colony where every Family lives as it were within it self, and by it self, for the propagating their Business; and where, tho' the whole Country is infinitely populous, yet, if you pass in the middle of the Day thro' the Villages, and by the straggling Houses on the Road, you shall hardly see any Body to ask the Way of: But if you go in the Evening, after working Hours, you are surpriz'd at the Multitude of the People every where to be seen.

HAVING taken a View of these Countries, let the same Person take a Tour through those few Counties in England, where Trade has the least Concern, and where the Inhabitants consist chiefly of Landlord and Tenant, the Gentry and Husbandmen; and tho' there you see no want of needful People to cultivate the Ground, or to dispatch the necessary Labours of the Place; yet the Face of Things differs extremely, and the following Particulars discover it.

1. THE Market Towns are few and small, compar'd with such as I have nam'd, and compar'd with the general Bulk of the smaller Towns, not fit to rank with those great ones nam'd; nay, the Villages in those manufacturing Countries, are equal to the Market Towns in these.

2. THE Villages are distant and remote, small and thinly inhabited; and as for the open Country, you see here and there a Farm-house, and a Cottage indeed, but nothing like the numerous Dwellings which spread the enclosed Counties mention'd above, and where the Roads as you travel are like one continued Street, for sometimes twenty or thirty Miles together, and full of Inhabitants.

3. In these unemploy'd Counties, you see the Women: and Children idle:, and out of Business; these sitting at their Doors, and those playing in the Streets; even in the Market Towns, and the most populous Villages, where they might be supposed to be employ'd, the Poor by the Rich, yet there 'tis the same, much more in the single scattering Villages, where they have no Business but their own.

WHEREAS, in the manufacturing Counties, you see the Wheel going almost at every Door, the Wool and the Yarn hanging up at every Window; the Looms, the Winders, the Combers, the Carders, the Dyers, the Dressers, all busy; and the very Children, as well as Women, constantly employ'd.

4. As is the Labour, so is the Living; for where the Poor are full of Work, they are never empty of Wages:; they eat while the others starve; and have a tolerable Plenty; while in the unemploy'd Counties it goes very hard with them: And whence is all this? Look to the Lands, and consequently to the Estates of the Gentry, the manufacturing Counties are calculated for Business, the unemploy'd Counties for Pleasure; the first are throng'd with Villages and great Towns, the last with Parks and great Forrests; the first are stored with People, the last with Game; the first are rich and fertil, the last waste and barren; the diligent Part of the People are fled to the first, the idler Part are left at the last; in a Word, the rich and thriving Tradesmen live in the first, the decaying wasting Gentry in the last.

THE Product of the first, tho' improv'd by Diligence and Application, is all consumed among themselves; the Product of the last, tho' not half what it might be, is carried away for want of Money to the Markets of the first; the first eat the Fat and the Kernel of all, and enjoy the Soft, being by their Diligence made able to buy it; and the last eat the Husk, the course, and the hard; pinch, and live miserable, being without Employment, except meer Drudging, and consequently without Money.

THE Reason of the Thing answers for it self; a poor labouring Man that goes abroad to his Day Work, and Husbandry, Hedging, Ditching, Threshing, Carting, &c. and brings home his Week's Wages, suppose at eight Pence to twelve Pence a Day, or in some Counties less; if he has a Wife and three or four Children to feed, and who get little or nothing for themselves, must fare hard, and live poorly; 'tis easy to suppose it must be so.

BUT if this Man's Wife and Children can at the same Time get Employment, if at next Door, or at the next Village there lives a Clothier, or a Bay Maker, or a Stuff or Drugget Weaver; the Manufacturer sends the poor Woman comb'd Wool, or carded Wool every Week to spin, and she gets eight Pence or nine Pence a Day at home; the Weaver sends for her two little Children, and they work by the Loom, winding, filling Quills, and the two bigger Girls spin at home with their Mother, and these earn three Pence or four Pence a Day each: So that put it together, the Family at Home gets as much as the Father gets Abroad, and generally more.

THIS alters the Case extremely, the Family feels it, they all feed better, are cloth'd warmer, and do not so easily nor so often fall into Misery and Distress; the Father gets them Food, and the Mother gets them Clothes; and as they grow, they do not run away to be Footmen and Soldiers, Thieves and Beggars, or sell themselves to the Plantations, to avoid the Goal and the Gallows, but have a Trade at their Hands, and every one can get their Bread.

(N. B. I once went through a large populous manufacturing Town in England, and observ'd, that an Officer planted there, with a Serjeant and two Drums, had been beating up a long Time, and could get no Recruits, except two or three Sots, who they had drawn in to be drunk, and so listed when they were not themselves, and knew not what they did.)

ENQUIRING the Reason of it, an honest Clothier of the Town answered me effectually thus, The Case is plain, says he, thus, there is at this Time a brisk Demand for Goods, we have 1100 Looms, added he, in this Town, and the Villages about it, and not one of them want Work; and there is not a poor Child in the Town of above four Years old, but can earn his own Bread; besides, there being so good a Trade at this Time, causes us to advance Wages : a little, and the Weaver and the Spinner get more than they used to do; and while it is so, they may beat the Heads of their Drums out, if they will, they'll get no Soldiers here; but let them come when Trade is dead, and the People want Work, and they may get Soldiers enough; the Gentleman Officer took the Hint, and went off with his Drums, to try his Luck in the Counties where there was no Manufacture, and there he pick'd up young Fellows enough, where they were Poor and Proud, Idle and Lazy, as among the Farmers, Horse-Breakers, Gentlemens Servants, &c.

IN a Word, 'tis Poverty and Starving that fills Armies, not Trade and Manufacturing; and therefore the Swiss and the Grisons, the Danes, and the Lunenburghers, the Hessians, and the Prussians, are glad when they hear the Drums beat, and rejoice when other Nations will hire their Troops, and entertain their Men for Soldiers; for their Numbers are their Grievance: And for the same reason, the

Scots and the French are found dispersed over all the Nations of Europe, and indeed of the World, to seek Employment, either as Soldiers or Slaves: (that is Servants) merely for want of Entertainment at Home; whereas on the other Hand, in England, in Holland, and Flanders, where the People have Manufacturing, and are well employ'd at Home, nothing is more difficult than to raise Men upon any extraordinary Occasion; it was found so here, in the late War with France, after a few of the first Campaigns had carried off the loose Fellows that a long Peace had left among us; then they were oblig'd to make Acts of Parliament to empower the Justices to send away all the poor Fellows they could pick up, and force them into the Service.

NOR would this do neither; in the next Reign the War being renewed, Men were so hard to be had, the Queen was oblig'd to hire Troops from all the neighbouring Princes, to form her Armies; such as Saxons, Hessians, Danes, Lunenburghers, and the like, few English could be had without the utmost Violence and Compulsion; even the Scots themselves, what with Disaffection, and better Business, were not able to supply any sufficient Numbers; the Reason was plain; Trade flourish'd, the Manufactures were in Demand, the Merchants gave out large Orders, and the Men were full of Business: Indeed what poor Man in his Senses, that could get nine Shillings, ten Shillings, and twelve Shillings a Week at his Loom, and at the Comb-Pot, or at the Clothworking, Dressing, &c. of the Manufactures, and live at home warm, easy, and safe, would go abroad and starve in a Camp, or be knock'd on the Head on the Counterscarp, at the Rate of three Shillings and six Pence a Week?

AND here give me Leave to remind you of a Piece of History recent in every Man's Head, and full to my Purpose. There was, one Year of the late War with France, a very terrible Scarcity of Corn throughout the whole Kingdom of France, such a Scarcity, that had it not been for the Merchants, who, as we might say, rumaged the World for Corn, many Thousands of People must have perish'd more than did, for many died of meer Want.

IT happen'd that there having been three terrible Blows given to the French King the Year before, and his Armies having been routed on several great Occasions, as at the Relief of Barcelona, the Battle of Turin, and the Battle of Ramellies in Flanders, all in one Campaign, the King of France found himself greatly embarrass'd with the Difficulty of recruiting his Armies, and it was the Opinion of most of the Confederates, that the Fate of France was come; that the Fall of the French Empire was at Hand, for that his Armies were ruined, his Country threatned on all Hands, and his People starving, and ready to cut one another's Throats for Bread, so that it seem'd impossible for him to restore his Troops.

IN this Distress the General Officers were almost affraid to speak to the King, the old Monarch unacquainted with Misfortunes, was so wayward, so fretful, and so full of Resentment, that none car'd to meddle with it, and yet they saw all was going to Wreck.

IN the mean Time, the King published several Orders, and employ'd People, and issued out Money every way for the amassing Corn, from all the Quarters of the World; even from the outmost Ports in the Levant, to Egypt, to Syria, to Cyprus, to all the Isles of the Arches, to the Gulph of Volo, to Salonichi, and even to Constantinople itself, and great Quantities of Corn were procured, which the King gave express Orders should be brought into the publick Magazines, for the supply of his Troops; but took not the least notice, nor spoke one Word about raising Men to recruit his Regiments, and replace the many whole Brigades that had been lost and cut off in the unhappy Campaign that was past; nor did he order his Financiers or Paymasters to issue out any Money for the Supply of that important Article, as he was always wont to do.

At last, some of the Mareschals of France, who presumed upon their great Interest in his Favour, and were greatly concern'd at the dangerous delay, as they look'd on it to be, resolv'd to move it to him: His Majesty foresaw the Errand they came about, but began with them pleasantly upon other Business, entertaining them so warmly with other Discourse, that he gave them no Opportunity to speak a Word about the main thing they came for, namely raising Recruits, and augmenting his Troops, his Discourse still running another Way.

PARTICULARLY, His Majesty enquired of them separately, how the People far'd in their Provinces, and in those Provinces he knew were particularly under their Government, with Respect to the want of Corn; and all agreed, that the Misery was inexpressible, and that many of the poor People perish'd for Want. But, says the King, How do my Troops fare? are the Orders I gave for supplying my poor Soldiers put in Execution? Yes Sir, says one of the Mareschals, and I think it was Monsieur Villeroy, such of your Majesty's Armies as are listed, are taken care of. I understand you, says the King, I have given no Orders for Recruits, nor do I intend it till next Spring, and with that spoke again of the Corn, Are my Magasins kept full? says the King. They answered, Yes, the Magasins were well supply'd, and were all kept full.

The Officers were surprized at what his Majesty had said about Recruits; but such was the fiery Disposition of the august Tyrant, that no body cared to make the least Reply to it: but with a profound Submission went away, as acquiescing with the King's Measures, tho' they thought them the most ridiculous in the World, and thought the King little better than stupid, or lunatick.

AT their going away, the King repeated his Orders to them, to take effectual Care that his Troops might be supply'd with Corn out of the publick Magasins in all the Provinces where they were respectively quartered, and told them he would have it publish'd that this was his Order, That so says the King, my good Soldiers shall know that if they suffer any Want, it is not my Fault, but the Fault of the Mareschals of France.

ACCORDINGLY, publick Notice was given in Print for the Encouragement of the Troops, that the King had given express Orders, that the Soldiers should be supply'd with Corn out of the publick Magasins, and the Regiments, whose Quarters were remote from the Magasins, were forthwith removed, so as to be near those Magasins for their supply.

THIS was no sooner done, and that it was every where known, that the Soldiers had plenty of Bread, but the Mareschals complimented the Wisdom of the King, which they did not understand before; for the poor starving Peasants run every where to the Army, and listed so fast, that tho' the Army wanted near 80000 Men, the Troops were fill'd up without any Expence, and twenty new Regiments were raised by way of Augmentation; and all this with a surprising Expedition.

THIS Story abundantly confirms what I have said, and for that Reason I told it, viz. that Poverty and Want raises Soldiers. Trade is a Friend to Peace, and provides for the People a far better Way: Trade sets them to work for their Bread, not to fight for it; and if we want Men in England, 'tis not that the Number is deficient, but because they live too well to go for Soldiers.

THIS also confirms what has been said above, namely, that as the trading, middling sort of People in England are rich; so the labouring, manufacturing People under them are infinitely richer than the same Class of People in any other Nation in the World.

As they are richer, so they live better, fare better, wear better, and spend more Money, than they do in other Countries; and I make no doubt 'tis the same in some other Places in their Proportion, as well as here; at least, in free Nations, where the People are not affraid to own their Circumstances, and to appear in good Condition when they are in good Condition: In short, the Tradesmen in England live in better Figure than most of the meaner Gentry; and I may add than some of the superior Rank in foreign Countries; nay, not to magnifie Things here, and lessen them Abroad, it is very evident that we have Tradesmen or Shop-keepers, of very ordinary Employments in London, such as Cheesemongers, Grocers, Chandlers, Brasiers, Upholsterers, and the like, who are able to spend more Money in their Families, and do actually spend more than most Gentlemen of from 300 to 500 Pounds a Year, and that with this remarkable Addition, that the Tradesman shall spend it, and grow rich, and encrease under the Weight of the Expence; whereas the Gentleman spends to the Extent of his Revenue, and lays up nothing.

How many Shop-keepers, Ware-house-keepers, and Wholesale Traders, (to go a Step higher) have we seen in London, such as Drapers, Iron-Mongers, Salters, Haberdashers, Blackwell-hall, and other Factors, &c. who shall spend 500 Pound a Year in their Housekeeping, and other Incidents, and lay up 500 Pound a Year more, while a Gentleman of a Thousand Pound a Year Estate, can hardly bring both Ends together at the close of the Year, and not live in a much better Figure than the Tradesman, and not at all in better Credit?

How do our Merchants in London, Bristol, Liverpool, Yarmouth, Hull, and other trading Sea-Ports, appear in their Families, with the Splendor of the best Gentlemen, and even grow rich, tho' with the Luxury and Expence of a Count of the Empire! so true it is, that an Estate is but a Pond, but Trade is a Spring.

BUT to look at the meaner People (for among them, generally, the Wealth of which I am now speaking is lodg'd, because their Number is so exceeding great) those, it is evident, are in England supported after a different manner from the People of equal Rank in Trade among other Nations; let any Man that has seen how the trading People, and the labouring Poor live abroad, make the Comparison, it is too evident to be disputed.

IT is upon these two Classes of People, the Manufacturers and the Shopkeepers, that I build the Hypothesis which I have taken upon me to offer to the Publick, 'tis upon the Gain they make either by their Labour, or their Industry in Trade, and upon their inconceivable Numbers, that the Home Consumption of our own Produce, and of the Produce of foreign Nations imported here, is so exceeding great, and that our Trade is raised up to such a Prodigy of Magnitude, as I shall shew it is.

I need not describe it at large, a few Words will give a Sketch of it and a great Volume will not line it out compleatly: They eat well, and they drink well; for their eating, (viz.) of Flesh Meat, such as Beef, Mutton, Bacon, &c. in Proportion to their Circumstances, 'tis to a Fault, nay, even to Profusion; as to their Drink, 'tis generally stout strong Beer, not to take notice of the Quantity, which is sometimes a little too much, or good Table Beer for their ordinary Diet; for the rest, we see their Houses and Lodgings tolerably furnished, at least stuff'd well with useful and necessary household Goods: Even those we call poor People, Journeymen, working and Pains-taking People do thus; they lye warm, live in Plenty, work hard, and (need) know no Want.

THESE are the People that carry off the Gross of your Consumption; 'tis for these your Markets are kept open late on Saturday Nights; because they usually receive their Week's Wages late: 'Tis by these the Number of Alehouses subsist, so many Brewers get Estates, and such a vast Revenue of Excise is raised; by these the vast Quantity of Meal and Malt is consumed: And, in a Word, these are the Life of our whole Commerce, and all by their Multitude: Their Numbers are not Hundreds or Thousands, or Hundreds of Thousands, but Millions; 'tis by their Multitude, I say, that all the Wheels of Trade are set on Foot, the Manufacture and Produce of the Land and Sea, finished, cur'd, and fitted for the Markets Abroad; 'tis by the Largeness of their Gettings, that they are supported, and by the Largeness of their Number the whole Country is supported; by their Wages they are able to live plentifully, and it is by their expensive, generous, free way of living, that the Home Consumption is rais'd to such a Bulk, as well of our own, as of foreign Production: If their Wages: were low and despicable, so would be their Living; if they got little, they could spend but little, and Trade would presently feel it; as their Gain is more or less, the Wealth and Strength of the whole Kingdom would rise or fall: For as I said above, upon their Wages it all depends; the Price of Provisions depends on the Consumption of the Quantity; upon the Rate of Provisions the Rent of Lands, upon the Rent of Lands the Value of Taxes, and upon the Value of Taxes, the Strength and Power of the whole Body: So that these are originally the first Spring of all the Motion.

IN like manner it affects foreign Trade; if the Poors Wages abate, the Consumption of Quantity also, as above, would abate; if the Quantity abates, the foreign Importation would abate, the Brandy, the Oyl, the Fruit, the Sugar, the Tobacco: For if the Poor have not the Money, they can't spare it for Superfluities, as those foreign Articles generally are, but must preserve it for Necessity; upon their Necessity depends the Consumption of the ordinary Food, which is the Home Produce; and upon their Superfluity depends the Consumption of their Extraordinaries, which is the foreign Importation. EVEN the Wine, the Spice, the Coffee and the Tea, after the Gentry have taken the nice and fine Species off, are behold-ing to the mean, middling and trading People to carry off the coarser Part, and the Bulk of the Quantity goes off that way too: So that these are the People that are the Life of Trade.

THE Silk Manufactures are indeed a Branch, the chief part of which the Gentry may be said to support, and to help out Trade in: As to the Linen, they take in-deed the finest Hollands, Cambricks, Muslins, &c. But the middling Tradesmen break in upon them, and follow them so at the Heels, that 'tis to be questioned, whether, as the Humour runs now, the Tradesmen by the help of Numbers do not out go them, even there also; not to mention the vast Quantity of Linens of other Kind, which they consume every Day, imported from Ireland, France, Rus-sia, Poland and Germany.

HAVING thus mention'd the Substance of our Trade, and the Support of it, it remains to examine a little the Magnitude of these several Branches, as well of Exportation, as of Importation, in Order to make this Discourse be according to my Title, a true Plan of the English Commerce; and here it is necessary to make some little Provisos, against the too forward Expectation of the Reader, as to Numbers and Calculations, in which it may be impossible to go the Length which may be unreasonably expected.

THERE are many Things in our Commerce, as well Abroad as at Home, in which no exact Calculation can be made; and yet perhaps our Estimates and Conjectures may not be so remote as some may imagine, or so, as that no prob-able Prospect, no rational View of the Commerce may be made from them: For Example,

IT is not possible to make any Calculation of the Number of Shop-keepers in Great Britain, or of the Number of Spinners, or of the Quantity of Wool, or of the Bulk of the woollen Manufacture; and yet, from what has been, and shall be said, I doubt not, we shall form just and rational Ideas in our Thoughts, of the Great-ness of our Manufacture, and of our home Trade; and so of many other Things which we cannot otherwise judge of, than by such general Estimates.

THE World must be left in the dark, concerning many useful Parts of Knowledge, if we were to take no Measures, and form no Ideas of Things from the Lights that are given; tho' it should be true, that those Lights do not amount to Demonstrations; and especially, in Matters of this Kind, where the Founda-tions are subject to various Changes, and where the whole is rather Matter of Observation, than real Intelligence of Fact.

WE may make an Estimate of many Branches of Trade, without being able to determine the Dimensions of either the Subject on which those Branches are founded, or of the particular Parts themselves: We may make just Estimates of the Returns of Treasure from the Spanish Indies, without enquiring into the Fund of that Treasure, (viz), how many Mines there are discovered, in which the Silver is found, or how much every Mine that is discover'd produces; and thus we may entertain a true Notion of the Magnitude of woollen Manufacture, and of the great Advantage of it to this Nation, without being able to know, to what Val-ue the Return of it amounts in a Year: We may give an Account of its being able to consume the whole Quantity of the Growth of our Wool in England, and of much from Ireland; and we may bring this in Evidence of the Magnitude of the whole Trade, without being able to cast up how much that Wool amounts to, and so of the rest.

WE may venture to say in Publick, that we are a most powerful Nation in Shipping, having the greatest Number of Ships and Seamen, of any Nation in the World, without being able to give a particular Account how many Ships we have, or how many Seamen we employ.

UPON the same Foundation, 'tis reasonable to say, we may judge of the Magnitude of our Commerce in general, by the several Circumstances of the particular Branches; for Example, the Encrease of the Consumption of such and such Goods imported, which are absolutely requisite for such or such a Manufacture, is a just Measure, by which to conclude the Encrease of that Manufacture: In other Cases we may have plainer Rules to judge from, and to make our Estimates by; and yet, even those Rules are not such, as that we can ascertain those Estimates upon that Foot, because of several Incidents in Trade, which cannot be accounted for, any more than they can be avoided.

WE may judge of the Consumption of Wines in England, because they are all imported from Abroad, and we can have an exact Account of the annual Importation from the Custom-house Books:; but we cannot positively ascertain the Consumption from that Importation, because, tho' all that are enter'd at the Custom-house, are imported and consum'd, yet all that are consum'd may not be enter'd at the Custom-house; clandestine Trade, and smuggling has a great Stroke in it; and the like of foreign Brandy: Of both which hereafter.

THUS again, we may judge of the Consumption of Spirits, by the Quantity of Malt distill'd, and the Spirits of the first Extraction gaug'd by the Excise-Man; but clandestine Concealments have so great a Share in that Trade, that we can never say our Calculations are exact.

UPON the whole, if our Calculations and Guesses are rational and probable, we hope in these Cases it may be allow'd to be sufficient, because it is as far as any Man can go. The Commerce of England, is an immense and almost incredible Thing, and as we must content our selves with being in some Cases in a difficulty as to Numbers and Figures; but in all such Cases, we expect the Reader will be content with the utmost possible Inquiry, and the utmost possible Discovery that we are able to make, and with such Reasons as may be drawn from what appears,   to   judge   of   what   cannot   be   fully   discover'd.

Chapter 3

Of the first rise, growth and encrease of the commerce of England

It is something difficult to adjust the Terms of our first Part of this Work, they are set down in general in our Title, viz. the Rise, Growth, and Encrease of our Trade, all which Words, as they imply a Progression, they necessarily imply a stated Period, like an Epocha of Time, from whence the Motion might be said to begin like the starting Post, or Place of a Race, where all that run, set out exactly upon an Equality, whatever Advantage is g obtain'd afterwards, being the Effect of the Strength and Vigour of the Racers, whether Horses or Men. I suppose all Nations had some Trade, and all People some Dealing with one another from the Beginning; that is, ever since they began to converse; when mutual Convenience guided them to enquire what they might either want from, or spare to each other for the Supply of common Occasions.

BUT this would lead us back into dull Speculations of the Nature and Original of Commerce; a dry useless Subject, and therefore carefully avoided in my Title, where it may be observ'd, that I do not call this Work a History of Trade, or a History of the English Trade; but a History of the Rise, Growth, and Increase of it; by which I mean as above, from the Time, let that Time be when you will, when standing upon the Square with the rest of the World, England gave it self a Loose, and got the Start of all the Nations about her in Trade; and having held it ever since, her Commerce is by that Means arriv'd to that Prodigy for Magnitude, which it appears in at this Time, and in which 'tis acknowledg'd by all her Neighbours, she out-does all the Nations in the World, as we shall see in the next Chapter.

How to fix this Period without running out into foreign Enquiries, and giving a State of Things tedious in themselves, and remote from our Design, is the Thing we are now to attend to; and tho' I shall do it my own Way, and may differ from the Opinion of some wiser than my self; yet, I shall endeavour to support my Opinion with such Reasons, as shall bring over such differing Judgments to agree with me; or I shall, for want of it, submit to theirs; so that either way the End will be answer'd, and the Magnitude and Encrease of the Commerce of England be confirm'd and describ'd, and the Time of it ascertain'd.

England being an Island surrounded with the Sea, and with neighbouring powerful Nations; her Converse in Peace, and at other Times her Wars with those Nations, made Shipping in particular exceedingly necessary to her; and we find upon many Occasions, the English Fleets not only very numerous, but very formidable; yet History is very barren on that Occasion, nor is there the least Fragment to be gather'd up, that intimates to us, when, how, or in what manner this Nation began their Acquaintance with the Sea.

WE gather some Negatives indeed from History, as to this Part; we are pretty well assured, that the Britains had no Knowledge of Navigation, nor do we read of any Ships in Use among them, when Julius Caesar landed here with a great Navy.

THAT the Romans had Ships, and that the Britans had none, or none considerable, will, I believe, be granted; and as the Romans afterwards conquer'd and possess'd the Island, as is evident from History, nothing then can be more natural, than to suppose, that the Romans first introduced the Knowledge of Navigation, and the Use of Ships in this Island.

IT is true, and we are told it from History, that the Phoenicians traded hither several Ages before the Romans, and with their best Ships, no doubt; but be that so or no, we do not find that the Britains learn'd any thing from them.

THE Danes, after this, came in great Fleets, and ravag'd the Coast, both of England and Normandy; what their Ships were, we know not; but 'tis evident, they were such, as neither the Britains or Saxons could cope with; so that even after the Romans were gone, the Knowledge of Shipping and Navigation seems to be much sunk and decay'd in England, and even in this whole Part of the World; for according to Mr. Cambden, the Saxons themselves came over in strange Boats; that is to say, in Boats or Vessels, as we may suppose, built of Wood; that is, of Timber and Boards, or Planks, and cover'd with a Tarpawlin, or Canvas dipt in Tar and Oil, which being nail'd upon the Plank, serv'd instead of Caulking, to keep out the Water.

IF this is true, the northern World, who at this Time so much out-do the rest of the Nations in the navigating Skill, came very late into the Knowledge, either of building of Ships, or of managing them when built.

THE Danes, we may suppose, had better Vessels, ' tho' not such as would now deserve the Name of Ships, and were neither fit for Fight or Freight, for War or Trade; only prepar'd to waft over a Parcel of Thieves and Rovers, who came in a desperate manner, to fight, plunder and destroy, without any View or Design of returning; and therefore, when they burnt their Ships, as sometimes they did, and sometimes the Britains or British Saxons rather did for them, they had no great Loss, for sending but one Vessel Express to Norway, or to the Coast of Juitland, they presently had as many more as they pleased; but all this while, here was no Shipping for Trade, no nor much Business for Shipping, if they had been furnish'd with Vessels to be employ'd.

ON the contrary, what Commerce there was carry'd on at that Time between Britain and any other Countries, the Particulars of which, it is very hard to know, was certainly carry'd on in foreign Bottoms, till the Encrease of Commerce brought the English to build Ships, or the Encrease of Shipping brought the Commerce; take it which Way we will, one is as probable as the other.

IT is true, that Julius Caesar transported his Army over hither in Ships and Gallies, from the Coast of France, from Gaul as he calls it in his Commentaries; but 'tis as true by the same Commentary, that he caused those Ships to be built by his own People, I mean, Romans; for we do not find that the Gauls, any more than the Britains, had any Ships before.

HE built the Ships it is said in about two Months, so that they could not be very great; and he tells something of it himself, that for the Gallies, when they were landed in Britain, they haul'd them up upon the Beach: What Ships were em-ploy'd for Commerce, we cannot tell; yet there was some Trade at that Time too; for Caesar says, the Britains had Intelligence of his Design to invade them, by Merchants who frequented their Coasts: See Ces. Com. Lib. IV. Cap. 9. But all this leaves us in the Dark, either as to their Commerce, or their Navigation; what they traded in, or what Vessels they traded with; 'tis certain, the Britains had very little Trade, and less Shipping, for we read of none of their Ships for many Ages after-ward.

WHETHER therefore in succeeding Ages, Navigation introduc'd Trade, or Trade Navigation, is a Dispute not much material here; 'tis probable it may stand thus, (viz.) Necessity produc'd the Converse of Nations one with another, for the Supply of their mutual Wants, exchanging the Produce of their respective Coun-tries, as their Wants severally directed.

THIS exchanging of the Produce of Countries, produced Commerce or Trade.

TRADE thus explain'd, necessarily required a Voiture or Carriage of Goods, by Land or by Water; the latter requir'd Vessels to carry them in, either to sail or to row, and this is Navigation.

IF I was to write a History of Navigation, I should go back here to the first In-vention of Boats to row, of which they tell us the Phoenicians were the Inventers; and of Sails to make use of the Wind, of which they tell us the Fable of Dedalus and Icarus is a Representation, viz. that Dedalus being a Prisoner at Cyprus, con-triv'd a Sail to his Boat, and taking his Opportunity when the Wind blew fresh from the Shore, put boldly out to Sea in the Sight of all the People; his Son Icarus doing the like in another Boat fitted out by his Father's Direction. That the People enraged to see them attempt their Escape even before their Faces, pursued them with Boats row'd with many Oars, laughing at the Madness of the Attempt. But that when they came out to Sea, Dedalus run two Foot for their one, as the Sea-men express it; the Sea also being rough, and the Wind blowing a fresh Gale; so he made his Escape from them all, which they called flying in the Air with waxen Wings. As for his Son Icarus, he outwent his Pursuers too, but impatient, and not content with his Escape, but willing to go faster, he crowding too much Sail, as the Seamen call it, or not having Judgment to fill, trim, and manage his Sails skil-fully as his Father did, he over-set his Boat, and was drown'd; which the Fable represents, by soaring too high, and melting his Wings.

BUT these Things would lead me out of my Way, I am not writing of Naviga-tion, but of Trade and Commerce: So I return to my Subject.

IT seems the Dutch, (for the Flemings were all called Dutch) a diligent and la-borious People were in Trade before us, and being in Search of proper Methods to improve and enrich themselves, fell to Manufacturing. In this the first of their

Improvement, as I am assured by good Authority, was making Linen, which they fell into by the Instruction of some Carthaginian Merchants, who fled into France by Sea from the Fury of the Wars between the Romans and Carthaginians, which War afterwards ended in the Destruction of their City.

IT is well known, that the Carthaginians were great Friends to Trade, and Encouragers both of Merchants and of Manufacture (that is a History by it self). These I say fled to France, and thence some of them to Flanders, where the Romans had not made so intire a Conquest as in France.

HERE they fell to Trade and Manufacturing, and having planted the Flax, which they found the Country very proper to produce, they of Course set the People to Work, instructing them how to dress the Flax, spin the Yarn or Thread, weave the Cloth, bleach it afterwards, and then to sell it; and this I take to be a true Account of setting up the Linen Manufacture in the seventeen Provinces.

(N. B. The Dutch had their Linen Manufacture from the Carthaginians, they from the Tyrians or Phoenicians, of whom they were a Colony, and they from the Egyptians; the fine Linen of Egypt is often mentioned in the Scripture History, and in others also, as the most antient.)

INDUSTRY seldom wants Business: The Flemings falling into the Manufacture of Linen, it led them as it were by the Hand into that of the Wool; and the same Carthaginian Refugees put them upon that also, for the old Numidians had Wool in great Plenty, and the Wool of Barbary is good to this Day.

BUT here they were put to a Stop, for neither Belgia (Holland and Flanders) or Gaul (France) yielded any Wool: This balk'd their Undertaking for a while; but the diligent Tradesman never tires; it was not long before, searching among the neighbouring Nations, they found that they had Wool in Britain, and that so fine and good, that no other Wool the World produced was equal to it, for their Business.

THIS encouraged them so, that they bought the Wool in Britain, manufactured it in Belgia, and supplied first themselves, and afterwards the neighbouring Countries with woollen Manufactures, to the great Encrease of the Wealth and Power of the Netherlands; especially by drawing infinite Multitudes of People to them, so that they soon became, from a few fishing Towns, and a poor labouring People, to be a most populous, rich, and powerful Nation.

THE Britains too, in their Degree, found the Sweetness of this Encrease of Commerce, and next to the Flemings had their Share of the Gain from the Wool of their Sheep: This Wool was but of small Value to them before; for instead of manufacturing it as the Flemings did, they wore the Skins of their Sheep with the Wool on: But now the Flemings eagerly calling for the Wool, and giving a good Price for it, the Britains were not only encouraged to preserve it, but to nourish and take more Care of their Sheep, in order to encrease the Number of them, that they might, in the Consequence, encrease the Wool.

THUS began the English Commerce, and thus it may be said began the Opulence and Greatness of the English Nation; for the Flemings took off their Wool in a prodigious Quantity, and gave also a prodigious Price for it.

(N. B. WE find in King Edward the III's. Time they gave 40 l. a Pack for the English Wool, which by the Way was more than 200 l. a Pack, as Money goes now; but of that in its Place.)

THIS filled the Nation with Money, the Merchants grew rich, the Staple of the English Wool was erected at Antwerp, 50000 Packs of Wool was the least that was carried thither yearly, and the Fleets of Ships which carried over the Wool, and which went generally from Southampton and London, were such, that sometimes Fifty, Sixty, to 100 Sail, went off at a Time.

IT is to be doubted indeed, the Ships were most of them Hollanders, that is to say Flemings, or in general Dutch, for I do not find, but that as they were before us in Trade and Manufacture, so they were also before us in Shipping and Navigation; tho' growing rich by the Wool, we soon fell in to building Ships too, especially as Trade encreased; of which hereafter.

AS the Quantity of the Wool was thus great, and the Price also, the Ballance of Trade was necessarily very great on our Side, I mean great to the Advantage of Britain; for the Britains bought but little of any Goods from Abroad, for many Ages after this, and their Wool was generally paid for in Money; nay, they had two several Products beside the Wool, which were peculiar to Great Britain, and which no other Nation in the World had, (viz.) their Block Tin, and their Lead.

WE have very good Evidence, that both these Metals were found and dug by the antient Britains, long before this, and especially that the Tin was fetch'd from Britain by the Phoenicians, many Ages before the Time I am now speaking of.

I take it, that at the first of the Trade with the Flemings, the Importations of Britain were so small, that the Export of Tin and Lead was sufficient to purchase all that they wanted from Abroad: So that the Wool was necessarily all paid for in Specie.

THIS I say enrich'd the British Nations to a very great Degree, fill'd them with ready Money, and especially the landed Men grew very rich and powerful by it, I mean the Barons, Knights, Gentlemen and other Degrees, for they were the Men that got the Money, the Wool and the Sheep being their own.

(N. B. WHEN I say other Degrees of Men, I mean plainly the Clergy, for the religious Houses had many, if not most of their Rents paid in Wool; and some had large Flocks of Sheep of their own, kept by their own Shepherds, for the Supply of the House, (that is the Fryars) and their large Attendants with Mutton, and for Supply of Money to their Coffers by the Wool; and we see the Clergy tax'd in King Edward the ILL's Time, in so much Wool to the King and his Wars.)

IT is almost incredible what immense Sums of Money came over yearly to this Kingdom for the Wool, and how rich and powerful England grew by this Means, even in the Time of the Normans Government; and had they not been so often exhausted by foreign Wars, peel'd and pol'd by their tyrant Princes, ravag'd and wasted at home by one another, I mean in civil Dissentions, and plunder'd and emptied by the foolish and ridiculous Zeal, or rather Fury, call'd the Holy War, they might have been infinitely richer than they were.

LET but any Man of Figures calculate the Commerce at that Time; the Wool only that was exported, at the Rate above mentioned, amounted to two Millions Sterling in Specie; an immense Sum, and more than Ten Millions per Annum would be now.

IT is indeed very strange, that when every Thing else was so cheap, the Wool should be so dear, and that now, when every Thing else is so dear, the Wool should be so cheap; we only are left in some Uncertainty as to what was then called a Pack of Wool, and how they could give such a Price for it; if the Pack was the same then as it is now, the Price was intolerable, perhaps it might be made up in such large Packs, as we still see sometimes brought into Norfolk, one of which loads a Waggon, and is called a Poke of Wool, or a Pocket; but that we cannot now determine: But be the Bulk what it will, the Number of Packs was the same.

AGAIN, the Pack of Wool must be much larger than it is now, otherwise the Quantity of Wool produced in England was but trifling; for as to 50000 Packs of Wool to be the whole Crop, or the whole Product, 'tis ridiculous to suggest it, 'tis evident we import more than twice that Quantity now yearly from Ireland, in Wool or in Yarn; the Wool of England is more likely to amount to five Hundred Thousand Packs, than to fifty Thousand; and we are assured, as you will see, by a just Calculation in its Place, that the Sheep fed in Rumney Mash only in Kent, make 2523 Packs of Wool every Year; which, were the whole calculated, is not a two Hundredth Part of the Wool of the whole Country.

BUT to leave our Guesses at the Magnitude of the Pack of Wool, I am ready to grant it must be larger than ours are now, which are but two hundred and forty Pound Weight to a Pack, and could never be worth forty Pound Sterling; but if a Pack was a Poke, and weighed twenty Hundred Weight, as the Poke of Wool still does, and is called in some Places a Load of Wool, because 'tis a Waggon Load, then indeed it might yield such a Rate (tho' dear too) and it also agrees best with the Growth or Crop of Wool in England, which would then be about 400000 Packs a Year, and it was an immense Business of its Kind too, for the Time of Day in Trade.

THAT this Trade was really a Prodigy for Magnitude, at that Time, appears by many Particular Circumstances; and especially by this, that great Increase of Wealth and People, which the Manufacturing of it brought to the Netherlands, that is, to the seventeen Provinces, whose Greatness, as well as ours, began here.

NOR is it SO long ago that this Trade receiv'd a Turn, that we should want Evidence of the Fact, for it continued in the same Situation to the Time of Henry the VII. and tho' we began then (by the Wisdom and Sagacity of the Prince) to break in upon the Flemings, and to manufacture much of our Wool at home, yet we find no Prohibition of the Exportation of Wool, till the Reign of Queen Elizabeth,; for the Fifth of Edward VI. we find a large Fleet of Flemings laden with Wool, sail'd from Southampton for the Scheld, being above sixty Sail, that Wool being sent to pay the King's Debts.

I have met with some who are of the Opinion, that the Trade of the Netherlands in the Woollen Manufacture, was much greater then, than it is now here, or than it has ever been since; and they give these Reasons for it,

1. THAT if they had not had a most extensive consumption, they could never have been able to have consumed such a Quantity of Wool; for England being not enclosed and cultivated then, as it is now, they suppose the Quantity of Wool was much greater, than it has been at any time since.

2. THAT they had no Rivals in the Trade; no other Nation, for many Ages, having any such thing as a woolen Manufacture among them; and this gave them such a Command of the Trade, as to be able to give a Price for the Materials, and to sell the Manufacture when wrought at a Rate in Proportion.

3. THAT by the same Rule they had all the Trade; and tho' it is true, they had not extended the woollen Manufacture into Turky, Russia, and to both the Indies, as it is now, and to several other remote Countries; yet, on the other hand, they had the whole Extent of France, Spain, and the German Empire, Poland, Sweden, and Denmark, to supply with Goods; none of those Countries making any thing of a Woollen Manufacture; and as at length, the Dominions of the Netherlands fell to the House of Austria, and that Spain, Germany, Italy, and the whole seventeen Provinces, were united under one Head, in the Government of that great Monarch Charles V. they were allowed an unlimited Commerce through all his Dominions, and had all possible Encouragement for their Goods, of which I might give many Particulars.

THESE things considered, it must be granted, that their Trade was exceeding great; whether it was equal or superior to our Trade of the same kind now, is what no body can make any Calculation of: And therefore I shall not attempt to form any Plan or View of Trade upon those remote Guesses.

THE Turn given to this Trade afterward, and the Wealth raised upon it in England in so short a Space, as was seen in Queen Elizabeth's Time, may give us some Idea of what it was before; and this part indeed cannot without a Breach in our Work, as it is proposed in my Title, be quite pass'd over; but I shall be as brief in it as I can.

THAT King Henry VII. was the first Prince that put the English upon the Thought of manufacturing their own Wool, must be acknowledged to his Memory; we should not do him Justice, if we did not mention it, as often as the Original of our Woollen Manufacture is spoken of.

HE had been a kind of a Refugee in the Court of his Aunt the Dutchess of Burgundy, being forc'd to make his Escape from Bretagne, where he first harbour'd; while he was here, he had opportunity to see as well as hear of the mighty Increase and Improvement of the Commerce of those Countries; how populous their Cities, how rich their Burghers, how great their Merchants, how all the People were busy, and employ'd; hardly a Child above five Years old, but could do something to gain its Bread; and particularly, it could not escape his Observation, that all this Commerce, all this Wealth, all this Imployment of the People depended entirely upon the Supply of the Materials, viz. The Wool and Fullers Earth from England; that they had not a Pack of Wool of their own in the whole

Country, and if that Source should by any Accident be stopped, they should be all ruin'd, their Trade would be at a full Stop, and in a Word, that the Manufacture could not be carried on without it.

To a Prince of such Penetration as he was, it could not but occur after he came to the Crown, that certainly England was much in the wrong, to let their Wool go out of the Country thus unmanufactur'd, and to let Strangers be made rich by the working of it, while his own People sat idle and unemployed, and consequently starving the Poor.

THAT without doubt, where the Principals and Materials of the Manufacture were only to be found, there Nature seem'd to direct the making of the Manufacture it self, and there it might be wrought with the greatest Advantage; that, at least, it would be an Advantage to his own Kingdom, and that he could see no Reason why that Advantage should be given away. In short, he resolved, that if he could prevent it, Strangers should no longer eat the Bread out of the Mouths of his own Subjects.

I need not enter here into the particular Measures the King took to put this happy Resolve of his in Execution; 'tis enough to mention it here, that in Persuit of these Observations, he immediately set about the Work, applied himself to the finding out proper Instruments for the carrying it on, and set the Manufacture of Wool on Foot in several Parts of his Country, as particularly at Wakefield, Leeds and Hallifax, in the West Riding of Yorkshire, a Country pitch'd upon for its particular Situation, adapted to the Work, being fill'd with innumerable Springs of Water, Pits of Coal, and other Things proper for carrying on such a Business, and where it remains and thrives to this Day.

BUT not, I say, to enter into the Particulars of this historically, which would be too tedious, 'tis sufficient to say, the anxious Care of this Prince for the Prosperity of his People has been followed with such a glorious Success, that the Example is perfectly fitted to fire the Breast of any succeeding Monarch, who desires the Good of his Subjects with the same paternal Warmth for the general improvement; and for this End I mention it, and for this End these Sheets are thus addressed to the supreme Powers of the British Government, and at this Time too; because, being assur'd that his present Majesty has the same Ardour and Affection, the same improving Genius, and the Advantage of a much greater Fund of Wealth and Power for the advancing the Interest of his People, nothing may be wanting to lay open the several Prospects for the farther improving the Commerce and extending the Manufactures of England which yet remain, and which perhaps have not been so thorowly consider'd of by any other Hand.

THO' King Henry acted with a Vigor becoming a Prince, and one that knew how to execute, as well as how to resolve, for the Advantage of his own Dominions; yet he knew withal, that it was an Attempt of such a Magnitude, as well deserv'd the utmost Prudence and Caution, that as it was not to be attempted rashly; so it was not to be push'd with too much Warmth: And therefore, tho' he did not fail to encourage his People in working and manufacturing, and at a considerable Expence, secretly procured a great many Foreigners, who were perfectly skill'd in the Manufacture, to come over and instruct his own People here in their Beginnings; yet he did not immediately prohibit the exporting the Wool to the Flemings, neither did he, till some Tears after, load the Exportation of it with any more Duties than he had before.

NAY, so far was the King from being able to compleat his Design, that he could never come to a total Prohibition of exporting the Wool in his Reign; he did indeed offer at it, but found, that if he had proceeded, his People were not Masters enough of the Trade to work up the whole Quantity of the Wool, and consume the Growth; that the Flemings were old in the business, long experiene'd, and turn'd their Hands this Way and that Way, to new Sorts and Kinds of Goods, which the English could not presently know, and when known, had not Skill presently to imitate: And that therefore they must proceed gradually.

BESIDES, if in some Years the English were able to supply themselves, and make Goods enough for the Home Consumption, so that they had no need to buy from the Flemings the Manufactures of their own Wool, This was a great Point gain'd, and was a Step sufficient for the first Ages of the Manufacture; whereas, to have prohibited the Wool being carry'd out while they were not able to supply the Markets abroad, was to ruin the Trade in general, and stop the Consumption of the Wool too.

ON the contrary, the King acted like a wise and warlike Prince, besieging a City, who tho' he attacks the Garrison, and batters the Out-works with the utmost Fury, yet spares the Inhabitants, and forbears as much as he can ruining the City, which he expects to make his own: So the King seem'd willing to let the Flemings keep up the Trade, till his Subjects were thoro'ly enabled to take it into their own Hands, and not destroy a Commerce, which he knew would one Time or other be his own.

UPON this Foot, I say, the prudent Prince went on by Measures perfectly well adjusted, and particularly adapted to the End which he aim'd at; and tho' he did once pretend to stop the Exportation of the Wool, he conniv'd at the Breach of his Order, and afterwards took off the Prohibition entirely, leaving the Success of his Undertaking, to the Industry of his People, who, he perceiv'd, to his great Satisfaction, went on with Courage and Chearfulness, improv'd daily, and would at last entirely carry the Business from the Flemings, by the meer Course of Things.

IN this Manner the Manifacture began, and thus gradually it encreas'd; nor was it much less than one hundred Years, before Englandcame to such a Perfection, h as to be able to claim the Property of it to themselves, and to prohibit the Exportation of the Wool, which was never effectually done, til the Spanish Tyranny under the Duke d'Alva finish'd the ruin of the Commerce of the Netherlands, by driving the Dutch into a Common-Wealth, to cast off entirely the Spanish Government; and by forcing the Protestant Flemings, who, indeed, were the chief Manufacturers, to take Shelter in England, where they presently erected all the several Species of the Manufacture, which were not set up before.

THUS it was, from the Year 1489, when King Henry VII. began to encourage the Manufacture in England, to the Year 1587, when Queen Elizabeth may be said to see it arriv'd to its Perfection, that this great Work was gradually encreasing and bringing forward.

IT is worth observing here, in how short a Time the Queen having fully stop'd the Stream of Wool which supported the Manufacture in Flanders, spread the Commerce of England, into the remotest Parts of the then known World, and carry'd the Trade of the woollen Manufacture of England, into every Part which the Flemings had supply'd before, and to many Places where they had no Business.

1. The Dutch, who were erected into a separate State under the Queen's Protection, and who breaking off from the Flemings, that is, from the Spaniards, had no Commerce with them, meddled no twith Manufacturing, but apply'd themselves to their fishing Trade, and to foreign Merchandize; and having before a very great Correspondence by their Rivers, viz. the Maes, the Rhyne, and other Rivers into Germany, they naturally apply'd to England for the woollen Manufacture, which they had formerly been supply'd with from Flanders, and were, as we may call them, our first Customers for them Abroad.

2. THE Queen heartily engag'd in the Interest of her People, and particularly espousing her Merchants, sent formal Embassies, with splendid Retinues, and in the most honourable Manner, for the opening the Sluices of Trade to her Subjects; 1. To the Grand Seignior; 2. To the Great Duke, or Emperor of Russia or Muscovy; 3. To the Great Mogul; 4. To the King of Persia, and in a Word, to every other Place, whither her enterprising Subjects desir'd her; for it was at that Time an enterprising Age, and the English Merchants spread the Seas with their Ships, as the Poet expresses it, every where as far

As Winds could carry, or as Waters roll.

3. UNDER her Majesty's Conduct, and by her particular Encouragement, her fortunate Navigators, her Merchants, and other Adventurers began to shew themselves, not experienc'd only in, but Patrons and Improvers of Navigation, beyond all the Trades of the World; they rang'd about the Seas having then no Rivals; searching the Globe for Discoveries, planting Colonies, and settling Factories in all Parts of the World; But I must come to speak of this Part again more at large.

BY this last Part of the Queen's Management, (viz.) prohibiting the Exportation of the Wool, the woollen Manufacture in the Netherlands receiv'd its fatal Wound; the Spanish cruelty scatter'd the chief Manufacturers, and the Prohibition starv'd those that were left; for now having no more Wool to work up, the Work it self stop'd at once, the Trade expir'd and dy'd: Nor has it been able since that to revive, no not in the least Degree; for as it depended before entirely, upon the Supply of Wool from England for its Support, when that Stream fail'd, when that Chanel stop'd, it could no more subsist, than a Body without Food, or Life without Spirits: In a word, the Flemings impoverish'd and poor, dispersed and fled; their great Cities, such as Antwerp, Ghent Lisle, and other Places wasted and decay'd; the People went away into other Parts to seek Peace and Employment; the populous Towns became thin of Inhabitants, compar'd to what they were; and the new establish'd Common-Wealth of Holland became populous and rich, out of their Ruins.

THE People who remain'd, and who are yet numerous, tho' not like what they were before, apply'd to other Works, such as Lace, Linen, and particularly fine Thread, fine Cambricks, and whatever else offer'd, for it must be own'd they are a most industrious People.

THEY are now further reduc'd in their Bounds by the French, who have taken from them the whole Province of Artois, and great Part of Flanders, and Hainault; and especially, the Port of Dunkirk, and the great Cities of Arras, Cambray, Doway, Lisle, St. Omers, and many others, so that the remaining Part, which is now call'd the Netherlands, is but small, compar'd to what it was; and their Trade is chiefly confin'd to the merchandizing Part, which they carry on by the River Navigation with Holland, on one Side, and with France on the other, and by the Manufacture as above, of Lace and Linen: As to the woollen Manufactures, they are oblig'd to give them over, and to buy them of their Supplanters the English, to whom they formerly sold them.

THIS being the antient State of our Commerce, and from which it deriv'd its Being, I thought it absolutely necessary to give this Summary of it, that we may have

no Occasion to look back any more, but begin the Plan of its subsequent Improvements at this general Epocha, as from its real Fountain Head, and as it is properly an English Commerce.

THE Improvements of our Trade from this Time are no less wonderful; its present Magnitude I call a Prodigy, and I think it well deserves that Name. How it come to arrive to such a Height, and how it may be farther improved and increased in Spite of all the Prohibitions and Encroachments of its Neighbours, remains to be discours'd of.

Chapter 4

Of the encrease of the English commerce, from the time of Queen Elizabeth's breaking with the Spaniard

IN the last Chapter, I mention'd the Inclination Queen Elizabeth had to propagate the Interest of her People; and especially, that of their Commerce. I must observe here, as an additional Remark, that this Warmth of the Queen their Sovereign, fir'd her Subjects with an inexpressible Ardor for new Discoveries, planting Colonies, finding out unknown Passages, settling Factories, engaging in new Correspondences for Trade, and the like; and in this Reign, and in pursuit of this new Principle, (for it was new at that Time), they began several of the present most flourishing Branches of our present Commerce, and where our woollen Manufactures are now best establish'd: For Example,

1. THE Queen sending an Embassy, as I have said, to Muscovy, the English Merchants obtain'd Licenses of the Great Duke for a certain Number of them to pass with their Merchandize thro' his vast Dominions into Persia, where they carried their English Cloth, Kerseys, Bays, Says, &c. and sold them to great Advantage, and brought back their Returns by the same Way 2500 Miles upon the River Wolga, 800 Miles upon the Dwina to Arch-Angel; besides crossing the Caspian Sea, and besides their Journey by Land to Ispahan. These were afterwards call'd the Russia Company, and indeed, they carry'd on a very noble and gainful Commerce, as well to themselves, as to their Country, till it was afterwards interrupted by the meer absolute Tyranny of the Muscovite Emperor or Great Duke, without any Offence given, and without so much as a Pretence of any.

THIS Journey, besides the Voyage by Sea, between London and Arch-Angel, then also newly discover'd, was five Times perform'd by one Merchant of London, whose Name was Lancaster, as may at large be seen in Huckluyt's Voyages.

2. THE Queen having by an Ambassador, as I have said, establish'd a Treaty of Peace and Commerce with Solyman the magnificent, the Great Emperor of the Turks; Her Merchants immediately follow'd with their Ships; and the Turky Company being by that means erected and establish'd, they settled their Factories at Constantinople, Smirna, and at Aleppo, where the Trade flourish'd and encreased to a very great Magnitude, and continues to this Day.

3. THE War with Spain encouraging her Majesty's Subjects to farther Adventures, partly for Reprisals upon the Spaniard, and partly for Discoveries, Sir Walter Raleigh, Drake, Smith, and others, upon the meer Account of Commerce, discover'd and planted the great, and now flourishing Colonies of Hudson's-Bay, New England, Virginia, and Burmoodas, with the Fishery of Newfoundland; the Magnitude and Commerce of which Countries, is not easily to be described; and to which are since then added, the Island Colonies of America, called in com-

mon the West-Indies, such as Barbados, Nevis, Antegoa, St. Christophers, &c. and at last Jamaica; and upon the Continent, New-York, with East and West Jersey, obtain'd by Conquest from the Dutch, and Pensilvania and Carolina, obtain'd by more modern and extended Discoveries.

To and from these, the Advantage of the English Commerce is such at this Time in the Consumption of European Goods sent thither, and particularly the British Product, and their Manufactures of Linen, Woollen and Silk; in the Numbers of Seamen and Ships employ'd, and in the Returns made from thence, as also the vast Wealth acquir'd there in Plantations, Buildings, Value of Lands, Slaves:, &c. that it is a Doubt not easily resolv'd whether is greater in real Value, the Silver return'd to Spain yearly by the Galleons, or the Sugars, Ginger, Tobacco, Rice, Furrs, Fish, and other Product of America returned to England, and to other Parts on English Account.

To such an immense Greatness is the Trade grown, such a Consumption is made of the English Merchandizes, such Cities and Towns are built, Countries, nay Kingdoms peopled and inhabited, and such a Fund of Wealth and Commerce is raised, that it is not to be estimated.

4. IN the same enterprising Times, was the Trade to the Gold Coast of Africa begun; a Trade founded upon the most clear Principles of Commerce; namely, the meanest Export exchang'd for the richest Return; a Trade carry'd on with surprising Success, while justly countenanc'd by the Authority which own'd its beginning; and a Trade still holding up its Head, tho' so strangely, unaccountably, and contrary to the true Interest of Trade in general, as well as of England in particular, abandon'd and forsaken at last! And I ask leave to say, I think 'tis the only national Advantage in Commerce, which seems to be neglected in England; it waits, however, for better Times; and I cannot doubt, but as it is capable (were it freed from the Invasions of Interlopers) of being made the most flourishing Trade of its kind in the World; so it will still recover it self, and flourish in a manner few People expect, because they do not see it possible; which however, I shall demonstrate, upon proper Occasion, to be both possible and easy.

5. BESIDES all these particular Steps taken for the Encrease of Trade, the Export of the English Manufactures to Holland, mention'd above, took its beginning in this Queen's Reign, by the natural Consequence of the commanding Influence the Queen had over all the Affairs, as well as in the Affections of the Dutch: The Hollanders ador'd the Queen, and esteem'd her, as she really was, their great Patroness and Protector, and in Return, they omitted nothing that would oblige her, or her People; and particularly the encouraging and propagating the Consumption of the English Manufacture was their particular Care, knowing they could do nothing that could oblige her Majesty more.

THIS Part was indeed one of the main Articles, in which the Growth of the Manufacture at that Time consisted; for as to the rest, tho' they were Foundations on which the future Greatness of the Manufacture of Wool was very much rais'd; yet, as I said of King Henry VII's Part, so it was here, it was many Years, and not till long after the Queen's Death, that the Harvest of that Spring Time of Trade was reap'd.

(N. B. THE Success of those glorious Attempts for the Encrease of Commerce, and the generous Care for the Prosperity of the Nation, tho' the Issue could not be seen, or the Advantage be reap'd till some Ages after, is a noble Patern for the Princes, and for the Legislature of the present Age; moving them to lay such Foundations, as present themselves for the future Advantage of their Subjects, tho' the Benefit should not immediately be felt, and tho' the Prospect be something remote, of which something farther remains in the Design of this Work.)

THESE, I say, were the Beginnings of foreign Trade in England, and from hence the home Manufactures rais'd themselves: These were the Beginnings, upon which the immense Business carry'd on in England at this time has been rai'sd: This was the Time, when (as I said above) England gave herself a loose in Trade, and got the Start of all her Neighbours, and like a strong Horse in a Race, who having shot a Head of the rest at their first setting out, by the Skill of the Rider, holds it all the way, bymeer Strength, as well as Speed.

THE Advantages gain'd by the War with Spain, gave England such a Start of her Neighbours in this single Reign, in matters of Commerce, as the whole World could never overtake her in to this Day; the Discoveries made in America are an Example of this; England began, and being early, carv'd for her self, nor did she lose her Time; the French put in as soon as they perceiv'd it, but found all the North Coast of America gone, and possest by the English, and were glad to take up with what was left, (viz.) to run into the great and dangerous Gulph of St. Lawrence, take up with the frozen and wild Countries of Canada, and plant behind the English, remote from the Sea, and out of the Way of Commerce, except by that one Port; by all which Inconveniences they have been always so crampt in Trade, they have made but mean Advances in a Hundred and fifty Years Possession: As to their Louisiana and Mississipi, it has indeed been made a Bubble at Home, and but little better Abroad, having only starv'd, or otherwise devour'd most of the People that have been sent over to it.

AMONG the Islands the French came a little more timely, and so got a better Share than any other of their Neighbours, except the English; for they got Martinico Guadaloup, Tortuga, and a part of St. Christopher's, and several other Places, which they profitably hold to this Day.

THE Dutch came last, got little upon the Continent, and lost that little they had got to the English, viz. New York, and East and West Jersy; so that they have nothing to call their own on that Side; no, nor have they one Island of any Consequence; they got a footing in the Brasils indeed, and held it above twenty Years, but were driven out of it again by plain Force, even by the Portuguese: Those very People, who on other Occasions they so much contemned, and who, in other Places, they drove before them, as Wolves disperse a Flock of Sheep.

ALL they have now left in America, is the two small Colonies of Surinam and Curacao, of no Import, or worth naming, and hardly worth their keeping, except for a clandestine Trade carried on there with the Spaniard on the Coast of Caraccas; which is now also likely to be entirely lost, and then the Intrinsick of the Product will be their only Benefit, which will appear very small.

ON the contrary, How are these Colonies of the English increas'd and improv'd, even to such a Degree, that some have suggested, tho' not for Want of Ignorance, a Danger of their revolting from the English Government, and setting up an Independency of Power for themselves.

IT is true, the Notion is absurd, and without Foundation, but serves to confirm what I have said above of the real Encrease of those Colonies, and of the flourishing Condition of the Commerce carried on there.

How great a Consumption of the British Manufacture has the Encrease of these Colonies been to this Nation? Let the yearly Export of all Kinds of Goods from hence to New-England, Virginia, Barbadoes, and Jamaica, besides all the lesser Colonies, be a Proof of it: Above a Thousand Sail of stout Ships are constantly running between England and those Countries, above another Thousand are employed in coasting and traversing the Seas between the Islands and the Continent, including the Fishing Trade; besides the Numbers of Sloops continually waiting upon the Trade in Virginia, which they tell us are double the Number of all the rest.

I have omitted the Trade to India, as an Article made so much less advantageous to England, by our own Mismanagement, than it might have been, that I see but little to boast of in it: But the general Commerce is my Business, especially in those Parts where our Manufactures are particularly concerned.

THE next to the Dutch, (with whom we carry on such an immense Trade, that it was affirm'd to the Parliament in a particular Debate upon that Subject, that they took off two Millions yearly of our Woollen Manufacture only) I say, next to these our Trade with Hamburgh and the Baltick has been carried on to such an exceeding Degree, and so encreased of late, that notwithstanding several Prohibitions and Invasions upon the Manufacture lately appearing in Germany, in Bar of our Manufacture, our Trade thither is yet superior to all the other Nations; and in a Word is so great, as perhaps is beyond all Conjecture.

THE Turkey Trade has been carried on in the most regular Manner imaginable, from its first Establishment spoken of above: Its Encrease is visible, and as the Returns are to be duly estimated, and we can make it appear to be encreased from thirty or forty Thousand Pound Sterling a Year, to upwards of 300000 l. Value in a Year.

THE Export of our Manufacture to Italy, France and Spain, and particularly to Portugal, how are they advanc'd upon the first Establishment made in Queen Elizabeth'sTime: It is true, France, by our egregious Folly, is lost to us in some Sense; but how it is in Portugal, by the Encrease of their Colonies in the Brasils, and on both the Coasts of Africa South of the Line; I say, how has the Consumption of the British Woollen Manufacture encreased among them; so that I am assur'd the Portuguese alone take off more English Woollen Manufacture at this Time, than ever Spain and France, put together, took off from us before.

THE Trade to Italy, especially to Leghorn and Genoa, Messina and Venice, is the same, and under the same Proportion of Improvement. To this Prodigy of Magnitude is the British Manufacture arriv'd, and all built upon the solid Foundations layd by that glorious Princess: She opened all these Doors, she sent out all those Adventurers, she planted all those Colonies, or made Way for the plant-ing them; she circled the Globe by her Mariners, she founded the Commerce of both the Indies, of Africa, of Holland, and Hamburgh, the Levant, and the Baltick Seas.

SHE did not live indeed to see the Animosity of the Spanish War abated, much less brought to an End, or the Haughtiness of that proud Nation humbled into a settled Friendship and Commerce, as was afterwards done; but it was all found-ed on her Conduct; for Example, ON the Foot of her Establishments, the Ameri-can Colonies are since brought to that flourishing State in which we now see they stand; on her laying the Foundation of the Turkey, the East India, the Hol-land, and the East Country Trades, they are grown up to what we now see them.

BUT above all, and what I have not mentioned before, the Naval Glory of Eng-land, is all raised upon her prudent exerting her Strength at Sea; she shew'd the Spaniard, that however superior his Forces were on Shore (and it must be al-lowed his Armies were at that Time formidable, and his Troops, as well as his Generals, the best in the World) yet, I say, her Majesty shew'd him, that her Wooden Walls were her sufficient Defence; that she built her Strength for War as well as for Commerce, upon the invincible Power of her Fleets, and the Courage and Bravery of her Seamen. By this she carried her Arms to the Doors of her Enemies, and visited them with her Terrors in their remotest Situation.

BY these she took Cadiz, burnt the Galleons, with twenty Millions of Treasure in them, insulted Lisbon, (then in the Hands of Spain) ravaged the Coast of Galitia, and in a Word made all Spain tremble: By these she seiz'd the Islands and planted the Continent, landed upon the Coasts, plundered the Cities, destroyed the Shipping, and took immense Wealth from the Spaniards in America.

IN a Word, she cover'd the Seas with her Men of War, and like King George, let the Enemies of England see, that they that command the Sea, awe the World, and that to be Masters of the marine Power, is to be Masters of all the Power, and all the Commerce in Europe, Asia, Africa, and America.

NOR was this all, but the Queen by thus exerting her Naval Power, encreas'd it; nay, she took the best and the only Way to enlarge and encrease it; the Success at Sea made Seamen, as her Success in Trade made Merchants: To speak the Truth, all her Subjects were fir'd with new Thoughts; the very Nobility, and first Rate Gentlemen, fell into it, the Cliffords Earls of Cumberland, Sir John Hawkins, Sir Thomas Cavendish, Sir Richard Greenville of the Devonshire Family, since Earls of Bath, the Earl of Essex, Sir Walter Raleigh, and Multitudes more: Some com-manded Ships, some Troops; some planted Colonies, some supply'd Stocks; some ventur'd their Lives, some their Estates; all something: The Trade, the War, the Sea, emulated one another; all the Nation was in a kind of Flame.

THE Seamen returned enriched with the Plunder, not of Ships, but of Fleets, Loaden with Silver; they went out Beggars, and came home Gentlemen; nay, the Wealth they brought Home, not only enrich'd themselves, but the whole Nation.

THIS made the People run to Sea, as Country Folks to a Fair; and all the young Fellows turn'd Seamen as naturally as if they had been born so: The Multitude of

Ships and Sailors in England grew so great, that, in a Word, they, as it were, covered the Seas; every Part of the World was visited, and the Queen reign'd as it were Mistress of the Ocean; nor do we learn by History or Tradition, that the Queen ever prest any Seamen; Her glorious Successes at Sea both in publick and private Adventures, animated her People so, that they crouded into the Service on all Hands; and whatever Adventure was on Foot, they never wanted Hands.

THUS the Queen, I say, by exerting her Naval Strength, encreased it; and that to such a Degree, that no Power on Earth, during her whole Reign, was able to match her at Sea; nay, I believe I do not carry it too far, if I say, she was at that Time able to have fought all the Maritime Powers of Christendom at Sea, had they been all in Confederacy together; and this I speak of the Number of her Seamen and Ships, not at all insisting on the Goodness of her Seamen: tho' it must be allow'd, that her Seamen, flush'd with Spanish Prizes, were the best and the boldest at that Time, of any Sailors in the World: But that is a Subject by it self.

I return to the Subject; as it is now, so it was then; Spain could not bring home her American Treasures, without her Majesty's Leave; and with this addition too, that almost as often as they ventur'd to do it, they miscarried; which has not yet been our Case.

HERE began the formidable Strength, as well as Trade of England, to shew it self, the World scarce ever heard of an English Navy till then; the Emperor Charles the fifth had powerful Fleets, when he carried on his Wars with so much Glory against France, against the Turks (then very formidable at Sea) and against the Rovers of Tunis and Algier; and his Son King Philip had indeed great Navies, when he carried on his Wars against the Dutch, not then form'd into a State; and when he fitted that terrible Fleet against England, called Invincible, and which had been truly invincible, had not Heaven and Earth, as it were, fought against it in Conjunction.

BUT the World scarce ever heard of an English Man of War (so by the Iniquity of Custom we call our Ships of War) much less of an English Navy till Queen Elizabeth.

WITH our naval Power grew up our Commerce, as if like Twins they were born together, and not to live asunder; What had been all her new settled Plantations, all her Infant Colonies? they had Difficulties almost unsurmountable in their very Beginning, Difficulties found in the very Nature of their Undertakings, and which follow'd in the Consequence of the Thing; (viz.) planting among the barbarous Nations, and lying at the Mercy of the Savages: How often famish'd, and frozen to Death by the Severity of the Climates, and Want of Supplies? How often massacred by the treacherous Natives? How often driven, to abandon the Settlements they had made? And had the Spaniard too been able to have attack'd them by Sea, had not the Queen always kept herself in a Condition to defend them, and to protect their Commerce, all the Discoveries they had made, and the Colonies they had planted, like ill Births had been strangled in the bringing forth; and all had fallen back to the Spaniard, by the meer Consequence of their Naval Power.

BUT the Queen was the Life of all that Glory; her adventurous Subjects found out the Places, planted and settled them, and as well as they could, fortified themselves against the Bow and Arrow Enemies, which they found in the Place.

BUT 'twas the Queen's Naval Strength that was their Security; by this she kept the Spaniards Hands full, that they had no Time to bestow in attacking the newly planted Merchants; nor had they Ships to spare, they were met with in every Corner, fought with on every Coast, and which was more, beaten almost as often as fought with, on whatever Occasion.

UNDER this Protection the Commerce encreased. Trade got Ground, the English Nation swelled into an Empire of Nations, and the English Merchants carried a general Negoce to all the Quarters of the World.

HAVING thus look'd back a little upon Things past, I shall say a Word or two to Things present, and conclude with Things yet to come.

Chapter 5

Of the present state of the English commerce, especially that part of it which relates to the woollen manufacture; the prodigy of its magnitude, and some enquiry into how it may be call'd great, and what that magnitude really is

BY what has been said, we are a little let into the Beginning of Things, and English Men of Trade may see their glorious Original; how they receiv'd Life, as we may call it, from the Powerful Influences, and Paternal Concern of their sagacious Princes; and how they became a trading Nation. Take a Summary of it again in the following Abstract.

HEAVEN bestow'd the Wool upon them, the Life and i Soul, the Original of all their Commerce; he gave it them and gave it exclusive of all the Nations in the World; for none comes up to it.

Their King (Henry VII.) open'd their Eyes to the Blessing, and put them upon manufacturing it, after they had, for almost a Thousand Years of Ignorance, sold it to the diligent Flemings; and even bought their own Cloaths of them again, after they were made with it Abroad.

Their glorious Queen, (Elizabeth) shewed them the Way to find a Market for it, when manufactur'd; she open'd the Sluices of Trade to them, and Trade open'd the Sluices of Money. In a Word, she made them a Trading Nation, and that has made them a rich Nation, as we see them at this Time.

BUT I am called upon to describe the Magnitude of this Commerce, and shew the World, that we do not boast of its Greatness without Cause; that Strangers may know what we say of it, is not made up of Bluster and Wind, and that even those that read it among our own People, may be able to support and explain what they shall, upon any Occasion, advance of the real Greatness of our Trade.

THE Funds of Trade in any Nation, and upon which the Commerce that is rais'd, is with Propriety said to be the Trade of that Nation, must be contain'd in these Two.

THE Produce of the Soil, and.

THE Labour of the People.

Now, if I make it appear, that in both these the Trade of England is greater than that of any other Nation, I hope I may be supposed sufficiently to have prov'd the Magnitude of it.

1. THE Produce of the Soil.

AND here, that I may make all Things plain and easy as I go, and leave as little Room for Cavil as possible, I demand to explain briefly the Term Product or Produce: By Produce, as to Trade:, I am to be understood to mean, not that Part of our Produce, be it of what Kind it will, that is consumed at Home, and is employ'd by our People; for this does not relate to the Trade of the Kingdom, as I understand Trade in this Discourse; that is to say. Our foreign Trade:: By this Exception I take out all the vast Consumption of Corn, Cattle, Coal, Fish, Fowl, or whatever of our own Growth is consum'd unmanufactur'd; and tho' this makes an inexpressible Sum, and employs a Multitude of those of our People we call Shopkeepers, Carriers, Coasting Sailors, with Servants, Labourers and Horses; Ships, Barges Boats, Carts and Carriages innumerable, and that a vast Wealth is raised by this part of Trade; yet, I say, this is not the Article, or Branch of our Trade that I am in particular now describing: But by the Produce of the Soil here, I mean such part of its Growth as is exported beyond the Seas. What is consum'd at Home, will come under another Head. This includes,

1. WOOL, the greatest and best of our trading Produce, the Soul and Life of our whole Commerce, and the Fund of all our Prosperity and Success in that Commerce.

2. CORN, so much as is exported only.

3. COALS and Leather, also exported.

4. TIN and Lead, Iron and Copper.

5. FISH and Salt. I suppose no thinking Man will object that Fish being the Produce of the Sea, and not of the Soil, is not to be call'd a Produce.

6. Tobacco, Sugars and Ginger.

7. Rum, Melasses, Indigo.

8. Cocoa, Pimento, and THE Produce of our Colon- Drugs.

9. Furrs and Skins of Thing as our own Pro-Beasts.

10. Turpentine, Rice, Cotton,

11. Timber, Masts, and Planks.

The Produce of our Colonies which the same Thing as our Produce

THE Magnitude of our Trade, founded upon these Productions, will appear, when they are considered apart, and when the Labour of the People, being added to the Value, shall so far double and redouble the Sum, as the Nature of the Things respectively shall admit.

THE Labour of the People is the next article. This is supposed to be rated according to the Thing they labour about, and is to be added to the intrinsick Value of the Materials; which being so join'd, the Work finish'd is call'd Manufacture.

1. The Wool, as it is the first and greatest Produce, so it is the first and principal Manufacture; an Estimate of its Value, as Wool, is as difficult to be made, as of its Quantity; the Numbers of People it employs are not to be reckon'd by Thousands, but by Millions; the Places in Britain where the Work is managed and carried on, are not to be measured by Towns, and Districts of Towns, Villages, or Lordships, but by Counties, Provinces, Parts and Quarters of the Island: As it is a Product every where; so every where we see more or less of the People employ'd in it: The best Measure we can take to give you an Idea of its Magnitude, is to tell you, that it works up, and consumes not only all the Wool produced by the Sheep of this whole Island, the Cattle upon a thousand Hills, but it calls for a prodigious quantity from Abroad.

(N. B. I suppose I am much within Compass, when I say, that in the Fleece and in Yarn, we import 100000 Packs of Wool every year from Ireland, besides all the Wool of Scotland, which, since the Union, is generally brought to England, to be manufactured; and whose Quantity, as represented at the Time of that Treaty, was rated in the Parliament there, to be worth 60000 Pound Sterling per Annum.)

They that would examine into the Quantity of Wool used in England, must make an Estimate of the Numbers of the Sheep fed here, which it would be very hard to do; but let them view the Country where those Sheep are generally rais'd and fed, or enquire of those who have view'd it critically, and let them see the innumerable Flocks of Sheep fed constantly in the several Parts of England, following.

I. Romney Marsh, an Extent of Land for about 20 Miles long, and 10 Miles broad, of the best and richest kind of Sheep Ground. I name this Place first, because I can give an authentick Account of its Extent, and from thence may give you likewise something more than a rough Guess at the Produce of it in Wool.

THE Flat Country, commonly call'd Romney Marsh, includes some other Lands of the same Nature, and lying all in the same Level, but of which Romney is the Chief, and therefore gives its Name to all the rest, the Quantities of Land they contain, and upon which they are rated in their Level Books:, stand thus.

Acres.

Romney and Walland Marsh-----------40000
Gulford Marsh--------------------------3000
Bromehill--------------------------------906
Denge Marsh----------------------------2912
New Romney Level----------------------292

──────
47110

The ordinary Bounds of this great Level, are by Estimation, from Rye Harbour, or Guldford Marsh, East to the Town or Port of Hithe West, 20 Miles, and from South to North; that is to say, from Lydon the Sea Shore South, to Warchorn North, which is suppos'd to be a Medium of the Breadth, at least ten Miles.

As all (or all to a Trifle of) this Land, is employ'd in breeding and feeding of Sheep, they reckon the stated Number of Sheep to Stock, the whole, that is to say, of Weathers and Ewes, which produce Fleece Wool, is three Sheep to an Acre.

(N. B. THE Lambs, of which a very great Number, are every Year sold off, are not included.)

So that the Number of Sheep, and consequently the Number of Fleeces of Wool raised in this Level, is 141330 Fleeces.

OF these 'tis usually reckon'd, that 14 Fleeces, one with another, make a Draft, and four Drafts make a Pack of Wool; so that 56 Fleeces make a Pack, each Pack weighing 240 Pound; and, thus

THE Total of the yearly Growth of Fleece Wool in this Level, is 2523 Packs 23 Fleeces.

I could give many more Estimates of particular Places after the like manner; but, as all together will not amount to an exact Calculate, I shall not trouble the Reader with Figures. This is sufficient to give you some just Ideas of the rest, after I have a little describ'd the Countries where the Principal Numbers of Sheep are kept.

2. THE South Downs; an Extent of Carpet Ground, reaching from Bourn in Sussex, to near Chichester, and with small Intervals to Poll Down in Hampshire, being at least 65 Miles in length, and generally 5 or 6 Miles broad at a Medium; all covered with Sheep of a smaller Size, but of the finest Wool; in which Compass I find there is estimated above 70000 Acres.

3. THE Downs and Plains, vulgarly call'd Salisbury Plains, but extending from about 10 Miles on this side Winchester, to the Devizes East and West, and from Andoveron the Edge of Berkshire, through the whole Counties of Wilts and Dorset to the Sea at Weymouth, North and South; containing all, or the most Part of the large Counties of Southampton; besides, as above, that of Wilts and Dorset, the Number of Acres not to be estimated, and the Sheep not to be guessed at.

4. THE Cotswould Hills and the Plains adjoining, in the Counties of Worcester, Gloucester and Oxford; all these last Counties breed an infinite Number of Sheep.

5. THE County of Surry breeds a very great Number on Bansted Downs; and also on the vast extended Commons and Heaths on the West Part of the same Country, towards Farnham, Guildford, and the Hind Head Hills, all to be seen on the Road to Portsmouth.

6. THE two rich feeding Counties of Lincoln and Leicester, where the largest Sheep in England are bred, and from whence comes that innumerable Store which supplies the Markets of London with their Flesh, whose Number admits of no Calculation.

7. Newmarket Heath, and all those Downs and Heaths adjoining in the Counties of Suffolk and Norfolk, which reach from Bourn Bridge on the side of Essex to Thetford North East, and on by Brandon and to Lyn North West, and to the Sea due North, where an innumerable Number of Sheep are fed, noted for having all white Wool, but black Faces.

I forbear to examine the Mountains of Wales, the fine Wool of Leominster, the Woulds in the East Riding of Yorkshire, the Bank of Tees in the Bishoprick of Durham, where are the largest Breed of Sheep in the whole Island; even larger than in Leicestershire, or Romney Marsh; and last of all the Northumberland Sheep, where, and in Cumberland their Number is so great, that they are brought Southward to be sold, even to London it self.

ADD to all these, that at least there is brought from Scotland 120000 Sheep every Year, with the Wool upon their Backs, besides Wool, as I said before, of all the numberless Flocks that are left behind in the Shires of Galloway, Air, Nithsdale, Tiviotdale, and other Parts of Scotland.

IT would be foreign to our purpose, to mention these particular Sheep Countries, if there were not something material in it, to those English Men who are acquainted a little with their own Country; and who by reflecting on the Quantities of Sheep, may make some Guess at the prodigious Quantity of Wool produced by them; as an illustration of which, be pleas'd to observe.

I. THAT at Dorchester, the County Town of Dorsetshire above mention'd, I was told by very grave and creditable Persons, Inhabitants of that Town, that upon a Wager decided, it was made appear, that within a Circle drawn round the Town, six Miles every Way; that is, twelve Miles Diameter, placing the Town exclusive in the Center, there were 600000 Sheep feeding at that one Time viz. in June, Anno 1673.

2. THAT at Salisbury, I received an Account from Persons alike grave and judicious, that there were sold, or brought to be sold, at one Time at Wey-hill Fair, 400000 Sheep; and at Burford Fair in Dorsetshire, the same Year, upwards of 600000.

THE Sum of this Account is, that as the Number of Sheep, which are constantly kept in this Island, is so exceeding great, and as we may say, numberless; so must the Growth of the Wool be yearly in Proportion; and how great then must be the Manufacture, which not only works the Wool always up, but receives such immense Quantities from Ireland and from Scotland?

THE next Consideration upon which, to form an Idea of the Greatness of our woollen Manufacture, is the Exportation of it, and the several Markets where it is sold: For Example,

THE Markets for English broad Cloths in Turky, viz. at Constantinople, Smyrna, Scanderoon, Aleppo, and at Alexandria in Egypt. THE Staple at Hamburgh, the Fairs at Leipsic and Frankfort au Main, and the Markets of Ausburgh, Nuremburgh, Ulm, and many of the most considerable Cities of the upper, as well as the lower Germany.

THE great Quantity of English Manufacture sold yearly at Lubec, Gottenburgh, Stockholm, Straelsand, Stetin, Koningsburgh, Dantzick, Riga and Petersburgh; and this, notwithstanding all the Prohibitions, and pretended Imitations of our Manufacture in Sweden, Prussia, Saxony and Switzerland.

THE incredible Vent for the woollen Manufacture of England, which is now actually in Holland, as well at Rotterdam as at Amsterdam; and from thence it is sent to all the Provinces and Counties of Germany; which, as I have said above, is said to amount to above two Millions Sterling per Annum.

THE lately encreas'd Market at Lisbon, where, notwithstanding all that has been said of the French supplying them, we have so great a Vent for the woollen Manufacture, that 'tis said, the Portugal Trade is at this Time the best, and most entire Trade we have.

THE Trade to Spain, as well old as new, and to Italy; however, the first has been interrupted, either by clandestine or Permission'd Traders: I say, it is very considerable; and it is observable, that our Importation of woollen Manufactures into old Spain, much over-ballances all the Goods we bring back from the Spaniard, their Bullion only excepted.

THE Trade to India, with all its Faults, in which the Company oblige themselves to export yearly, the Value of 100000 Pound in woollen Manufacture.

ADD to all this, the Consumption in our own Colonies and Plantations, which, as has been already observ'd, is beyond the reach of all Calculation.

THUS far relates to the first Article of the Employment of Labour of the Poor, viz. the woollen Manufacture only.

THE Silk Manufacture; this is encreas'd in England within a few Years to such a Degree, that whereas it was asserted by the late Dr. d'Avenant, and others, that in the Years 1680, 1681, 1682, there was imported yearly, by a Medium of three Years, above 1200000 Pound per Annum, Sterling in Value, in wrought Silks from France and Italy; I am assured, that at this Time, there are not twelve thousand Pounds first Cost, imported in a Year from France, and from Italy less than ever, except what may be run in by Smuggling, which, we have Reason to believe, is not considerable: It is true, this is a Manufacture wrought from foreign Materials; but it has two Particulars attending, extremely advantageous in Trade, and which ballances all that can be said against it.

1. THAT the foreign Materials are such as are imported manifestly in Return for our Manufacture exported; as particularly the Raw-Silk from Turky and the Levant, and the Thrown-Silk from Italy and Sicily.

2. THAT the Labour of our own People is employ'd on the making those Goods, which, however they may be consum'd at Home, yet, would otherwise be bought from Foreigners with our Money; so that by this Labour of our People, the Sum of more than a Million Sterling per Annum is sav'd; if it is not gain'd, 'tis kept at home, instead of being sent abroad, and the Ballance of our foreign Trade turn'd so much the more in our Favour.

THUS far the Consumption at home is made a Branch of our Gain; and the Labour of the People, tho' expended by the same People, is made a means to keep a Million of Money at home, which would otherwise go abroad in Levity and Trifles.

BUT I return to foreign Trade.

3. THE Labour of our People is concern'd in foreign Trade, in all our Hard-Ware Manufactures, so far as those Hard-Ware Manufactures are exported; and this, it cast up in Form, and containing all our wrought Iron, Copper and Brass, and wrought Pewter, is a very great Article in the general Commerce; besides the many thousand Families employ'd in the Mines, in digging Lead, Tin, Iron, Copper and Coal, for Exportation; that is to say, the Lead in Sows or Pigs, call it as you please, the Tin in Blocks, and the Copper in Bars and Plates.

4. THE Labour of the People in the Fishery of all Sorts, in which, tho' we do not come up to the Dutch, who they tell us employ 10000 Seamen every Year in the Whale Fishing, and 10000 more in the Herring Fishing, and 10000 more in all their other Fishing, including the fetching Salt from St. Vvies; yet, it is certain, that next to the Dutch, we have more Men employ'd in the taking and curing of Fish, including the Newfoundland, and New-England Fishing, than all the World besides.

5. ADD to this, that England employs, without Question, more Shipping than any other Nation, even than the Dutch themselves; and consequently more Seamen, and Builders of Ships; for tho' the Dutch have an infinite Number of small Craft, such as Galliots, Hoys, Busses, and Bylanders or Hoys, for their River Navigation, in which they and the Flemings out-do all the European World; yet for great Ships, and Ships of Force for the Merchants Trade, they cannot come near us; our coasting Trade for Coals, our West-India, Spanish, and Straits Trade, which is all carry'd on in large Ships, carrying from ten to thirty Guns, or able to carry so many, and some 36 to 40 Guns, especially the Trade to Virginia, Jamaica, Barbadoes, Spain, Italy and Turkey, in which many Ships are employ'd, which, in times of a sudden Rupture, have been hir'd and taken up for Ships of War, and are very fit to be so.

HERE the Strength, as well as the Wealth of this Island, is discovered; and I need not add, that out of this extraordinary Number of Ships employ'd in our Commerce, the Government, with very little Compulsion, and less now than ever, is able to man any Squadron of Ships of War; nay, if need be, the whole royal Navy with unexampled Expedition.

And this is another unanswerable convincing Argument to prove the Magnitude of the English Commerce, (viz.) that if the King wants 20000 to 30000 Seamen for the Fleet, they are always to be had; the Trade supplies them, and the continued Train of homeward bound Ships produces them, and yet the Merchants always find Men for their Business; on the other hand, if Peace returns, and the Royal Navy lies up, if 20000 Seamen are dismiss'd and paid off, they are gone in a few Minutes, they find a Birth, (as they call it) in Trade, the Merchants fit out the more Ships, and good Seamen never want Business.

THIS could never be, if the British Trade was not a Prodigy for its Magnitude; what Difficulties was the late King of France, a Prince born to surmount all Difficulties, I say, what Shifts was he put to to find, or rather to make Seamen to man his Ships at the beginning of his late fatal Greatness? How did he oblige all his Merchant Ships to carry more Men than their Complement (or Compleatment) to Sea upon every Voyage? and besides that, a certain Number still more upon the King's Account, and paid by the Royal Treasury, that those Men being inur'd to the Sea, might be afterwards fit for his Service.

How did he invite foreign Sailors, especially Irish and Scots, to serve in his Fleet, by Offers of Preferment, and extraordinary Wages:, manning his best Ships with such, because he found them better and more experienc'd Seamen than his own Subjects?

EVEN the Dutch themselves, if a War presents, as was the Case more than once in their former Wars with England, and was in 1689, and 1690, areoblig'dto stop their Greenland Fleet, and even sometimes their Herring Fishery, or, at least, to shorten the Number, in order to man their Fleets.

WHEREAS the English, some small Embargoes excepted, for a Week or ten Days at a Time, never put a full Stop to any general Head of Trade, for want of Seamen; on the contrary, in the hottest Press, and when Seamen are wanting on any sudden Expedition, yet they grant Exemptions and Protections, upon the ordinary Representations of the Merchants and of the Citiesand Towns; as, to the Coal Trade, from Newcastle, the Mackrel and Herring-Fishing Smacks in their Seasons, and to their outward bound Merchants on many Occasions: And this was done in the late King William's Time, even when the Government required 40000 Seamen to man the Fleet, and when two or three Hundred Ships at a Time were employed in the Transport Service to Ireland, and other Places.

How could this be, if the Magnitude of the English Trade was not, as I have said, a Kind of Prodigy in the World, such as is no where now to be equalled, or was ever before heard of?

THESE I take to be solid Proofs of the general Proposition; they are no Rhodomontades or Boasts; the Case does not want such mean Helps to set it out; the Thing is not private and conceal'd, for a few to know and be called upon to give in Evidence, the whole World are Witnesses; where to the Southward of our Channel is the Port or the Place of Trade, in Europe, Africa or America:, where among all foreign Ships that enter their Harbours, the English are not the most in Number? at Lisbon, at Cadiz, at Malaga, at Messina, at Leghorn, at Genoa:, at Zant, at Venice; read any of the publick Advices, there is ordinarily more

English Ships, not only than of any other Nation, but generally more than of all the other Nations put together. The last Account I saw went thus,

Lisbon	French Ships	18
	Dutch	5
	Swedes	2
	Hamburghers	1
	English	50

Cadiz	French	12
	Dutch	3
	Hamburghers	2
	Swedes	1
	English	18

Legborn	French	5
	Dutch	2
	English	8

AS for America, we see hardly any French or Dutch in any of the Ports or Places of the Country, except the French Bankers off of Newfoundland, and a few Ships at Canada; the Dutch, with all their powerful Commerce, have scarce any Thing to do there.

THESE I call Demonstrations of the Greatness of our Commerce in general; 'tis true it is not a Detail of Particulars, neither is it needful to our Subject.

I have met with some who have pretended to be critical in those Things, and have made Estimates of the Value of the Woollen Manufacture in the whole; and they have told us, that they allow it to be five Millions Sterling exported, and two Millions Sterling the Home Consumption. These Calculations I take to be much of a Piece with those general Guesses formerly made at the Value of our old Coin; some would have it to be three Millions, and others four; and the last pretended to speak with Judgment, and with a Kind of Authority, and took upon them to make the World believe they knew something more than common.

FROM this assuming positive Way they went on, to make a Judgment of other publick Things, as the Proportion of People, the Value of Lands, the Number of Acres in England, and what such and such Taxes might raise; by all which it past with the World as a just Calculation, that the current Coin was 4 Millions of Silver Money; and when upon these Presumptions they adventur'd upon that great Work of reforming the Coin, and calling in the old Money, they found the Sum nearer to twelve Millions than to four; which Mistake plung'd the famous Mr. Montague, afterwards Lord H-----x, into unexpected Difficulties, which required his utmost Skill to go thro', and which a Genius less than his, would have been in Danger to have been sunk under.

CALCULATIONS in Cases where there is no Principle to calculate from, no given Number or Rule to begin at, should never obtain too much upon us; the judging by or from such Calculations leads Men, of otherwise great Penetration, oftentimes into fatal Mistakes, such as at least touch the Reputation of their Understandings and Judgment; and sometimes such as expose them to Contempt ; such were the Guesses of that great Pretender to politick Arithmetick, Sir William Petty, whose Calculations of the Numbers of the Houses, and Families, and Inhabitants in London, and other populous Cities, were not erroneous only, but we may say have been since prov'd absurd, and even ridiculous.

I give therefore no Heed to those Guesses of five Millions and two Millions, in the Account of the Value of our Manufacture, there being no Rule or Foundation to make such an Estimate upon, and it may be too little or too much, none knows whether.

BUT all this, without Impeachment of my general Proposition, viz., that the Magnitude of our Woollen Manufacture is a Prodigy in Trade.

I must therefore be allowed here to enter into some Comparisons, and to talk by Allusion in Behalf of this particular Branch of our Commerce, and that is, that it is not only prodigious great, but that it by far out-does, and goes beyond any single Branch of Trade, or any particular Manufacture of any other Nation, at least in these Parts of the World.

IT is true, the Linen Manufacture is a Thing so universally useful, so wanted and called for in all Parts, that if any Thing in the World out-does our Wool, it is the Flax, and this I might grant, without Prejudice I say to my general Proposition.

FOR this is not a national Manufacture, but a Manufacture of many Nations; and I might almost say of all Nations, even from Egypt in the Levant, where we have Reason to believe it began, to Russia at the Bottom of the Baltick; whereas the Woollen Manufacture, as now describ'd, is a Nostrum, a Peculiarity to England, and to no other Country in the World, except Ireland, which is our own.

THE Wool, as I have said, is an exclusive Grant from Heaven to Great Britain, 'tis peculiar to this Country, and no other Nation has it, or any thing equal to it in the World; and the Manufacture is of Consequence singular to us also; nor do all the Depredations made upon it by Imitation, by Application for the getting Wool either from us by Stealth, or from remote Countries, as Saxony, Silesia, Poland, Barbary, and the like, amount to much; far from so much as England need be concerned at them; while she has the Wool, her Trade is invulnerable, at least no mortal, final, destructive Blow can be given it; of which I shall say more in its Place.

AGAIN, the Callico and the Silk Manufactures in the East Indies are (at least for Asia) an universal Manufacture; so great, that spreading into Europe, they become a general Grievance, and are already prohibited from being imported in several Kingdoms and Countries in Europe, the Quantity is so great.

BUT these again are the Manufactures of many Nations, Kingdoms, nay Empires of Nations, such as the Empire of China, and of the great Mogul, the Kingdoms of Golconda, of Siam, of Cochinchina, and many more, too long to reckon up.

BUT the Woollen Manufacture, as above, is singular to our Nation, no People in the World can come up to us j in the Workmanship, or have the Materials; not that I am, or will be partial to my Countrymen, as if they were the Nonparels of the World for manufacturing of Wool; 'tis evident, other Nations would go a great Way with them in it, if not outdo them, if they had the Wool, the main Principle of the Manufacture to work upon; but it cannot be, they have it not, nor can have it, the whole World cannot supply it; they may get some Wool in one Country, and some in another, and too much they get clandestinely from England, and much too much, from Ireland; and with this the French make some Things very well, nor should I deny this Justice to that diligent Nation to own, that considering the Shifts they are put to for Wool, they shew themselves but too good Manufacturers in making such Things as they do.

BUT what does it amount to? they supply themselves perhaps, and 'tis a great Step, if they can do that; but it must be remembred, that it is because their Government obliges them to make Shift with it, and to wear their own Works, however defective; a Wisdom we cannot arrive to, tho' we have the Manufacture in its utmost Perfection : Of which in its Order.

BUT after all, they do not supply themselves neither, and in Spite of the severest Prohibition, in Spite of Tyranny, and the Terror of an absolute Government, they do, and will get English Manufactures in, and do import very great Quantities too, as I could demonstrate by undeniable Evidences of Fact.

WHAT else means the great and sudden Export of English Goods to Leghorn, more just after the Stop of the English Commerce with France than ever before? what the continued Export of the same Goods to Dunkirk? and above all, what means the Commerce between Holland and France by the Maes and the Sambre, and by the Lys and the Scheld?

AND why? if the French make their Manufactures equal to others, I say, Why is it, that when the French Gentlemen make a Tour over hither to see the Country, or to visit the Court, they bring no more Clothes with them, than those on their Backs, but make them more Clothes as soon as they come hither, and always carry several Suits of Clothes Home with them ?

ON the contrary, if an English Gentleman goes Abroad into France to travel, he always makes himself new Clothes, and carries them with him; I speak now of the Gentlemen of Quality that do not want Clothes, or Money to buy them.

THE Reason is plain, the Frenchman can get none so good at Home as he can buy Abroad, and the Englishman can get none so good Abroad, as he can buy at Home.

IT is the like with the Linen and Lace in Holland and Flanders, if an English Gentleman travels into Flanders or Holland, he carries as little Linen as possible out with him, but gets all he wants made there; and when he comes back, he is sure to make himself two or three Dozen of fine Shirts, and to lace them at the

Neck and Hands with fine Bone Lace. ON the contrary, if a Dutchman, or French Gentleman comes over to England, he is always well furnish'd with Linen and Lace before he comes.

THE Reasons are just the reverse of what is said above; the Dutch-man or Fleming can get none so cheap Abroad as he can buy at Home, and the English-man can get none so cheap at Home, as he can buy Abroad.

I give this Instance of the French, because they are the People who are said to have made the most considerable Advances in the Woollen Manufacture; and much has been said, and much fruitless Pains taken to insinuate,, that the French make our Goods to Perfection; nay, some will tell you, the French out-do us, and undersell us at Market; which is a great Mistake, and even in the Turkey Trade, which is the Top of their Performance, and the Goods they send thither are certainly the best of their Performance; yet I appeal to the Men of Experience even in that Trade, whether they out-do us; whether, as is mention'd in our first Chapter, a Bale of their Cloth will weigh as much, or sell for as much at Market, as a Bale of English Cloth? and whether in general, the English Cloth is not rather bought, tho' at a dearer Price, by the Turkish and Armenian Merchants, I mean those who are the chief Dealers in those Goods, than a Bale of the French.

It is true, there are in all Markets a sort of Buyers, who take up with the Goods of an inferior Quality, for the Sake of a cheap Price, and these will buy the French Cloths: And the worst Goods will find a Chapman, as well as the best, if the Price be accordingly.

IT is true also, the French Cloths carry as good a Face as the English, are as well drest, as well pack'd and set off, and the Colours are as fine; so that it is not hard to deceive the unexperienc'd Buyer: And this is not the only Example of the superficial Performances of that Nation, who are very rarely wanting in Outsides, whatever they are within; but the Substance is wanting, the real intrinsick Worth of the Goods is found in the English Cloths, and in them only; there is all the Beauty of Colour, and the Ornament of Dress, and the Substance too; and this, whether the first Buyer can discover it or no, the last Buyer and Consumer, the Turkish or Persian Gentleman, Aga or Bassa that wears it, finds it out presently; one will wear firm and smooth, and solid to the last; the other wears rough, light, spungy, and into Rags; and when this Man buys again, he calls for English Cloth, he will have no more French Cloth, for it did him no Service, it did not wear well.

IF I did not speak this from the Experience and personal Knowledge of those that have been upon the Spot, and been Witnesses to the very Fact, I should not take upon me to affirm it thus positively; but I may appeal for the Truth of it to unanswerable Evidence, nor is there Room to dispute it; the Nature of the Thing speaks it, the French Cloth, with all its superficial French Gloss upon it, is fine, but thin and spungy, and will do the Wearer neither Credit or Service, while the English Cloth wears to the last like a Board, firm and strong, and has a kind of Beauty even in its Rags.

HENCE I infer, we have no such Reason to terrify our selves with the Apprehensions of other Nations ruining our Trade, and out-doing us in our woollen

Manufacture ; let us but keep our Wool at Home, and we need be in no Pain for our Manufacture any where: But of that hereafter.

I return to the Magnitude of our Woollen Manufacture; which, as I have said above, I insist is the greatest single Manufacture, and occasions the greatest Trade both Abroad and at Home, of any Manufacture that is to be found in any particular Nation in the World, be that Nation otherwise as much greater, richer, or more populous than we are, as you will.

BUT there is yet another thing to be considered in the English Woollen Manufacture, which is above all our Boasts; and were we to use the utmost Partiality, and the utmost Art to compliment our own Country, and set out the Beauty and Usefulness of our Manufacture, nothing could be equal to this.

IT is not only great from the prodigious Quantity of the Wool, the Numbers of the People employ'd in it, the vast Quantity of Goods made and the, Beauty and Perfection of the Performance: But the Extensiveness of its Consumption, is another Prodigy in Trade; and I cannot pass it without some Notice: I'll be as brief as I can.

LINEN is a Thing universally worn and wanted; and few People of any tolerable Figure or Fashion in the World are, or can be without it: But then, more or less, all the Nations of Europe make it; and all they have to do, is only as it were to exchange Sorts with one another.

THE Silk Manufacture is very great, and in all Nations some or other of it is made use of; but then, 'tis made in many Countries, and is exported from one to another in Trade several Ways, the French, the Italians, the Venetians, the Dutch, the Flemings, and now the English, make all their own, and carefully exclude the East Indian Silks from their Countries.

THE Russian and Turkish Empire are supply'd from Persia, and the Spaniards and Africans South, and the Germans and Swedes North, from India,, the Variety spreads as the Situation of the Countries, and as the Commerce directs.

THE Callicoes are sent from the Indies by Land into Turky, by Land and Inland Seas into Muscovy and Tartary, and ab.out by long-Sea into Europe and America:, till in general they are become a Grievance, and almost all the European Nations but the Dutch, restrain and prohibit them.

BUT take our English Woollen Manufacture, and go where you will you find it; 'tis in every Country, in every Market, in every trading Place; and 'tis receiv'd, valued, and made use of, nay, call'd for and wanted every where. In a Word, all the World wears it, all the World desires it, and all the World almost envies us the Glory and Advantage of it.

NOR is it the Dress of the Mean and the Poor in the several Countries where it spreads, but of the Best and Richest: The Princes, nay, at this Time I may say, the Kings of the Earth, are cloth'd with it. I appeal to all his Majesty's Servants, who have had the Honour of his Commission as Ambassadors, and Residents in foreign Countries, and the Courts of Princes throughout Europe, whether they have not seen the Czar of Muscovy, the Kings of Sweden, Denmark, Prussia, Poland; nay, even the Emperor of Germany himself, cloathed in English Cloth.

THE King of Spain vouchsafes, even on his Days of Ceremony, to appear in a Bays Cloak; the Grand Seignior; Lord of the whole Turkish Empire, has his Robe of English Cloth, and the Sophy of Persia, amidst all his Persian and Indian Silks, wears his long Gown of Crimson Broad Cloth, and esteems it, as it really is, the noblest Dress in the World.

As it is with the Princes, it is, and ever will be with the People, the Nobility, the Gentlemen, and in a Word, the Burghers, the best and wealthiest of the People are generally cloath'd with it; nay, so far has it prevail'd, that in Russia and Sweden, and other cold Climates, it has been known, that those who could not go to the Price of English Cloth, have bought the Lists of it which the Taylors cut off, sewed them together, and lin'd them with Furs, to make them long Robes or Garments, which they wore in that Country, till the late Czar cut them shorter for them.

AND this brings me back to the Imitations which the People of these several Countries are said to run into, to the Prejudice of our Manufacture. 'Tis true, the Swedes, the Prussians, and several other People, do imitate the English Manufacture, and would gladly do it universally for the Advantage of their People; and we cannot blame them; nay, even this alone is a Document, an authentick Voucher to the Truth of what I have said: For if our Woollen Manufacture were not necessary to them, they would not buy it of us; and if not profitable, they would not attempt to mimick and make it.

BUT what does it all amount to? they are able indeed to make the coarsest and meanest of the Manufacture, and that just enough to cover and cloath the Boors, and most despicable of their People; those whose Clothing was our coarse Duffells, Wadmill, Half thicks, and in general a kind of the coarsest Kersies, but a Degree or two above Blankets; or perhaps, the meanest of our Dozens, and what we call Yorkshire Cloths: And even this is done but indifferently neither.

BUT in all these Countries, the People of Fashion still cloath with our English fine broad Cloth; and 'tis ordinary to have a Ship bound to Gottenburgh, or to Stockholm, carry 500 or 1000 Spanish Cloths at a Time into Sweden; by Spanish Cloths I mean the fine medly Cloths, such exactly as we wear here, which are mix'd with Spanish Wool in the Making, and therefore call'd Spanish Cloths.

IT is the same at Stetin and Koningsburgh, Straelsund or Dantzick, notwithstanding the Kings of Prussia and Poland, prohibiting our Cloths, and setting their own People to Work.

To conclude; our Manufacture is the general Wear, for therein the Argument is forcible; 'tis not that some of it is to be had everywhere, for so might be said of several other Things, as of the French fine Stuffs, Silks and Druggets, and other light spungy Manufacture of Hair and Silk mingled with Wool, &c.

BUT the English broad Cloth is the general Wear; the Druggets, Serges, Duroys, Kersies:, Camlets; in a Word, the Woollen Manufactures of Great Britain are the general Wear in all the Countries in Europe.

THE Muscovites, as I have said, wore them formerly in their long Vests, the Germans, the Poles, the Swedes are clothed with them universally; witness the great Marts or Fairs, of Leipsick and Frankfort, where such exceeding Quantities of them are sold every Year, as is said above, and witness the Cities of Hamburgh, Lubeck, Bremen and Embden, by which all the Provinces of the lower Germany are supplied.

NOT a capital City in the Empire, but you may find the Shops of the Tradesmen stor'd with English Cloth, as far as the Navigation of the Elb, the Oder, or the Weisselcan convey them; the Rhine, the Maes, the Moselle, the Saar, the Main, the Neckar, the Danube, they all assist to hand it on, not at Prague only, not at Vienna, not at Munich, but even at Buda and Belgrade, it is to be sold; and the best Gentlemen in the Country buy it, if they do not, 'tis for Want of Money, and not for Want of Will.

FROM the Empire, and the northern Countries, come away into the Mediterranean, I have mention'd the Turkish Court, there you see the Bassas, the Agas, the Kadilescharsy and even the Grand Seignior, cloth'd with English Cloth, even in their Habits of Ceremony.

FROM thence you come to Italy, 'tis the same there, and the great Fair at Messina is an undeniable Evidence of it, where there is seldom so little as an Hundred , Thousand Pound Value, sold in our English Woollen Manufacture every Season, such as Druggets, Duroys, Sagathyes, Camlets, with all other Sorts of Mens Stuffs, and broad Cloth it self; and tho' they have wrought Silks in such Abundance, and so cheap, yet you see the Italians generally clothed in English Cloth or thin Stuffs; the Clergy in black Bays, the Nuns are vail'd with fine Says, and Long Ells, and even the noble Venetians wear our fine Cloth for their best Dress.

AT Rome it is the same, the foreign Princes and Ambassadors, and the Italian Princes themselves, wear it at Mil/an, at Turin, at Naples, even at Rome; 'tis all the same: As to France, I mention'd it already, and I scarce need name the Spaniards and the Portuguese.

WHAT one Manufacture like this can boast of so general a Reception, or of being the Favourite Dress of the whole Christian World? If we should go over to America, whether to the Brasils, the flourishing Colony of the Portuguese, how many Hundred Thousand Moyd'ors a Year do we receive from thence, for the English Manufactures worn and consumed there, notwithstanding the intense Heat of the Place? 'tis the same Thing at Mexico, the most luxurious, extravagant, and profuse City and Country in the World; even there the utmost Pride of the proudest People upon Earth, is to be clothed in the English Cloth, and to have their Wastcoats and Breeches of fine Camlets, and other Stuffs of Crimson and Scarlet; and over all, a Cloak of our Essex Bays.

'Tis the same at Cartagena, at Panama, at Lima and St. Jago, the Capital richest Cities of their several Countries; some of them situate within ten Degrees of the Equinox, and where the Heats are almost unsufferable; which I mention to observe to you, how well our Manufactures are adapted to all Countries, Climates, Persons, and Qualities; not too thin for the frozen Laplanders, Swedes, and Russians, or too thick for the scorch'd Americans and Inhabitants of Peru and Brazil; not too light for the Germans, or too heavy for the Italians.

IN Value 'tis the same; not too cheap for the Nobility, no not for the Kings and the Emperors of the World; not too dear for the Burghers and the Tradesmen, no not for the Boors, and the Peasants; not too gay for the Men, not too grave for the Ladies: We find in common, the British Manufacture is the general Wear, as well of Poor as rich; the highest Sovereign, and the most retir'd Recluse; 'tis the best Habit of the best of their People, in every Nation in Europe, Asia, Africa and America:; the only Country where it is not so, is that Part of Asia, which we call the East Indies, where the infinite Variety of their own Manufactures, and the little Time that the English have traded among them, has not yet made its Way; yet we find it begins to be received in China, and also at the Court of the Mogul; and as the Number of Europeans encrease in the Indies, there is Room to believe the British Manufactures will gain Ground among them too; It is evident, that at Melinda, and the other Portuguese Settlements on the East Coast of Africa, beyond the Cape of Good Hope, where the Portuguese have brought the Natives to wear Clothes, even within five Degrees of the Line; there the British Manufacture, carried by the Portuguese to them, are the general Habit, as well of the Natives, as of the Portuguese, among whom they dwell.

WHAT can be more plain than these Facts, of which the whole World are Witnesses? And what can be a clearer Proof of the Magnitude of our Woollen Manufacture? I think I need say no more about it.

WHAT Wonder then, that the several Nations endeavour to set their own People to work to make it? How could any other be expected? That also is a farther Testimony of its intrinsick Value, and the Necessity of it in Use.

1st. IT appears, that they cannot be without it.

2dly. THAT it is to be had no where else.

1. THEY cannot be without it; if any other Sort of Goods would supply, if their Linens would cloath the Germans, or their Silks the Italians; if any Thing of their own Growth would be equivalent to them, why do they not prohibit ours, as they do the Silks and Callicoes of India? I mean in general, as the Spaniards most ridiculously did a few Months since, without having any thing for their People to wear in the Room of them; which made their very Women laugh at them, and ask their Husbands where they would get Cloths.

IT is true some Princes have prohibited some of our Manufactures; that is to say, such particular Sorts as their own Wool, and their own People can make; but where is the Prince or People, Kingdom or Empire in the World, the Indies excepted, who will, or indeed can be wholly without our Woollen Manufacture?

2. THAT it is not to be supplied from any other Country, is as evident as the other; for where is that Country, and why are they not as rich, as opulent, as powerful at Sea, and on Shore, as England is ?

WHERE is the Country? if there is not a Country, as I have prov'd above, that has or can have an equivalent Manufacture, or that does not buy from us. How should there be a Country that can supply its Neighbours ?

BUT why do not some of the Nations, who envy the Profits and Advantages of this Manufacture to us, and who would be careful to keep at home the immense Sums of Money, which this (to us happy) Article draws from them; I say. Why do they not publish a general Prohibition, not of this or that particular Sort of our Goods, but of all Woollen Goods whatsoever, and from what Country soever?

Is it possible, that they can find out no Equipment for themselves? Might not the Men in Italy and Spain cloath themselves in thick Silks, Velvets, and strong Paduasoys? and in the North, might not the Poles, the Russians, the Swedes, the Danes, the Prussians, the Saxons dress themselves in rich Furrs, Skins of Beasts, such as the Sables and Ermines, Beaver, Otter, and black Fox Skins, the latter more valuable than Ermines?

METHINKS the Germans, and Italians, who are such Masters of the Linen and Silk Manufactures, and have the Advantage of such Quantities of Furrs as the Russians could furnish them with, might improve them into some Form, and turn them into some Shape, so as to supply their Want of Clothes, and not impoverish themselves and their Country to buy Foreign Manufactures : The reverend grave Sables, and the royal Ornaments of Ermines, might serve to gratify their Vanity, and make them all, like those Corporation-Princes, called Aldermen; and they might cloath as rich in Furs and Foxskins as they pleas'd, if the Outside was plain, the Inside would be great and rich, and the Climate would reconcile them to the Warmth of the Dress.

BUT 'tis impossible; it will not do; nothing can answer all the Ends of Dress, but good English broad Cloth, fine Camlets, Druggets, Serges, and such like; these they must have, and with these none but England can supply them; Be their Country hot or cold, torrid or frigid, 'tis the same Thing, near the Equinox, or near the Pole, the English Woollen Manufacture clothes them all; here it covers them warm, from the freezing Breath of the Northern Bear; and there it shades them, and keeps them cool from the scorching Beams of a perpendicular Sun.

LET no Man wonder, that the Woollen Manufacture of England is arriv'd to such a Magnitude, when in a Word it may be said to cloath the World; there are but three Sorts of People in the World that do not use it.

1st, THOSE that cloath altogether with Callicoes, and Silks, as in India; the Manufactures of their own Country.

2dly, THOSE that living in some hot Countries, wear no Cloths at all. And,

3dly, THOSE who are so very poor and despicable, that they cannot get it.

Chapter 6

Of the magnitude of the British commerce, as it respects the consumption of foreign goods imported from abroad, as well as of our own product and manufacture at home

As Manufactures, and other Exportations are thus great, and the Consumption and Export of our own, whether Product or Manufactures, are so much a Prodigy for their Magnitude, and are thus extended to all Parts of the World, our Importations are no less prodigious; and this the rather, because of the great Consumption of those Importations among our selves, as well as their Exportation as Merchandize.

IT must be acknowledg'd, that the Trade of the Dutch by foreign Importations, is also very great, and may be said to exceed the Importations of England; and I believe in many Articles they do so, if we consider their East Country Fleets, their Greenland Fleets, their East India, their French Wine, and their Herring Fleets, and all their other Branches of Trade to Turky, and to the Mediterranean; and especially their Importations of woollen Manufacture, Sugars, Tobaccos, wrought and other Plantation Goods; Lead, Tin, Iron, and Brass; Drugs, Dye Stuffs, Corn, &c. from England.

BUT then the Dutch must be understood to be as they really are, the Carryers of the World, the middle Persons in Trade, the Factors and Brokers of Europe: That, as is said above, they buy to sell again, take in to send out; and the greatest Part of their vast Commerce consists in being supply'd from all Parts of the World, that they may supply all the World again: Thus they supply some Nations with Corn, others with Ships, or Naval Stores for Ships; others with Arms and Ammunition of all kinds; such as Powder, Shot, Shells, Lead, Iron, Copper, Cannon, Mortars, &c. others with Fish, others with woollen Manufactures, and the like; and yet, they have neither Corn, Hemp, Tar, Timber, Lead, Iron, Arms, Ammunition, woollen Manufacture, or Fish of their own Growth; the Product of their own Land or Seas, or Labour of their own People, other than as Navigators and Seamen, to fetch, find, and carry them.

NOR is their home Consumption of foreign Importations great, except of Corn and Woollen Manufacture; their People are few, compar'd to foreign Nations, tho' many compar'd to the Country where they dwell; their Way of Living is sparing, their Excesses few and mean, and their Ostentation or Gayety very low priz'd.

BUT in England, the Country is large, populous, rich, fruitful; the Way of Living, large, luxurious, vain and expensive, even to a Profusion, the Temper of the People gay, ostentatious, vicious, and full of Excesses; even criminally so in some Things, and too much encreasing in them all.

HENCE comes as a Consequence, a vast Importation of foreign Growth of every kind, either for Eating or Drinking, for Fancy or Fashions, and this so great, as not to be equall'd in any Part of the World; the Fact seems a Charge, tho' not design'd as such, but to illustrate the Subject: But I must descend a little to Particulars, to make it out.

I am credibly inform'd, and firmly believe it to be true, that take all the maritime Nations of Europe, where no Wine is made, and cast them up together, they do not import so much Wine as the Subjects of Great Britain do, for we have not a Drop of our own Growth; and this, notwithstanding a very great Consumption of Malt-Liquors, Malt and Melasses Spirits, brew'd and distill'd at Home; and notwithstanding a vast Quantity of Cyder and Perry, Mead, Rum, and other Liquors; much of it spent in meer Extravagance and Profusion; and in spite of a most excessive Duty upon the Importation of the Wine, as well as an Excise upon the Consumption of the brew'd Liquors of our own. THE Importation of Wines of all Kinds, and Brandy included, from abroad, have been often calculated by just Mediums of Years, and is lately cast up for the Year 1721, at 60000 Pipes, or 30000 Ton per Annum.

BUT then let me add by Way of Supplement, That as I understand it,

1. ALL this Account is exclusive of the Wines and Brandy imported in Scotland and Ireland, and the Isle of Man; and of all the Madera and Canary Wines imported in our Colonies, the Madera Wine being at least 1000 Ton per Annum; and the Wine imported in Scotland and Ireland, &c. cannot be so little as 3000 Ton more, which makes it 40000 Ton in all.

2. IT is exclusive of all the French Wines and Brandy run on Shore by the Smugglers, in all the three Kingdoms, and especially in Scotland and Ireland, where I have some particular Reasons to believe, not 1-6th Part (of the Brandy, especially) pays the Duty.

3. IT is exclusive of all the Rum distilled in the West India Colonies, and consum'd in those Colonies, as well in the Islands, as on the Continent.

THESE are all to be call'd Importations, and the Sum total is prodigious; let any Man that may think me severe, in saying we are a luxurious, expensive People, calculate the annual Consumption of Wine and strong Liquors in his Majesty's Dominions at this Time; and then judge impartially, whether I do Justice to the People or no.

WERE Wine the ordinary Drink of the People, or were strong Beer and Ale the needful Table-Liquors for the Support of Life, it were quite another Case; but if Wine were the ordinary Drink, it would be mingled in the drinking with Water, as it is in the usual drinking of the Countries where it grows, as in Spain, Italy, France, &c. where scarce any Wine is drank without Water, and very little to Excess.

(N. B. IN France and Spain, Wine mingled with Water, is the ordinary Beverage or Drink for meer Necessity, as Food; but if they take any Thing to exhilerate or raise the Spirits, it is Brandy; which yet, they very rarely drink to Excess; whereas here; all, as well Brandy as Wine, and all our strong compounded Drinks, such as stout Ale, Punch, Double-Beer, Fine-Ale, &c. are all drank to Excess, and that to such a Degree, as to become the Poison, as well of our Health as of our Morals; fatal to the Body, to Principles, and even to the Understanding; and we see daily Examples of Men of strong Bodies drinking themselves into the Grave; and which is still worse. Men of strong Heads, and good Judgment, drinking themselves into Idiotism and Stupidity: But that by the way; I return to the Discourse, as it is the Subject of Trade; Wine, and all the strong Liquors mention'd above, are not our Drink, but our Excess; not our needful, but our superfluous Drink.)

ON the other Hand, our Table Beer, which is the wholesome, useful, and necessary Liquor of the Country, made for Family-Supply, and used as such by the sober Part of our People, is excluded from the Account: Nor is there a Gallon of Water mingled with a Hogshead of Wine, one with another, for all the Wine we drink.

I am not going to launch out here into a Satyr upon our Country, or to dip into the Scandal of our common Vices; the immense Greatness of our Trade is the Subject; but our Vices are so unhappily mingled with our Interest in Trade, that as a late Author, writing on that Subject, says well. Our Luxury is become a Virtue in Commerce, and our Extravagancies are the Life and Soul of our Trade.

As I proposed to judge of the Greatness of our Manufactures, by the Quantity of the Wool which is consum'd in making them; so we may take some View of the Consumption of Liquor among us, from the Quantity of Malt consum'd in Great Britain and Ireland, that being the Fund or Principle from whence they are produc'd.

I shall not enter here into a Cloud of Figures, to deduce the long Account; but tell you in the Gross, and at one View, that calculating the Quantity of Drink brew'd from the Quantity of Malt made, and taking that from the Foot of the Excise, or Duty paid on the Malt, called in general the Malt Tax, I venture to affirm, there are forty Millions of Bushels of Malt brew'd or distill'd in his Majesty's Dominions every Year, exclusive of what is exported in Trade to foreign Countries.

IT remains only to deduct out of this Reckoning, the small Beer; that is to say, the Quantity yearly made Use of in Table Beer for Family-Uses; and should I take out one fourth Part for necessary Beer, as I call it; that is, small Table-Beer, which, I think, is a great deal too much, there would still remain thirty Millions of Bushels to be brew'd in strong Beer, which it must be acknowledged, is much of it Luxury and Extravagance, much of it Vice and Intemperance.

REDUCE this again into Drink, and allow three Bushels of Malt to every Barrel of strong Beer; this makes no less than ten Millions of Barrels of strong Beer consum'd at Home, in this sober Nation in a Year.

THE only Exception to this Account that I can meet with, which has any weight in it, is, that some of this Malt is distill'd into Spirits; and suppose I allow 200000 Quarter per Annum, so consum'd, that is, one Million, 600000 Bushel; it will be answer'd, 1st, That this is of the worst of the Malt, and of a Kind which would not make good Beer, if it was brew'd, and that much of it is not fit to be brew'd at all: But then, 2d, It will be said, that this cannot be plac'd to the Account of our Temperance, or taken off from the Luxury spoken of, since 'tis generally brew'd into a worse Liquor, and apply'd to worse uses, which it is not my Business at this Time to talk of, and which it would be better, were it entirely forgotten (if that could be) than spoken of at all.

IF this Consumption of Liquors in the King's Dominions were to be calculated in the whole, and the Value were to be cast up in Money, what an immense Sum would it amount to? And what an Article would it make in the Magnitude of our Trade?

1. TAKE the Wine and Brandy consum'd in the whole, and suppose the Quantity to be no more, than what is legally imported, not reckoning the so much greater Quantity of what is clandestinely run on Shore by Smuggling, and other Frauds: If the legally imported Quantity of Wine and Brandy amounts to 40000 Ton, the Rum consum'd in the Plantations not included, which is very great Quantity.

LET this be brought to the Pint Pot; that is, to the Retailer, and reduce it thus, 1. The Price of almost all Sorts of Wine and Brandy, is at least to a Consumer, sold at two Shillings per Quart; the French Wine, the Canary, the Rhenish, the Sherry, all at more than two Shillings; and the Brandy by retail, generally at double the Price: But take it one with another, at two Shillings per Quart, which is eight Shillings per Gallon, and make a reasonable Allowance for Bottoms and Leakage, as usual; yet to what an immense Sum does the Consumption of imported Liquors in the British Dominions amount to?

252 Gallons is a Ton, this at 8s. per Gallon, (the Retailers Price) amounts to 100 l. 16 s. per Ton; but abating 12 Gallons in every Ton for Bottoms and Leakage: And suppose it to be but 240 Gallons Nett Wine per Ton, at 8s. per Gallon, it is 96 l. per Ton.

Ton. 40000 of Wine and Brandy imported yearly at 96 *l.* per Ton, amounts to 3,840,000 *l.*

(N. B. THERE is no need at all of the Abatement for Bottoms and Leakage, the Vintners making effectual Provision for it in their short Measure; and if that is not taken out, it amounts to just four Million Sterling per Annum; besides all the Wine and Brandy really imported in the dark; that is, by clandestine Trade, Smuggling, &c).

THUS much is calculated upon the legal Importation; and as we may call it, the known, and avow'd Consumption of Wines and Brandy in the Dominions of Great Britain; what we may suppose to be clandestinely brought on Shore, is hard to determine: But they who know as I do, how common, how plentiful Brandy is, I mean French Brandy, known and acknowledg'd to be such on all the Sea Coasts of England, in all Parts of Scotland and Ireland, and how much it is us'd. They who'd know, that but a few Years ago, 5000 Ton of Brandy was said to be brought into the Isles of Jersey and Guernsey, from France in one Year. They who have had any Knowledge of the prodigious Quantity of Wine and Brandy constantly brought to, and manag'd (so it seems 'tis call'd) in the Isle of Man, for some Years past, and by which that whole Island is visiblyenrich'd, to a surprising Degree: I say, those who have had any Insight in these Things, will not think it unreasonable to allow, at least one fourth Part more of Wine and Brandy to this Account.

BUT it is enough to mention it only; I believe, it will be readily admitted, that what is said above, is very likely to be true, viz. That the British Dominions import more Wine, than all the Countries of Europe, who are without Wine of their own Import, put them all together.

IT may be true, that some of those Countries import more Brandy than we do, in Proportion to their Trade; but it is to be allow'd, only, because we have loaded the foreign Brandy with heavy Duties, in order to encourage the Consumption of our own Malt Spirits.

2. I might in the next Place calculate here the Value, as I have already the Quantity of our home Consumption of strong Beer and Ale, among our own People; and it would not be difficult to do it, either from the Quantity of Malt consum'd in the whole, (as well for Sale, as for private Use), as also from the Rate of Excise: But the Sum would be so great, it would surprise the Reader.

IT is true, the Beer, or Ale brew'd in Gentlemens Houses for private Use, does not cost so much as the Beer brew'd for Sale, because of the Excise; but then, if we should abate reckoning the Beer and Ale retail'd, at the Price paid by the Consumer, which is the manner of Reckoning we are now going upon, and is the true way, when we are to examine the Magnitude of an Expence, on the Foot of Trade; I say then, if we should abate the retailing Price of the Beer and Ale retail'd, in Ballance of the Quantity consum'd in private Families, which I think is giving up a very manifest Odds; upon this Equality, we might bring it to a Head, by rating all the strong Beer, and Ale consum'd in England, at the Rate of twenty Shillings, upon every three Bushels of Malt. If there are any Objections to be made against the Calculation, I believe they would be easily answer'd; but if they cannot, they may be ballanc'd by Abatement; for as by this Calculation, the Consumption of strong Drink amounts to no less than ten Millions Sterling per Annum, if we should abate a quarter Part of it; 'tis an immense and almost incredible Sum, and what no other Nation in the World can expend in one single Article.

Now to examine this a little another Way, let any Man that is admitted to such a Liberty, cast up the Books: of the Excise, and tell us how much the Excise upon strong Beer amounts to in Great Britain and Ireland, and from thence some Estimate may be made.

SUPPOSE then, for Example, the Duty as collected; for in this Account, we are not to cast up and deduct the Charges of the Collection, the Establishment of the Office, the Incidents, &c. but how much is collected from the Brewer; I say, suppose this amounts in England, Scotland, and Ireland, and all his Majesty's Dominions, where the Excise is payable, to 800000 l. per Annum. I doubt not, but it amounts to much more; but let the critical Enquirer do Justice on that Account, as he finds the Case will demand; I have good Grounds to say it may be cast up thus, till a Reason is produc'd why it should not.

IF the Excise then, at four Shillings and nine Pence per Barrel upon strong Beer, collects 800000 I. per Annum; the Beer being sold to the Retailer, at twenty Shillings per Barrel, must then amount to above four Times the Sum: We need not in such a conjectural Estimate as this, cast up the Fractions of three Pence per Barrel, it would but add to the Sum, which you may evidently see, I do not seek to make greater than it is. THIS then brings the Value of the Beer, as sold to the Retailer, to be three Millions two hundred thousand Pound per Annum. ADD to this then, the Value of the strong Beer brew'd for private Families, which, as before, I take to be equal to the other, (under the Disadvantage of its being underrated, viz. to the Retailer, and not to the Consumer) but to avoid Cavils, I'll state it at half that Sum: The Expence then of strong Beer in these Dominions, rises to four Millions nine hundred thousand Pounds per Annum.

I could support these Estimates, by a stricter comparing the Quantity brew'd, with the Quantity of Malt made; but 'tis needless here, there is a manifest Difference between exact critical Examination, and a general Estimate, after the manner of an Hypothesis; it is the latter that is before me now; wherein, however, the Advantage is so great, that it fully answers the End of the Argument, if I should throw in a Million or two of Pounds Sterling, in the whole, and take it at so much less than it really amounts to, as I am well assur'd I do in this Account: For Example, if according to the proposed Principle, I am casting up the Value of the strong Liquors which the Nation consumes, and ought to take it (for the purpose) at the Rate it cost the Consumer, as I did in the Wine, it would stand thus. Every Barrel of strong Beer retailed by the Victuallers, measures him out by the Quart Pot 36 Gallons; this sold at 3 d. per Quart, the ordinary Price, (tho' the general Rate is now 4 d.) is 36 s. the Barrel, besides the Advantage of the selling much of it at 2 d. per Pint, and besides the Half, which the Victualler finds in short Measure.

(N. B. THIS is evident in the Suttlers and others, who draw Drink in Garrisons; and the Tapsters, who take Cellars and Tap-houses in great Inns, who frequently allow the Governours and Masters of such Houses, 30 to 35 s. and some 40 s. per Barrel for the Drink they draw under them; so that if I calculate all the strong Beer at the Rate of but 20 s. per Barrel, it will allow for all the Objections that can be made against any other Part, seeing it cannot amount to much above half the Value which the Consumer pays.)

UPON the Whole, I take upon me to say, without any Hazard of being confuted, that there is consumed in his Majesty's Dominions, of all the following Liquors, exclusive of small Beer, no less, reckoning it at the Value paid by the Consumer to the Retailer, and including the strong Beer brew'd for private Use, than the full Value of eight Millions per Annum.

THE Liquors included in this Account, are as follows.

WINE of all Sorts,
BRANDY, Imported.

STRONG Beer, and all
CYDER and Perry, Brew'd at Home

MALT and Melasses Spirits
CYDER Spirits Distill'd at Home

RUM distill'd from Sugar and
BEER and Ale brew'd in the Plantations.

THE Plantations, as being Part of our selves, are always in Accounts of Trade, to be cast up with our other Accounts; and as their Produce is esteem'd our own: So their Consumption should be also, and is so in all just Calculations; and for this Reason, the Importations from thence are not reckon'd as foreign Importations, but as a Home Produce.

THE next Article of the Importation of foreign Goods is Linen, and this, it must be acknowledg'd, relates more especially to England, and to the Consumption here, and in the English Colonies in America.

OF this Consumption, it may indeed be said it is a Prodigy; and tho' there is a considerable Quantity of Linen made in some Parts of England, especially in the North Parts, as in Lancashire, Cheshire, Yorkshire, and the four other Northern Countries, insomuch, that at one Market in Lancashire 'tis said, there is the Value of 500 l. a Week sold in Hukabacks only; yet this Quantity is so little worth mention, that this sort of Linen is scarce seen at London; but England does as it were ravage the whole spinning World for Linen and Linen Yarn and Lace, which is Linen also.

THE principal Importations of Linen are indeed from our neighbouring Countries; but such is the exceeding Consumption of Linen here, that it seems as if all the World were not able to supply us; and this not only of the coarser Kinds of Linen from the Northern Nations, but such is the Demand of fine Linens, Hollands, Cambricks, and the finest of other Country Linen, that it is advanc'd to me for a certain Truth, by a Person experienc'd in those Trades, that England alone wears and consumes as much fine Linen; nay, his Words are. More of the finest Linen than all the Kingdom of France, the Austrian Netherlands, and the united Provinces put together, where the fine Linen is chiefly made.

I need not enter critically into the Enquiry whether this is literally true or no; but when I come to look in to our Custom-house Entries, and see by the Books: the exceeding Quantity of Linen, as well fine as coarse, imported into England from all Parts, it is really surprising. For Example,

COARSE Russia Linen, properly so call'd, from Petersburgh and Narva, Revel, Riga, &c. Canvas and Polish Linen from Dantsick, Koningsberg, Stetin and Straelsund, &c. and Diapers, Damasks and Lawns; from Silesia and Lusatia, and Saxony by way of Hamburgh; also other Germany Linens, including a multitude of Sorts of middling Finess, such as are the Manufactures of several Countries upon the Elbe, imported likewise from Hamburgh.

(N. B. THE Quantity of German Linen imported from Hamburgh, is past all Calculation, and is supposed to amount to many Hundred thousand Pounds Sterling a Year, something more than two Millions.)

COARSER Linens, such as Hessens, Osnabrigs, Hinderlands, and several other Sorts from Bremen and Embden, the Manufacture of the Circle of Westphalia, and the Countries of Osnaburgh, Hannover and Lunenburgh.

FINE Hollands for Shifts and Sheets, and such like fine Uses, of all Prices and Denominations, from 1 s. to 12 s. per Ell; as also the best Sail Cloth, call'd Duck, all from Holland.

FINE Ghentish Hollands of several Sorts from Bruges and Ghent, generally from 2 s. to 4 s. 6 d. and 5 s. per Ell.

FINE Cambricks and fine Lace from Lisle, Brussels, Valentiennes, Mecklen, all the upper Flanders, and the Paiys Conquis the Cambricks to such a Degree of Trade, that England and Ireland are said to take off just now above 200000 l. Sterling per Annum in Cambricks only, the Quantity exceedingly encreased by the Wear of Muslin growing out of Fashion.

DOWLAS Lockrams, and Vitry Canvas from France, the Quantity formerly prodigious great, not less than 100 Ships Loadings a Year, and now encreasing again, notwithstanding the high Duties, it is imported from Morlaix, and several other Ports in Normandy and Bretaigne.

ALL these, besides Irish and Scots Linen, the Quantity of which, especially since the Encouragement given to their Importation, by the printing of Linen, is so much, that the Importation of Irish Linen, amounts to at least 2000000 Yards in a Year, and is still exceedingly encreasing; being so in Demand, that if the Ships are but a little Wind bound, there is frequently not a Yard of Irish Linen to be had in the Town.

LET any one judge, whether we do not as it were ravage the World for Linen, and whether I have exceeded in saying, we import more Linen than any one Nation in the World.

IT is true, that a very great Quantity of Linen of all Kinds is ship'd off again from hence. But it is answered, That it is chiefly, if not wholly to our own Colonies in America:, which, as I said above, is justly to be esteemed our own Consumption, as being all consumed by our own People.

IT is indeed impossible to make an Estimate of the Quantity of Linen imported from all these places into Great Britain and Ireland: For notwithstanding the Quantities made either in Scotland or Ireland, there are yet great Quantities of fine Hollands, Cambricks, and other Sorts imported in both those Countries. I say, there can be no Estimate made of the Value. But having thus describ'd the Trade in its several Branches, I leave it under this General, namely, that there is more Linen as well in Bulk as in Value imported from other Countries, into the British Dominions, than any, or than all the Nations of Europe put together import besides us.

I could run over all the Kingdoms and Provinces of Europe by Name, and from their particular Circumstances give Reasons to prove this. It is certain, that thro' all the German Empire, Italy, France, Flanders, Holland, all those Kingdoms, and Provinces, either make their own Linen, some small Quantity of particular Sorts excepted, or make more than they use, and send it abroad.

IT is also certain, that those Countries where the Linen they make is of an inferior Quality, as in Poland, Russia, Prussia, Pomerania, &c. Either they use a very little Quantity of Linen, compar'd to what is made Use of in England, or make Shift with the meaner Quality and Kinds, which their own Countries produce; and except the Courts and Princes in those Countries, they call for very little from abroad.

FOR Proof of this, we are able to give a known Example of all the Northern Parts of the Empire in Particular; where 'tis evident, tho' they buy neither from Holland, France, or Flanders, they are in no Want; but the Gentry, and even the Princes and Nobility are supplied with fine Linen, at least the finest that they use from their own Manufacture; that is to say, from Silesia, and the Provinces of Lusatia, Bohemia, Moravia, and the Countries adjoining; so that all that Part of the World may be said to make Linen even more than sufficient to themselves.

NOR can we desire a better Evidence of this, than is to be found in the two following Articles,

1. THAT as I said above, we import into England a great deal of fine Linen from those Countries, such as fine Lawns, equal to some of the Cembricks which are made in Flanders, also fine Diapers and Damasks; and it cannot be doubted, but those Provinces which supply those Sorts to us at such a Distance, are able to supply themselves; for I call all the German Provinces on that Side, themselves; being all the Dominions of the same Sovereign, speaking the same Language, and lying contiguous to one another.

2. THE Dutch themselves, who make those fine HOLLANDS which we import here, and which we give such a Price for, buy the finest of the Yarn, with which those Hollands are made, from those very Provinces; and it cannot be question'd, but that the Silesians, who supply the Dutch with such fine Yarn, are able to supply themselves, and the Provinces about them, with all the finest Sorts of Linen they have Occasion to buy.

THIS Example is sufficient, and for this Reason I bring it; to prove that all these northern Countries supply themselves with Linen sufficient for their own Uses; no Nation but Britain, nay, but England, buys and imports the Gross of their Linen from Abroad; and yet at the same Time, no People in Europe wear and consume so great a Quantity of Linen, and that Quantity so fine in its Quality, as the English do.

IT is true, that Spain and Portugal import great Quantities of Linen, having very little of their own; but 'tis not worth Mention, in Comparison with England; nor do the Spaniards wear any Proportion in Quantity to the English; as may be determined from the Certainty and Sameness of their Dress: So I need say no more to that Part.

AS to Italy in all its Parts, from Naples to Turin, Rome and Venice, they not only do not use so much in Proportion as the English; but what they do make, they (especially the Venetians) make in their own Countries.

INDEED it cannot be supposed, that the Venetians, who for so many Ages were famous for making the finest Lace, and consequently must have a sufficient Quantity of the finest Thread, could want a Manufacture of the finest Linen; and it is known, that they do not want it, but on the contrary, export it to the Islands in the Archipelague, and other Parts among the Greeks, who have much Cotton, but little or no Flax.

THUS I think I may have accounted for all the Linen-wearing World; that every where but in Italy and Spain, they wear less Linen, or make more than in England; and in most of those Countries, make sufficient for their own Use: There might be some Exceptions to this general Head, that is to say, that in Sweden, Norway and Denmark, they do not make any large Quantity of Linen, and that the City of Lubec carries on the Linen Trade to Sweden, as the City of Hamburgh does to England; but the Objection is not worth the Answer; it is provided for before; I do not say no other Nation imports any Linen, or use any, but what they make of their own; but I do say and insist on it, that all those Nations put together, do not import the Quantity that England and the other British Dominions do import.

I have quitted this Article, without mentioning also, that besides the Quantity of Linen we consume, which as above, is beyond all Calculation, we import from Holland, Hamburgh, and especially of late from Russia, very great Quantities of Linen-Yarn, for our own People to manufacture, and weave into Linen at Home; much of which Yarn is made use of in the Home-made Cloth, which as I have said, our People make in the northern Parts of England; and in the Linsey Woolsey Manufactures at Kidermintter, Manchester, &c.

NOR is this Importation small and inconsiderable, tho' in Comparison of the Linen it is so indeed; but all oin together, to let us see what a Prodigy of Trade, the. Consumption of Linen in this Nation really is; the Account of which is, without Doubt, many Millions yearly

(N. B. WHEREAS I omit the Turks, and all the eastern and southern Nations in Europe, in the Account of the Linen Trade Abroad; the Answer is, That all those eastern Nations are supplied with Cotton and Callicoe, instead of Linen, and very little Linen is used among them.)

THE next Capital Head of our Importation I call FRUIT, and this consists of a great Variety of small Articles, which however, being put together, will appear to be not only very considerable, but in a Word exceeding great in Trade.

PERHAPS I may be cavill'd at for the Term FRUIT, the Product being so various, and in its Appearance trifling; but as 'tis just to bring all such smaller Articles under one general Head, as they are a Merchandize; and that they are all really the Product and Growth of the Plants, which come under the Denomination of Vegetables, I think it will be a needless Objection: The Particulars are as follows, viz.

1. Raisins,
2. Currants,
3. Figs,
4. Oranges and Lemons,
5. Almonds,
6. Oyl.

THESE are all, except the Oyl (which notwithstanding is so too) usually called Fruit, by the Merchants that import them; and even all these have this Particular attending them, as a Trade, viz. that they are used in no Nation in Europe, in Proportion to what is used in England.

. N. B. THESE are brought from several Countries, but chiefly from the Mediterranean, viz.

Raisins from   { Alicant / Malaga / Lipari   and some small Ports adjacent

Raisins from	Alicant Malaga Lipari	and some small Ports adjacent
Currants from	Zant Cephalonia	and small ports in the Morea
Figs from	Algarve, sc. Faro and Figuera, and from Barbarry	
Oranges and lemons	Malaga Sevillia Lisbon Oporto	and some from Genoa:
Almonds from	Barbary, Spain.	
Oyl from	Lisbon and Oporto Faro and Figuera Sevil and Cadiz Leghorn and Gallipoli	

Coffee	All from Mocca or Mocha in the Red Sea, either by way of Alexandria, or about by Long Sea, round the Cape of Good Hope.
Tea	All from China or from Japon by Way of China
Cocoa	From Jamaica, the Coast of Caracas, the Gulph of Honduras, and other Parts in the West Indies.
Nutmegs Cloves Mace	From the Indies by Way of Holland, and (as it happens) no other Way.
Cinnamon	From Ceylon by the same Hands.
Pepper	From Malabar, Sumatra, by our own Shipping.

Piemento	From New Spain
Pickles such as Capers, Olivers &c.	From Leghorn Lucca and Seville.
Add to these Anchovies	From Leghorn; tho' this indeed a Fish, not a Fruit, and is the only Fish we import from any Part of the World, except , Sturgeon; but I add it here, as not sufficient for a Head by it self.

THEY that at first Sight look upon this Article under the Head of Fruit, will perhaps think it a trifling Thing, and that Oranges, Lemons, Raisins, Almonds, &c. are all Trifles.

BUT let them go thro' all the Articles, and bring them into one Head of Importation, and they will have three Things to observe, which bring them to our present purpose.

1. THAT they are really so far from being small, and of little Importance, that on the contrary, they are very considerable, and that many Ways.

2. THAT no Nation in Europe imports an equal Quantity of any of them, much less of all of them together, as we do.

THEY are a wonderful Testimony of the Greatness of the British Commerce, in that those twelve Articles of petty Trade, (as they may, and would be esteem'd any where else) are by our Consumption of Quantity made so considerable; that as I am assur'd by those who have made Estimates of the Value, the Coffee, Tea, and Chocolate only, are equal in Trade, to the Spices of the Dutch.

IT is worth Notice also, what Numbers of stout Ships these particular Articles, tho' small in themselves, constantly employ; for besides the Pipiners, as they call the running Fregats, and which are a little Fleet of small Ships, that in the Season fetch Oranges from Sevil, and Lemons from Malaga; I say, besides these, the Trade for Raisins and Currants only, does not freight less than forty to fifty good Ships every Year from the Coast of Spain and Italy, including the Island of Zant.

THE Oyl from Gallipoli fourteen or fifteen more; and so in Proportion those Things which do not come single; as the Coffee and the Tea, and all the smaller Kinds of Goods from Leghorn, and other Ports, tho' they are little separately, yet together, are very great Articles in the Freight of Ships, and encourage and support the Navigation in its most considerable Parts.

IT would be surprising, if the Consumption of those few Articles once thought so trifling, and formerly so entirely unknown, were cast up into Money, and their Value brought together, what Sums they would amount to: To cast up the Tea, Coffee, and Pepper only, three Articles of the East India Trade; how often do we see in the Cargoes of the East India Ships 500000 l. Weight of Tea in one Ship, six or seven hundred thousand Pound Weight, when two Ships come in together? We cannot suppose this sold cheaper than from 10 to 16 s. per Pound to the Retailer; 300 to 400 Tun of Coffee comes frequently Home in one Ship; Pepper indeed is of less Value, and not much of it consum'd in England; but the Quantity is great, and the Chocolate makes up the value of the rest to be a monstrous Sum, considering it all as a Superfluity.

THE Importation of Silk is an Article of home Consumption, grown up now to a prodigious Height, and is the more profitable to this Nation, in that,

1. IT is all manufacture within our selves; and as it is now grown up to such a Magnitude as was never known before, employs abundance of our Poor, who, by Decay of other Branches of Commerce, began to be threatn'd with want of Employment.

2. AND especially, as it now supplies the Nation with those fine Silk Manufactures, by the Industry of our own Poor, which it has been publickly prov'd, cost us (as above) Twelve hundred thousand Pounds a Year to purchase them of the French, the Flemings, the Dutch and Italians.

THIS Importation of raw Silk, and thrown Silk has been lately calculated to amount to about 500000 l. a Year from

Turky,
Italy, and
India. ,

HERE I should mention, and I shall but mention it, the great Importation of Drugs and Dye Stuffs, in which, put together, no Nation can consume, or does import alike Quantity as England, such as,

Brasil, and Brasilletta Wood.
Fustic.
Logwood,
Sumach,
Red-wood,
Red Earth,
Gauls,
Madder,
Woad,
Indico,
Turmerick,
Cocheneal,
Cantharides,
Bark Peru.
Gums of many Kinds,
Civet, Aloes, Cassia.

Turkey Drugs,   ⎤
African Drugs,   ⎬   Innumerable.
East India Drugs,   ⎦
Rhubarb, Sassafras, *cum aɩɩs.*

I might go on here to mention the other Importations from India; and the late Addition made to our Commerce by the Trade to the South Seas; but as the last is only an Abatement of Commerce in one Part of the World, for an Encrease in another, the Assiento Contract only excepted; and the other, an unhappy Trade, to say no worse of it, and especially made so, by being unhappily managed, I shall omit entring upon them in this Part of the Discourse of Trade, as being no Addition to the Magnitude of the British Commerce in general, whether it be not a Lessening and Abatement of the Commerce, or, at least, injurious and ruinous to it, I shall not enquire here.

BUT I must not omit another Branch of Importation, which is great in it self, and necessary too: And this is the Importations of Naval and building Stores from the East Indies, and North Seas, such as,

Tar. Hemp, Flax From the Russian Dominions,

Iron,Copper, Deals From Sweden, and some of the first from Spain.

Deals, Timber and Fir (small) Wood, Masts, &c. From Norway.

Canvas, Sail Cloth East Country Plank and Clap-Board Wainscots From Dantsick Momel and Koninsbro

Oyl, Sulphur or Brimstone Rosin From Greenland. From (Denmark) Isceland and Italy.

To make an Estimate of the Value, or of the Consumption of all these Things, would be in some Measure to enquire into the Number of our Shipping, of Ships built yearly, (and which is still more as to the Consumption) Ships repairing and fitting out; an Article, when join'd together, too great to make any Calculation upon.

I might mention here, how unaccountably to blame we are in this Trade; that whereas a full Supply might be had of all those things, I may say, Every one of them from our own Colonies, the Product of the British proper Dominions, the Labour of the British People, and which is equal to it, all brought by our own Ships, to the vast Encrease of the British Navigation, it should miserably be neglected or omitted, and the Goods be bought with our ready Money, great Part of them brought Home in foreign Bottoms, and the whole Trade managed in a wrong Place; or, as we may say, running in a wrong Channel, to the infinite Advantage of the Danes, Swedes, Poles, Prussians and Muscovites, and to the enriching the (otherwise) poorest and most worthless, and I had almost said, the most beggarly Nations in the World. But I shall speak farther of this by it self.

I have not in all this Account mentioned any thing of our Importations from Holland, except only that Particular of the Spice Trade, and Linens, which I call their own.

BUT this is not, that our Importations from thence are not exceeding great, only that we do not import any thing material or considerable from thence, that is of their own Growth or Manufacture; but that by importing from them, we only bring in the Goods of almost all Countries in the World thro' their Hands: So that, tho' we are said to sell them the Value of two Millions per Annum, in our own Manufacture; yet 'tis certain, we take off again a prodigious Quantity of Goods of other Nations thro' their Hands; so that 'tis hard to determine which Way the Balance turns, either for us, or against US, and I make no Difficulty in affirming, that it may be sometimes one Way, sometimes another.

PARTICULARLY, suppose a dear Year of Corn in England, so that the Exportation comes to be prohibited. This putting a Stop at once to so considerable a Branch of our Exports to Holland, would go a great Way in shortning our Credit, in the general Account of Trade with the Dutch for that Year, and consequently might give a turn to the Balance; we at the same Time not abating our Demand of foreign Goods from them.

AGAIN, suppose for a further Example, a Scarcity of Sugars and Tobacco in the British Colonies for the same Year; for at the same Time that a common Sterility, or failing of the Crop of Corn should happen in England, the Crop of Sugars might (as it often does) fail in Barbadoes, Jamaica, and the other Islands and Colonies of America, and the Crop of Tobacco also in Virginia.

ADD to this, that in such a Year, it being probable the distilling of Corn might be forbidden in England, as no doubt it would for such an Occasion; the Consequence of which would be the allowing a greater Importation of Brandy from Holland, which they would pour in upon us, infinitely to their Advantage, we being pleased at this Time to allow the bringing in Brandy by way of Holland, at the same Time loading it with an insupportable Duty, if directly brought from other Places, tho' we might perhaps put all the Gain which the Dutch make now of it, into our own Pockets.

IN these, and many other Cases, it is easie to suppose, that the Ballance of Trade may, and sometimes does turn against England, by our general Commerce with the Dutch.

NOR can it be doubted, but that even at this Time, tho' the Exportation of Corn, and of Sugars, and Tobacco, has no Interruption; yet the late Encrease of the Importations from Holland, such as fine Hollands and Linen of all Sorts, and admitting Brandy from thence, as above, has infinitely encreased the Debt of Trade on our Side, and at least turn'd the Ballance very much in favour of the Dutch.

THE Sum of all these Explanations, and more, which might be mentioned, may be drawn up into these Heads.

1. THAT the Magnitude of the English Exportations as they consist only of our own Growth and Manufacture (including that of our Colonies as our own) is greater than that of any other single Nation in the World.

2. THAT the Consumption in England of foreign Importations, and of the improv'd Product of our own Country; that is to say, our Woollen and other Manufactures, is likewise infinitely greater than the Home Consumption of any other Nation.

FROM both which Articles, as they have been explain'd in the last two Chapters, I think I have sufficiently made out what I said in my Title, of the Magnitude of the English Commerce, and that it is a Prodigy of its Kind, the like of which is not to be seen any where in Europe, if it may be in any Part of the World.

THERE are some other Heads of Trade necessary to be spoken to, in order to make this Work a compleat Plan of the British Commerce.

I. WITH Relation to Home Trade, I should make some Estimates of the natural Product of the Land and Sea in this Island, viz.

The Corn, The Mines, The Timber,

The Cattle, The Minerals, The Stone.

HERE I should describe the Manner of breeding and managing our Cattle, the prodigious Consumption, especially of their Flesh, and the Employment of them; that is, of Oxen and Horses in Labour for the carrying on of Trade.

(N. B. ALSO I might assert, and (fully prove my Assertion by unanswerable Reasons) that notwithstanding in general, it is the Advantage of Commerce, to have all Things done as cheap as possible; yet that as it is the grand Support of Wealth and Trade in England, to have our Product consum'd, and in order to it, to have our People and Cattle employ'd; So, it is not always the Advantage of England, to lessen the Labour of the said People and Cattle, by the Encrease of River-Navigation; and some Examples which might confirm this might be brought, which amount to a Demonstration.)

2. WITH Relation to the Shipping and Navigation of England, the Number of Ships built and employ'd in Great Britain, and in that Article two other, viz. (I.) the Number of Trades depending upon the building and repairing, fitting and furnishing of those Ships, (2.) The Number of Mariners who are bred up and employ'd in those Ships, to the great Encrease of Navigation, and furnishing a constant Supply of able Seamen, the Strength and Glory of the whole Nation.

IN both these Heads, I have still the same General to maintain, and that without the least Boast, (namely) that England out-does the whole Trading World, and that there is no Nation, except Great Britain, that can carry on such a Trade; and this that I may not be suppos'd to speak in the Gross, and leave it unsupported, I shall explain in the Particulars following.

(N. B. BEFORE I descend to these Particulars I am to note, That I think it is no Boast to insist upon the Article of Shipping as an extraordinary Branch of our Commerce, not only as it is exceeding great, but as so great a Quantity of the Materials are of our own Growth and Produce, and almost all of our own Manufacture, whereas the Shipping in Holland has hardly any Thing belonging to it produced at Home, no not the Provisions which victual the Ships.)

HERE follows a Repetition of the Particulars in the Trade, in which I insist it is already proved that we exceed other Countries. Take it as follows, viz. That there is not any one Nation in Europe,

1. THAT consumes the like Quantity of Flesh Meat, and Malt Liquor.

2. THAT having no Wine of their own Production, consumes the like Quantity of Wine imported from Abroad.

3. THAT having so little Linen of their own Product consume the like Quantity of Linen imported from Abroad, or that wear so much Linen, especially of the finest that is or can be made.

4. THAT have such a Prodigious Quantity, or so good a kind of Wool.

5. THAT export an equal Quantity of, or Value in any one Manufacture of their own, let it be of what kind it will, as England does of her Woollen Manufacture.

6. THAT build and employ in their own Business a like Number of Ships, and maintain a like Number of able Seamen.

7. THAT have a like Variety of Nature's Productions, singular to themselves, or so singular, as that they are not to be had in Quantities for Commerce in any other Country; such as

1. Block Tin, 2. Lead, 3. Coal, 4. Lapis Calliminaris, 5. Allom. 6. Wool, &c.

I cannot enlarge on every Particular.

Chapter 7

Of the magnitude of our trade, as it relates to our other exportations, and particularly what we call re-exportation, or exporting by certificate; including the exports of goods first imported from our own colonies, and factories abroad

Tho' all I have said of the Greatness of our woollen Manufacture is prov'd, and how great soever the Consumption of it is in the World, I would not be understood to mean, that this was the whole of our Commerce, either one Way or other: On the contrary, this is but one Branch of it: It is true, it is the most considerable Branch; that I must always grant, and is indeed the Wheel within the Wheel of all the rest; That which sets all the Wheels of Trade in Motion; I mean of the British Trade; 'tis the Life of all the rest.

BUT we have several Branches of Commerce, very considerable besides this, and that for Exportation too: For Example,

THE Exportation of Corn, Salt, Fish, and Flesh, I put these four Articles together, for Reasons which we shall see in the Course of this Work; they are all very great Heads of Trade and Employ in Great Britain, a great Number of our Ships, more perhaps than will be thought probable at first Sight.

THIS Article, indeed, includes Ireland, of which I have yet said nothing; tho' as we are one Government, the Trade of the whole ought to come under one Head of Commerce: However, I shall not meddle with the Trade of Ireland here, any farther than as it is blended with the British Commerce, and carried on together, as in this Article it is, and is inseparable from it.

CORN is chiefly exported from England to Holland; tho' Great Britain, which may truly be call'd a Corn Country, is always ready to send it, wherever they can find a Market; so that wherever the Harvest happens to fail abroad, whether in France, Spain, Portugal, or even in Italy it self, we are always at Hand to supply them; it being very rare that England and Scotland has a general Scarcity, so as to stop the Exportation.

As it is certainly true, that whatever Corn can be spared for Exportation out of Great Britain, above what is necessary for subsisting our own People, is clear Gain to the publick Wealth of the Nation: So this Article of exporting Corn, is one of the most advantageous Parts of our Commerce, in Proportion to its Magnitude.

NOR is the Dearness of the Price of Corn at Home, any real Detriment to the Generality, or any Abatement of the publick Stock, provided we admit none from Abroad; for tho' it may be a Damage to some particular Persons, and may pinch the Poor, who yet, for ought I see, are always alike poor, in Plenty, as in Scarcity; of which hereafter; yet, I say, 'tis no loss to the publick Stock, because it is all paid among our selves; The general Body of the People have but one publick Stock of Wealth, whereof every individual is trusted with a Part; and what they pay to, or get from one another, no way lessens or encreases that Stock, only lessens and encreases the particular Part, which this or that particular Person was so entrusted with; as if ten Men, having each a hundred Guineas in their Pockets, go together into a Room or House to play; i st, take the Room in which they play, to contain a publick Stock of the whole thousand Guineas; suppose then, after some Time of play, one or two of the ten win all the Money, and break the rest; There are eight Men left empty and poor, and two Men grown full and rich; but the Money is all in the Room still, the thousand Guineas are not diminish'd at all, the Stock they play'd with is neither lessen'd or encreas'd.

THIS is too plain to dwell upon: It is the same Thing in the Rise and Fall of the Rate of Corn consum'd at Home.

ON the other Hand, if Corn bears a great Price in Portugal or Spain, or any where Abroad, all that Advance of Price, except only the Labour of the People in carrying it, is clear Gain; and even all their Labour too, except the Provisions which they consum'd in the Voyage, is so much added to the publick Stock.

I am a profess'd Opposer of all fortuitous Calculations, making Estimates by guess Work, of the Quantities and Value of any Trade or Exportation, where, as I said before, there is no given Number or Rule to raise those Estimates upon; and as this is one of the Cases, in which there is no Certainty to calculate from, and especially having not the Custom-House Books to refer to, I therefore decline it.

AND yet, I would not have been without some probable Grounds of Calculation from the Custom-House Books:, if I had not found that there is no judging of the Exportation of one Year, from the Quantities exported in another, for the Reasons following.

I. BECAUSE our Exportation of Corn depends upon the Crop we have had the Harvest before, and by Consequence on the Price the Corn bears at Market, whether dear or cheap, according to which the Merchant is limited from, or encourag'd to the Exportation.

2. BECAUSE likewise, tho' the utmost Encouragement was given at Home for the Exportation, the Quantity exported will depend also upon the Plenty or Scarcity of Corn Abroad. It is true, that dear or cheap. Corn always finds a Market in Holland: But then, 'tis as true, that if the Dutch find a forc'd Exportation, they, like all expert Merchants, will buy cheap, and perhaps to loss, or not buy at all: So that in short, it is no Market at all: To sell to Loss, is not to be call'd Trade, but a Stop or Check to Trade; for the Seller finding no Profits, is sure to come there no more, till he is satisfied by his Intelligence of a better Market.

THE Quantity exported therefore depending upon such precarious Circumstances, it would be of no Importance to make Calculations upon Uncertainties, that is to say, upon such evident Uncertainties; There may be 500000 Quarters of Corn Exported in one Year, and not one Bushel the next; as was the Case among our selves but a few Years ago, when there was not less than a Thousand Quarters of Wheat a Day entred at the Custom-house in London for a great while together, to be exported to Ireland, besides an immense Quantity shipt off on all the West Coast of England, from Chester Water as far North as the Clyde in Scotland, A great Scarcity happening that Year in Ireland.

IT would be laying a preposterous Foundation to calculate from hence what might be yearly exported that Way, when perhaps for twenty Years before, Ireland, which generally is more able to spare Corn, than likely to want it, had not called for a Quarter of Corn, and perhaps may not again, for twenty Years to come.

IT may be the like in France, and often is, that in one Year they shall take two or three Hundred Thousand Quarters of Corn from England, if they can get it; and the next Year or two would give nothing for it (speaking comparatively) if you would carry it them.

UPON the whole, I say there is no Calculation to be made of the Quantity of Corn exported; only that in general it is always very great, (except as before.)

THE East and South Coast of Britain is chiefly concerned in this Trade from the Firth to Edinburgh, to the Mouth of the Thames; more especially the Ports of the Humber, the Coast of Norfolk, from Lyn to Yarmouth, and the Coast of Suffolk also, from Yarmouth exclusive, to Ipswich inclusive.

2dly. THE Fish; there is something more of Certainty in our Calculations of the Exportation of Fish, than of most other Goods; particularly of the Herring, Pilchards, and white Fish, and to take this by the Merchants Calculations, rather than by that of the Customhouse, because the former can give an Estimate where the latter cannot, I mean Abroad. To begin North,

THE Scots are said to cure sixty Thousand Barrels of Herrings for Exportation, one Year with another, including the West of Scotland as well as the East Side; I think they that calculated the Scots Herring-fishing at sixty Thousand Last, which is ten Times the Quantity, had no Guess with them, but spoke by Way of Bluster, (tho' in Print) it being more than the Dutch take one Year with another; at least in their first Part of the Fishery: Sixty thousand Barrels is a large Quantity.

THE next Part of the Herring-fishing on the British Coast is at Yarmouth, for the red Herring Trade; the Towns of Yarmouth and Leostoff are supposed, if they have a good Fair, as they call it; that is a good fishing Season, to cure four Thousand Last of Herrings, that is, n forty Thousand Barrels a Year, the greatest Part of which is exported to Holland, France, Spain and Italy.

NEXT to Yarmouth, the Fishing for Herrings for the London Market comes in, and for present Consumption, and this is a considerable Article; but being all for Home Business, it weighs nothing in the Scale of our foreign Commerce: These Fish are ordinarily taken in the Mouth of the Thames.

IN the West of England, on the Coasts of Dorset and Devonshire, and sometimes of Cornwal, the Pilchards are a particular Fishery, singular to that Coast, and found no where else in those Seas, or in this Part of the World; it is computed, that the usual Quantity of Pilchards cur'd in those Seas in a Year, are from a Thousand to twelve Hundred Last.

ADD to these the Herring-fishing in the Bristol Channel, about Bidiford, Barnstable, and those Parts, where in a good Year they usually cure about the same Quantity of Herrings, as the other Side cures of Pilchards.

THIS is the Sum of the fishing for Herring on the several Coasts of Great Britain, the Merchants of Belfast, and of London-Derry in Ireland, have, as we are told, a considerable Share also in this Herring-fishing; but I have not learn'd any Thing of the Quantity they take.

UPON the whole, the British Fishing (for Herring and Pilchards only) amounts not to less than fifteen Thousand Lasts, or a Hundred and fifty Thousand Barrels, besides the Home Consumption of the Fish uncur'd.

THE next Branch of our Fishery is the white Fish, which may be divided into four Parts.

1st. THE English Fishing for Cod in the North Seas, and which are therefore called the North Sea Cod; the Fish taken here is generally brought to London, and to the Sea Ports on the Coast, and is used principally in victualling of Ships, Coasters, and others, for short Voyages; as also for home Consumption: So that this I take no notice of in Trade.

2. THE second is, The Scots white Fish, as they call it, which is the same kind of Fish, and are taken upon the Eastern Coast of Scotland, from Heymouth to Dunbar, and into the Mouth of the Firth: But neither is the Quantity great on this Side.

3. THE Third is, The Fishing for Cod on the North West: of Scotland, and among the Westward Islands, which lie about the Lewze and the Orkneys, where the Glasgow Merchants, as also the London-Dery Merchants take them; and these are usually exported to Spain, but not in great Quantities, that Fishery being not improv'd to the Extent, as it might be, for want of sufficient Adventurers.

4. THE Fishing for Cod in Newfoundland.

5. THE like Fishing on the Northern Coast of New-England.

THESE Fisheries cure a very great Quantity of Fish; and if we may credit their own Accounts, there are not less than 200000 Quintals of Fish cur'd by them every Year: Most of which is sent to Bilbo in Spain, to Oporto and Lisbon, to Cadiz, and to all the Ports of Spain and Italy in the Mediterranean, but especially to Leghorn, and also to our other Colonies in America:, besides what is sent to the Canaries, Maderas, and Cape de Verde Islands.

THERE are two remaining Fisheries belonging to Great Britain, I mean for Trade, and these are,

1. THE Whale Fishing carried on, for some Years on the Coast of Long Island, and Rhode Island, and New York; and now, within about three Years, by the South Sea Company at Greenland.

2. THE Salmond Fishing for barrelling up and exporting them: And this is done,

1. AT Aberdeen in the North of Scotland.

2. AT Berwick upon Tweed on the Border of England towards Scotland.

3. AT Newfoundland (that is) within the Rivers on the Island of Newfoundland, where they take pretty great Quantities, and the Trade encreases every Year: But neither of these are yet very considerable.

THUS far the Fishing Trade in which the Dutch are said to go beyond us as to the Herrings and the Whales, but not to come near us in that of the white Fish.

(N. B. THE white Fish or Cod is a very improving and encreasing Trade, and employs at least 200 or 300 Sail of Ships or Ketches, besides small fishing Vessels, without Number.)

AS for the Exporting of Flesh; it consists of two Parts, (viz.) The Exporting of Beef from Ireland, as well to our Colonies in the West Indies, as to France.

2. THE Exporting barrelled Pork from Aberdeen, chiefly brought by the Dutch for victualling their Ships to the East Indies, and other long Voyages.

3. THE Exporting of Tallow, Butter, and Hides from Ireland to Flanders, by the Ports of Dunkirk and Ostend, these are properly annexed to the Flesh, as being Part of its Substance.

THESE, put together, amount to a very great Sum, especially the Irish Beef, of which we can make no Estimate here.

3. OUR next considerable Article for Exportation, is the Product of our Colonies; that is to say, such of them as being first imported from the English Plantations in America, or from the British Factories in the East Indies in our own Ships, and having been already assistant to our Navigation; but being more than our Home Consumption calls for, are exported again by Certificate. The Goods this imported, are, chiefly

1. From the East Indies. Pepper, Coffee, Painted Callicoes, Tea, Wrought Silks, Indigo, Drugs,

2. From America:. Hides, Molasses, Logwood, Virginia Tobacco, Cotton and Indigo, Sugar, Ginger, Rice, Drugs, &c.

OF these the main Articles for Re-exportation are,

1. PEPPER, most of which is exported again; our Home Consumption being small, 'tis exported chiefly to Italy, viz. to Leghorn, Genoa: and Venice, and to France, the Quantity used at Home, is about 6000 Bags a Year. The rest is sent Abroad.

2. TOBACCO, the Quantity exported by Certificate, generally speaking, may be estimated at about 30000 Hogsheads, and the Quantity consum'd in Great Britain and Ireland, to 50000 more, in which I am sure to be a great deal within Compass. We are told, that since the late Peace, France alone has taken off 10000

Hogsheads of Tobacco in a Year, and sometimes more; the rest is exported to Holland, to Germany, Norway, and the Baltick.

(N. B. By the Word Germany, I am to be understood now, and at other Times, when speaking of Marine or Trading Affairs, the Coast of Germany, from the Embs to the Elb inclusive, which takes in the Cities of Embden, Bremen, Hamburg, and all the Ports in and between those Rivers, with the Coast of Holstein or Holsatia, the River Eider to Husum, and the Coast of Juitland.)

3. SUGARS, Indigo, Ginger and Rice: These, and the Tobacco also, as they are the Growth of the British Colonies, and the Returns for all the Exportations thither, not from England and Scotland only, but from Ireland, and from the Coast of Afric also, are in the Language of Trade, to be esteemed as Exportations from Great Britain, and are, without Dispute, Branches of the British Commerce; The Value of these is hard to determine; the Quantity of Sugar and Rice is exceeding great, the Sugars especially which are shipp'd off to Holland, and Hamburgh, and Venice, where they are us'd by the Sugar Bakers, as we simply call them; for they ought to be called Sugar Boilers, but are more properly called Abroad, Sugar Refiners.

WE are supposed to export more than 40000 Hogsheads of Sugar a Year, one Year with another; some times much more, as the Crops of Sugar Abroad may yield, which are often very different.

As to the Rice, it is a new Trade, being the Product of one Colony only, namely of Carolina, and has been brought over in Quantity but a few Years; but it is an encreasing Trade, and is now spread into Pensylvania, and other Places: But be the Quantity what it will, it goes most of it Abroad again, and is a very acceptable Merchandize to Holland and Germany, (understood as above) and is likely to be a very great Article in our American Returns.

4. WE must not omit here the African Trade, as it regards the exporting Slaves from thence to the British Colonies in America, particularly to the Islands, and to Virginia, for the other British Colonies do not much make use of them, I mean, New-England, New-York, Carolina, &c. As these Slaves are the Produce of the British Commerce in their African Factories; they are so far a Branch of the British Exportation, just as if they were first brought to England, landed here, and then sent Abroad again, or exported by Certificate (for it would be the same thing) to the West Indies, or by the South-Sea Company to New Spain.

THE Number of these is very great, and the Value of them very considerable. The Rate of Negroes: in America:, as it is of late Years risen in all the Colonies, is from 20 to 25 to 30 l. a Head, according to the Age, the Growth, and the Sex of the Negroes; and if we allow 30000 to 40 and 50000 Negroes a Year to be carried away, as (if the Trade was uninterrupted) would be the Case; then the Value of this Trade at a Medium of 25 l. per Head upon all the Negroes, amounts to no less than One Million two hundred and fifty thousand Pound per Annum.

THIS is a Trade of infinite Advantage, considering that these Negroes do not cost in the Country above 30 to 50 s. per Head; and if the Trade was uninterrupted, as it might, and I think indeed merits to be, we should, no doubt, including the Assiento, carry 40 to 50000 Slaves : a Year from the Coast of Africa, and find Business enough for them all in our encreasing Colonies.

THERE are several other Branches of Commerce which might enlarge the Subject, but I strive to contract it; and therefore say no more to that Part.

PART II

Chapter 1

A solid enquiry into that important question, whether our trade in general, and our woollen manufacture in particular, are sunk and declined, or not

We have been very much alarmed of late with publick Complaints of the Decay of our Trade; I think the People who thus complain, ought to be seriously asked to explain themselves, and to tell us,

1st, WHETHER they mean in general, that the Bulk of our whole Commerce is lessened and decayed, and that there was any Time formerly, when it was greater than it is now.

2dly, OR whether they mean in particular, that any of our Manufactures are under Decay, that their Consumption is less now Abroad, or at Home, than it has been; or that there is any Appearance that it may be so.

IF they mean the First, they ought to tell us when that Time was, and how they prove the Fact? Then we might enter with them into a calm Examination of the Thing, judge of the Calculations they make; and by the Particulars, as they shall lay them down, determine whether they complain with Reason, or without.

WHILE instead of this, they content themselves with a meer Suggestion, making a Complaint in general, claiming to have it be believed in the gross, as they bring it, without farther Enquiry. This seems to be a Kind of Popery in Commerce, demanding our implicit Assent to what we cannot believe, or they demonstrate; begging the Question in the grossest Sense, and in short is rather a Clamour than a Complaint, and ought to be treated as such.

IF I should deal with these People, as they deal with us, I ought to answer them also in gross, and affirm, which I believe I am much better furnish'd with Arguments to prove, that the English or British Commerce is at this Time so far from a Decay, that it is encreased to a Magnitude far greater than it ever was before, and is still encreasing more and more; in a Word, that our Trade is in a more flourishing Condition than the Trade of any other Nation in Europe, perhaps in the World.

IT is true, that as this is affirming without Evidence, so it is answering without Proof, and is only paying them back the same Kind they bring; but I shall descend to Particulars in its Place; and explain my self at large; at present I must go on with the Complainers.

IF they mean the second, that any particular Branch of our Commerce is decay'd, as especially our Manufactures, which is what they seem to point at, they ought then to have descended to the Particulars of those Manufactures which they say are decay'd, seeing 'tis evident some of our Manufactures are exceedingly encreased; nay, the Trade or general Term, our Manufactures, or the British Manufactures, are encreased; and we call several Manufactures our own, and justly too, which never were so before: Of which also in its Order.

(N. B. HERE I should observe, that we ought to distinguish thus between the Decay of the general Commerce of a Nation, and the Decay of any particular Branch of it; because some particular Manufacture may decay, and even wear out, in a Country, and some other may rise up in its Place; as the Custom, Fashions, and Fancies of the Times may influence and direct, and of which many Examples are just now to be seen among us; and yet at the same Time the general Commerce may not at all be decayed or decreased.)

BUT to bring the Complaint mention'd above to a Point, and to understand it, as I suppose the Complainers would be understood, however lamely they express it: By the Decay of our Trade, they seem to mean this, and no more, namely, a Decay of the English Woollen Manufacture.

THIS they alledge is in a declining Condition, and they tell US for Proof of it, That the Consumption is lessened, both Abroad and at Home.

1. THAT 'tis lessen'd; this they say is evident, by other Nations falling into the Way of manufacturing their own Wool; imitating our Manufacture to great Perfection; their People underworking ours, and their Tradesmen therefore underselling ours in Price at Market; their Governments respectively, for Encouragement of their own Poor, pressing the Consumption of those Manufactures among themselves, and prohibiting the English Manufactures being imported into their Dominions. This they think amounts to a Demonstration of the Decay of our Trade.

To clear our Hands of Things, as we go, I shall answer this briefly, the Fact is true, but the Inference is false.

1st. The Fact is true, (in part, tho' not in the whole) the Wealth of England having been so visibly raised, by the Improvement of our Woollen Manufacture, (not forgetting our loud and impolitick Boasts of that Wealth too, and how the Woollen Manufacture has been the only Cause of it). This has set other Nations at Work as far as they can, tho' the farthest has been but little, to imitate those Manufactures; to work up their own Wool, and employ their own Poor; and we have no Reason to blame or reproach them with it at all; we do the same.

2dly, FOR the Encouragement of the People to do thus in those particular Countries, their Princes have, generally speaking, prohibited the English Manufactures, especially such Kinds, as their Subjects can make, from being imported into their Dominions; nor can we blame the said Princes for this, for we do the same. Thus far I say is true.

3. BUT the Inference is false, the Trade, no nor the Manufacture is not decay'd for this; these Prohibitions and Imitations: amount to no more than this, that the People of those Countries do make some woollen Goods there, such as the course Wool of Saxony, Poland, Bohemia, &c. will admit; and thus the poor People in those Countries may be said to be clothed with their own Manufacture; but it seems to be little more, than instead of the rough Sheep-Skins, which, 'tis known, the Boors in those Countries wore before: For we find the very coursest

of our Kersies, Dozens, Duffells, and Yorkshire Cloths, which are the meanest of our Manufacture, are exported even to those northern Ports (where they were used to go) in as great Quantities as ever: As for the fine Medly broad Cloths, and Spanish Cloths, which England is so particularly noted for, they do not so much as pretend to imitate, or to prohibit them; but the Quantity exported to Hamburgh, to Gottenburgh, to Dantzick, and to all the Baltick, is as great as ever, and perhaps greater; and if I were to go thro' all the Ports of Europe with the Enquiry, it would be hard to shew where the Decay lyes; but that if one Place sinks, another rises; and if one Kind of Manufacture declines, another advances.

(N. B. THESE Prohibitions have been, some of longer standing, such as in France, Prussia, Sweden, &c. and some of a shorter Date, as now lately in Silesia, in Austria, in Piedmont, and several Parts of Germany, and at last in Spain; and we may expect the like in other Parts.)

UPON the whole, admitting all these Prohibitions of our Manufactures, and all their being imitated and set up in foreign Parts, as above, yet it is not easy to prove, neither can I see Reason to allow, that the Exportation of the woollen Manufacture of England is at all lessen'd, and consequently, the Consumption Abroad is not abated, or the Trade in particular decay'd: What Abatement of the Consumption may have happen'd in this, or that particular Part of the World, is not the Case, nor is it worth our Debate; all Nations are, and ought to be at Liberty to set their own Poor at Work, if they can, and to prohibit what foreign Manufacture they please for their Encouragement: But as the woollen Manufacture of England is an Article the most extended in Trade, of any other Thing of its Kind in the World, it cannot be expected, but it may sink in one Place, and rise in another; flourish here, and decay there, and the demand alter, as as the Customs of Countries alter, and yet the Gross of the Trade may be the same; As the Sea, they tell us, gains in one Place upon the Land, and the Land encroaches in another Place upon the Sea; and yet, neither the Sea or the Land abates or encreases in Quantity, only vary in their Situation: And thus it is in our Trade, the Consumption of the Manufacture spreads in one Place, and draws back in another; one Nation opens the Door to it, and another shuts the Door against it; but still the Quantity goes away, it is exported abroad, bought, sold, and consum'd; and we do not find any Age pass, when more of it, either in Quantity or Quality, was ever sent abroad, than is now, or so much by a great deal: How then is the Trade under a Decay?

3. THE next Branch of the Complaint, is, that the Consumption of our woollen Manufacture is lessen'd at HOME.

THIS indeed, tho' least regarded, has the most Truth and Reason in it, and merits to be more particularly enquired into: But I might ask the very Complainer himself here, supposing the Fact to be true, Why do we not mend it, and that without Laws, : without teising the Parliament and our Sovereign, for what they find difficult enough to effect, even by Law? I say, Why do not the People of Great Britain, by general Custom, and by universal Consent, encrease the Consumption of our own Manufactures, by rejecting the Trifles and Toys of Foreigners, why do we not appear dress'd in the Growth of our own Country, and made fine by the Labour of our own Hands?

ALL the Kings and Parliaments that have been or shall be, cannot govern our Fancies: They may make Laws, and shew you the Reason of those Laws for your Good; but two Things among us are too ungovernable, viz. our Passions and our Fashions; the first is at present out of my Way, but the second is directly to my Purpose.

SHOULD I ask the Ladies, whether they would dress by Law, or clothe by Act of Parliament, they would ask me whether they were to be Statute Fools, and to be made Pageants and Pictures of? Whether the Sex were to be set up for our Jest, and the Parliament had nothing to do, but make Indian Queens of them? That they claim English Liberty, as well as the Men, and as they expect to do what they please, and say what they please, so they will wear what they please, and dress how they please.

IT is true, that this Liberty of the Ladies, their Passion for their Fashion, has been frequently injurious to the Manufactures of England; and is so still in some Cases, as I shall observe again in its Place; but I do not see so easy a Remedy for that, as for some other Things of the like Nature. The Ladies have suffer'd some little Restraint that Way, as in the wearing East-India Silks, instead of English; and Callicoes, and other Things, instead of of worsted Stuffs, and the like; and we do not see they are pleas'd with it.

BUT as I am talking in this Article to the Complainers, I would have them direct their Complaints where they ought to be directed; the King and Parliament have restrain'd those Things by Law, and farther they really cannot go; we must: turn the Complaint to the People themselves, and entreat them to encourage the Manufacture of England by a more general Use and Wearing of it. This alone would encrease the Consumption, and that alone can encrease the Manufacture it self, as we shall see in its Place.

AND yet, if even this Part were examin'd critically, it would appear, that the Complaint is not right plac'd; the Manufacture is not in its self declin'd so much, as the Consumption is divided into several Manufactures, which perhaps were not known before, but under one Denomination; such as the Cotton Manufacture in Lancashire and Cheshire, the Linen Manufacture in Scotland now become our own by the Union; and the Linen Manufacture much encreas'd of late in England it self, and the same in Ireland, which tho' not our own, we find it much for our Interest to encourage; if by the Consumption of these the Consumption of the Woollen Manufacture is divided, I cannot say this can be call'd a Decay of our Trade, at least as the Use of these Goods is now brought on, not in the Room of our Woollen Manufacture, but in the Room of the Callicoes, the Use of which was lately prohibited; They are not therefore the Reason of any present Decay of the Woollen Manufacture; but if there was a Decay in the Consumption of the Woollen, it was done by the said Callicoes before; of all which I shall speak as I go on.

UPON the whole then it does not appear, that our Manufactures are lessen'd, or that the Consumption of them is abated either Abroad or at Home, but rather the contrary; and that our Trade in general, and even our Woollen Manufacture in particular, is greatly encreas'd, and is at this Time arriv'd to such a Magnitude, as it was never at before. And here it occurs to notice a particular Thing, which may be of Use to us in its Kind, on several Occasions, viz. That the Magnitude of the Manufacture is really at present its only Grievance, being encreased to such a Degree, by the Ignorance and Wealth of the Manufacturers, that it is too great for its self; the Quantity too great for the Consumption, or at least too great for the Market, tho' the Market was intirely open, and uninterrupted by any Rival Manufacture, or any Prohibition whatsoever. And here I ask to be spared a Word or two of the present imprudent Encrease of the Woollen Manufacture of England, by the ill Conduct of the Manufacturers in particular Cases; and how unjustly a Check of that Encrease is called a Decay of the Trade.

As the Veins may be too full of Blood, so a Nation may be too full of Trade; the fine fresh Rivers, when they run with a full and gentle Stream, are the Beauty and Glory of a Country; they water the Meadows, moisten the Earth, drive our Mills, fill our Moats and Canals, carry our Vessels, and enrich the whole Nation; but when swell'd by sudden and hasty Showers, they turn rapid in their Course, overflow their Banks, and rise to an undue Height; then they turn frightful and dangerous, drown the Country, and sometimes the People; carry away Cattle, Stacks of Corn, Bridges, Buildings, and whatever stands in their Way, leaving Mud, and Sand, and Stones among the Grass, and rather starve the Land, than assist to make it fruitful, and thus they become a Grievance, not a Blessing to the Publick; on the other Hand, when by long Drought their Sources are withheld, the Streams fail, the Rivers are dry, the Mills stand still, the Boats lye a Ground, the Lands are parch'd up, and the whole Country suffers.

OUR Manufactures of Wool in this Nation, bear a just Analogy with this Case, like a Stream, they are in their prosperous Course the Wealth and Glory of the Country: While the Trade flourishes Abroad and at Home, and the Consumption makes a moderate current Demand, the Manufacture goes on at a steady, chearful, even Pace, the Wool is consum'd and wrought up, the Poor are employ'd, the Master Manufacturer thrives, the Merchant and the Shop-keepers go on with their usual Strength, and all the Trade flourishes.

1. UPON some sudden Accident in Trade here comes a great unusual Demand for Goods, the Merchants from Abroad have sudden and unusual Commissions, the Call for Goods this Way or that Way encreases, this makes the Factors send large Orders into the Country; and the Price of Goods always rises according to the Demand: The Country Manufacturer looks out sharp, hires more Looms, get more Spinners, gives more Wages, and animated by the advanc'd Price, is not content to answer his new Orders only, but he continues the Excursion he had made into the Country for Spinners, &c. runs on to an Extremity in Quantity, as far, or perhaps farther, than his Stock will allow: and in a Word, gluts the Market with the Goods.

2. THE Accident of Trade, which from Abroad fill'd the Merchants Commissions, and the Factor's Orders being over, those Demands are also over, and the Trade returns to its usual Channel; but the Manufacturer in the Country, who had run out to an unusual Excess in his Business, without Regard to the Circumstances of it, having not stopt his Hand as his Orders stopt, falls into the Mire; his Goods lye on Hand, the Poor which he call'd from the Plow and the Dary to spin

and weave, are cast off again, and not finding their Way presently back to their old Drudgery, lye and starve for Want of Work, and then they cry out Tradeis decay'd, the Manufactures are lost, Foreigners encroach upon us, the Poor are starv'd, and the like.

WHEREAS the Sum of the Matter is, the Manufacturer went mad, his Stream run over into a Flood, he run himself imprudently out of Breath; and upon a little Start of the Trade, willing to furnish the Orders all himself, and loth to let a Neighbour come in with him, run himself out, drag'd the Poor into his Business, nay perhaps robb'd his poorer Neighbour of his Workmen, by giving high Wages:; and when the Trade stops a little, he runs a-ground; so the Poor are starving, and ready to mutiny O for Want of Work: And this we call a Decay of Trade, whereas the contrary is manifest several Ways.

TRADE must certainly decay, if we will run it up to such a Length, as to make more Goods than the World can consume: But it is not to be justly call'd a Decay of Trade, 'tis only abating of the Flood; the Waters were out, and now they are down again, and reduced to their old Channel.

LET us examine a little such Accidents as may raise or sink our Manufacture as above, or as perhaps have done so at this Time, and see if it does not hit exactly with this Account.

1st, THE late Accident of a Plague in France. Upon that sad Occasion, the Commerce being entirely stop'd between France and Spain, and indeed all other Parts of the World, the Manufactures of the City of Marseilles in particular, and the Country adjacent, being wholly interrupted, occasion'd a very great Addition to the Trade of Great Britain; particularly for such Manufactures as the French used to send to Turkey, to Spain, and to Italy; and the Merchants Commissions from Abroad were visibly enlarged hither for near Two Years, upon that particular Occasion: It was plain they cou'd have no Goods from France.

THE like Occasion added to the Encrease of our Trade, upon the concluding of the Treaty of Utrecht, after the Confusions in Spain had put a Check to the Trade between England and that Country, for several Years; as likewise again upon the Accommodation with Spain, after the Surrender of Sicily, when Trade breaking out like the Sun after an Eclipse, the Demand for our English Manufactures, Bayes, Says, Perpetts, broad Cloaths, Serges, &c. was such, that the Manufacturers thought they could never make too many.

THESE Excursions are not to be cast up in any View of the real Magnitude of the Trade, or of the Manufacture, any more than the true Channel of a River is to be judged of, or its Waters measured by the overflowing of a Winter's Rain, as above.

NOR on the contrary is the Stop of those sudden high Demands, by any extraordinary Check of the Call on like Accidents, to be esteemed a Decay of the Trade, any more than the dry Bottom of a large River, when the Stream withheld by a Summer's Drought leaves the Channel empty, can describe the usual Dimensions of that River, or Quantity of its Waters.

SHOULD we ever see here such a fatal Time as that was in France, when Heaven sent the Infection among them at Marseilles, or as was here in 1665, God preserve us from it, what a general Stop would it make to all our Trade? who would send any Commissions hither for English Manufactures, when they did not know but every Bale would have a Plague pack'd up with the Goods, as certainly as the Bales of Wool or Hair brought it from Cyprus to Marseilles?

YET this would not justly be call'd a Decay of our Commerce; it would indeed be a Wound, and a very desperate Blow to it for the Time; but as it was an Accident to the Trade, so the Cause being removed, the Trade would revive, return to its former Channel, and be the same as before.

IF now (to return to the Case before us) the Manufacturers of Britain, upon any such hasty Demand from Abroad, shall run rashly out into Extremes in their Business, seek out of their usual Bounds for Spinners and Weavers, and other working People, and draw them by Thousands, and Hundreds of Thousands, as was lately the Case, from their other Imployments, shall they call the Stop of these hasty Demands a Decay of Trade? 'tis a Mistake, it is no Decay, it is no more but a Return of the Stream to its usual stated Bounds, bringing Trade into its right Channel again, and to run as it did before: And this I take to be the State of our Manufacture at this Time.

IT is indeed something difficult to make an exact Calculation, and judge between the antient and the present Bounds of Trade, and especially of the Woollen Manufacture; but I'll make a brief Essay at it.

THE Wooll is the principal Fund of the Manufacture, 'tis the Stock upon which it is carry'd on. Now, be the Quantity more or less, 'tis the fixt Boundary of the Trade: The Manufacture cannot outrun this Tether; the Maker can go no further than he has Wooll to work on; sometimes indeed one Year may borrow: a little of another, but that is generally not so much as Trade demands more or less, but as the Stock of Wooll appears to vary: But when there is an apparent Decay or Advance of the Trade in general, then it is to be seen in the Wooll. And thus, I remember, before the Stop was put to the free Exportation of the Irish Woollen Manufacture, the Quantity of the Wool of England was too great for the Manufacture; and I have heard the Farmers complain of having two or three Years Stock of Wooll before-hand, and that they could not pay their Rent, because they could not sell it off.

THEN it was our great Study to get the Wooll consum'd, as appears by the Acts of Parliament for burying in Woollen; you may see by the Preamble to that Act, that it was thought to be a publick Good to waste and consume the Wooll.

SINCE that, we find all the Wooll in England too little for the Manufacture; so that now we bring in all the Wooll of Scotland, which is in short an immense Quantity, tho' coarse, and which went formerly most of it beyond Sea, and yet call for at least the Quantity of an Hundred thousand Horse Packs from Ireland every Year. This is but a very odd Testimony for the Decay of our Manufacture; on the other hand, I think it is an unanswerable Proof of what I have advanced, (viz.) that our Woollen Manufacture is very much encreased: But of this hereafter.

THEY that tell us of the Encrease or Decay of the Woollen Manufacture, should fix a Standard of the Trade, from a Proportion to which, to denominate this Encrease or Decay: To tell us it is sunk from what it was just at such or such a Time, as upon a Peace, after a long Interruption by a War, or after a Plague or the like, is to say nothing at all. But let them take six or seven Years together, and make an Estimate from the Medium, take the Exportation at a Medium, or take the Rate of Wooll, and the Consumption of the Quantity at a Medium, and then their Guesses (for they can be no more) may at least be probable.

IF formerly we could not consume all our own Wooll; and now, we not only consume our own, but all the Wooll of Scotland, and an Hundred thousand Packs a Year from Ireland; then either England must produce less Wooll than formerly, or the Consumption must be so much the greater. I think, that way of Reasoning is liable to no Exception, except it be the running it away clandestinely to France, which is trifling, and I shall make it appear in its Place, that this Channel is much smaller than it was formerly, when our Wooll lay unsold, as above.

As to the Growth of our Wooll being alter'd, and that England produces less Wooll than formerly, 'tis time enough to argue upon it, when there is, or can be one probable Reason given to suggest it, much less Evidence to prove it; yet I must not wholly pass it by neither, because, as above, it is the only Exception.

IF there is any thing to be judg'd of from Probability, it is on the other Side, (viz.) 'tis rather probable the Quantity is encreased by the innumerable Number of Acres of Land improved and enclosed within these few Years, especially in the North-west Parts of England, and which breed and feed greater Numbers of Sheep than ever, and those of a larger Breed which are prodigiously encreased in England.

I might run out here very profitably upon this Subject, and give Reasons from the general Way of Sheep-keeping in England at this Time, by which it wou'd easily be proved, that the Quantity of Wooll is encreased by the Encrease of the large Breed of Sheep which are raised now, not on the Cotswold Hills of Gloucestershire, the South Downs, Salisbury Plains, and such open Counties, as formerly, where the Soil is poor, and the Sheep small, and the Fleeces light, tho' fine, and of a short Staple in Proportion to the Creatures: But in the rich"enclosed Grounds of Leicester and Warwickshire, the Fens of Lincolnshire and Norfolk, the Isle of Ely, the Marshes of Rumney in Kent, the rich Lands on the Bank of Tees and on the Wier in the Bishoprick of Durham, and thro' all the Counties of Northampton, Huntington, Hertford, and Bucks; for the Truth of which, I need do no more than appeal to the Knowledge of the honourable Representatives of those Countries.

As the Encrease of these Sheep is manifest, and that one of whose Fleeces is equal to three of the western Counties, 'tis very improbable the Quantity of Wooll should be declin'd in England; and if the Wooll is not declin'd, then the only tolerable Objection is removed, and my Argument stands granted, or at least fully confirmed, of which this is the Abstract.

WHEN the Growth of our Wooll in England was much less than it is now, yet there were frequent Difficulties in having it be consumed by the Manufactures.

Now the Growth of Wooll in England is encreased, yet it is not sufficient to supply the Consumption of it by the Manufactures.

I think the Consequence is natural then, namely, that the Manufactures must be encreased.

To bring all this to our present Purpose,

THE Manufactures are prodigiously encreased, whether prudently, or rashly, beyond a due Proportion to the Demand, it matters not upon a Stop or Check of that Demand, we complain of a Decay of Trade; the Question is, whether that Complaint is just?

I insist, that it is not, nor does it prove any thing of a Decay of Trade; only, that the Manufacturers having rashly made immense Quantities of Goods more than the Trade of all Europe ever did or, can call for in a constant Demand, the Trade is returned to its natural Channel, after an imaginary and casual Start out of it by the Accidents of foreign Commerce.

IN short, upon the Occasions mentioned above, the Manufacturers have made their good Fortune in Trade a Bubble upon themselves, and having over-run the Market with their Goods, it returns upon them like the late South Sea, and every thing goes back from its imaginary to its intrinsick Value.

THE Demand abates the Advancement, the Price sinks, the poor Spinners and Work-folk are dismiss'd to starve: But the Cause is not in the Trade, but in the Workmen, not in the Manufacture, but in the Manufacturers; the Quantity of Goods made are too many for the Consumption, and the Market is perhaps glutted for a Year or more to come; and thus and no otherwise the Commerce is abated; that is, there is no real Abatement of the Trade, only it must have Time given to waste the over-made Quantity.

FROM the whole we may observe here how many Ways the launching out a Manufacture to an undue Extent may be prejudicial to a Nation in general; 'tis like a Tradesman that over-trades himself, and runs out beyond the Compass of his Stock; the Consequence is, that upon the least Accident in Trade, his Credit is stagnated and shaken, and the Man is undone; and 'tis a just Observation in the Tradesmen of this Nation, that there are many more ruined by too much Trade, than for Want of Trade.

IT is very unjust and unfair Dealing by the Publick, first to glut the Market, and over-run it with Goods, and then complain that the Market is dull: How should the Respiration of Trade be preserved, when 'tis choak'd and suffocated with Goods? When Blackwell Hall is empty, the Trade breathes; but when we see it piled up to the Ceilings; the Yards, the Passages and Staircases throng'd, Trade suffers, it is oppress'd with Quantity, and must die if not relieved.

LET the Trade of Great Britain go on in its usual Channel, the Magnitude of it is sufficient of it self; all Excesses hurt it; I do not think Trade receives any Advantage from those sudden Starts and Advances of Price, as hinted above, but what the Manufacturer makes one Way, he loses another, and the Poor lose by it both ways.

I remember after the late Plague in France, and the Peace in Spain, the Run for Goods was so great in England, and the Price of every thing rose so high, that the poor Women : in Essex could earn one Shilling to one Shilling and Sixpence per diem by Spinning: What was the Consequence, 'twas too plain to be conceal'd.

THE poor Farmers could get no Dary-Maids; the Wenches told them in so many Words, they would not go to Service for Twelve-pence a Week, when they could get nine Shillings a Week at their own Hands, as they called it; so they all run away to Booking, to Braintree, and to Colchester, and other Manufacturing Towns of Essex and Suffolk.

THE very Plowmen did the same, and the Ale-houses in the great Towns were throng'd with them, young Fellows and young Wenches together, till the Parishes began to take Cognizance of them upon another Account, too dark to talk of here.

WHILE this Hurry lasted, the BayeS were call'd for in prodigious Quantities, and the Price rose from 12 d. per Ell to 16 d. besides the Advance upon the Parcels, an Article particular to that Business.

As soon as the Demand slack'd from Abroad, all these loose People were turn'd off, the Spinners went a begging, the Weavers rose in Rebellion, and the Parishes were left throng'd with Bast: ards, which was all that we might say was got by that Bargain.

WHEREAS, had the Merchants been obliged with the Goods as fast as the ordinary Numbers employ'd in the Manufacture could have wrought them, the Market had held the longer, the Merchants had had their Goods the cheaper, and the Markets Abroad would have been supplied at last too.

BUT, by that unadvised rash Hurry, nothing follow'd but Confusion; the Demand stopt; yet the Makers run on as long as they were able, the Bayes were pawned in every money'd Man's Hand in the Country, and the Price sunk to 11 d. per Yard at London; so that a considerable deal of Money was lost by every Piece made, the Bay-Makers broke by Dozens, and thus they went on; and now they as well as the West Country Men tell us, that the Trade is declin'd.

Now is this to be called a Decay of Trade? no not at all; there is still a moderate Demand, and the Trade, were the Glut of Goods taken off, would be where it was: But the Run has ruin'd them; the Money to be gotten blinded the Manufacturers, they could not keep within the Compass of their own Grasp, and so sunk in the necessary Stop of the Trade that follow'd.

To judge then of the Decay of the Trade, we must bring it back, as I said, to a Medium of Years, and see how it was carry'd on, and to what Degree, in such a Time, for 10, or 20, or 30 Years ago, and then compare it with its present worst Circumstances, and I venture to say, we shall not find the Trade decay'd at all, but rather encreased in all the Manufactures of England.

I have dwelt upon the encreasing Exportations of our own, and Importations of the Goods of foreign Growth, in the three last Chapters, as an Evidence of the Magnitude of our Trade. If our Trade is declining, why do our Importations and Exportations encrease? And if they do not encrease, let the Opposer of this Part tell us the Time when they were greater, or even equal to what they are.

SOME have attempted this Part, and indeed 'tis the only way to convince us, that our Trade is declin'd; for if neither our Importations or Exportations are decreased, which Way will they go to Work to shew the Decrease of our Commerce.

I might enquire of these phlegmatick Computers, first, Whether is our Shipping decreas'd or not? I confess, I have not yet heard it so much as suggested; and tho' it is true, that it is not easy to determine that Point, yet I think I am upon a Square with the Complainers, when I say, that when ever they please to enter into the Computation, I shall be ready to begin an Enquiry on the other side, which I believe will be convincing; in the mean time, let me refer the Reader to a View of the Western Coast of the Island, and let them look narrowly into the Encrease of Shipping at Bristol, Liverpool, Whitehaven, Dumfreis, Glasgow, and all the smaller Ports on that Side from Pembroke Haven to the Firth of Clyde, and tell me if there are not a thousand Sail of Ships more employ'd on that Side, I mean Merchant Ships, besides Fishing Boats and small Craft, more than were ever known before. I might go round the Island, and make like Observations; but, as before, I meet with no body that makes any Objection of that kind.

WE have two Trades, they tell us, which are evidently declin'd, and the Shipping, which was usually employ'd in them, apparently lessen'd; and these are first, the French Trade, and secondly, the Fishing Trade.

FOR the first, 'tis true, the French Trade is lessen'd; but 'tis a Truth so evidently, and I might say so infinitely, to our Advantage, by our having made almost all their Manufactures (of which we took off such exceeding great Quantities) our own; that no Man can with Justice call it a Decay or Declining of our Trade in general, that our Trade with France is lessen'd; on the contrary, 'tis no more than this, all that Part of our Trade, which we lost by, is lessen'd, and all that Part, which we gain'd by, is or might be, if we pleas'd, encreased and preserv'd; whoever considers the Importations of wrought Silks, Brandy, Paper, Hats, Glass, and several other Manufactures, for which we paid France two Millions a Year, turn'd all upon their Hands, and all those things supply'd at Home by the Labour of our own People. For even the Gross of the Brandy, formerly French, is now supply'd by the Distillers of Malt Spirits at Home, which, as to the common Consumption, is turned all into the meanest of Liquor; but however, 'tis such as the People eagerly close with, and by that the Importation of Brandy is certainly reduced from nine thousand Ton to less than two thousand Ton a Year.

ALL the rest of the French Goods, which were formerly imported from thence, so much to our Loss, being now made at Home, I hope no Man can be so weak as to call that a Declining or Decrease of our Trade; on the contrary, 'tis a happy Encrease of it, for that the Consumption is at least the same, and our own People have the Profit of the Making; the Consumption is the same among the rich, and our own Poor take the Money instead of the Poor of France.

As to the French Wine Trade, the Question answers it self, the Stream only is turned from France to Portugal, the Quantity of Wine consumed is not the less; and as it is farther to fetch, the Shipping is rather encreas'd by it than abated; the Ships not being able to make so many Voyages as they did before, there must be the more Bottoms, or the more Tonnage in larger Ships employ'd, and either of them are an Encrease to the Navigation.

As to the Fishing Trade being decreased, it is begging the Question in a notorious Manner, and I think needs no Answering. On the contrary we see it lately encreased by a very great and probable Undertaking of the Greenland Fishery; we see also several Proposals on foot for farther encreasing the Scots Fishery, and our other Fishing must be necessarily encreased by the Addition of our Dominion in Newfoundland, by the late Peace, where our Room for encreasing the Fishing is greatly enlarged. And it cannot be deny'd, but that the English Fishing on the Banks also is actually encreased: We must therefore be allow'd to say that Part needs no Reply till the Fact be prov'd.

LET us next enquire what one particular Trade in all our Foreign Business is impair'd, what Goods of Foreign Growth are they which lye by us unsold, and with which our Markets are glutted, or which our Merchants give no more Commissions for, being not able to consume them at Home, or export them to other Places Abroad.

I shall be very brief in the Inquiry.

I begin with the East India Company; their Trade has been crampt by Prohibitions at Home, and by new Invasions from Abroad; their Silks and Callicoes forbidden to be worn, in Favour of Rival Manufactures of Linen and Silk; their Commerce invaded by a Rival Company at Ostend; yet we see last their Sale amounted to almost eleven Hundred Thousand Pounds Sterling, which allowing it to be half yearly, as really is the Case, can very ill be called a sinking Commerce.

TAKE our Plantation Trade, the Island of St. Christopher's being our own by the late Peace, we see improv'd and increased to such a Degree, that the Return of Sugar, Ginger, &c. is now as great from thence as from Barbados; and the Plantations in Jamaica are so evidently encreas'd, that we are told in a few Years they will raise ten Thousand Hogsheads of Sugar and Cocoa more than ever they did before.

IN a Word, whereas formerly we had a Glut of Sugar from our Colonies, and were distress'd for a Market to dispose of the Overplus, 'tis now evident, that since the great encreas'd Consumption of Coffee and Tea in Great Britain, all our Colonies are hardly able to supply the Consumption; and from Thirty Thousand Hogsheads of Sugar which formerly we imported, 'tis certain we now import from seventy to eighty Thousand Hogsheads in a Year, from all our Colonies, not reckoning the extravagant Bulk of the Hogsheads, which now generally contain from seventeen to eighteen hundred Weight of Sugar in each Hogshead, one with another, some of them much more.

IN like Manner, the Plantations in Virginia and Maryland are encreased to such a Magnitude, that I am told they produce now from eighty to an Hundred Thousand Hogsheads every Year; a Quantity so great, compar'd to what has formerly been produced, that if it be all disposed of, no Man can say the Virginia Trade is not infinitely increased; besides the great Export of Provisions from Virginia, that is to say, from Cheseapeak Bay, which they send to our Island Colonies, more by some Hundreds of Sloops Loading a Year, than ever they sent before, which is one great Cause of the Virginia Planters falling lately into the Trade of buying Negroes from the Coast of Africa, which they never used to do formerly.

As our Island Colonies are thus mightily increas'd and improv'd, as it is most certain they are; their People encreasing, they necessarily demand a much greater Supply of Provisions from our other Colonies on the Continent of America:, than they had before; and this encreases the Trade of those Colonies, such as of New-England, New-York, New-Jersey, East and West; Pensilvania, Carolina, as also the Trade from the Canaries, Maderas, &c. Cape de Verd Islands for Salt, and the Coast of Guinea for Negroes: So that here is a manifest Encrease of all the Commerce of both the East and West Indies.

WHERE then shall we find a Decay? where is there a Stagnation, what Trade languishes, and where is it that we drive less Business than we did before?

Portugal will not pretend to it: I might say the whole World is Witness to the manifest Encrease of our Trade with the Portuguese, who alone 'tis plain take off more of our Woollen Manufacture, since the late Encrease of their Commerce to Brasil, than both the Kingdom of Portugal and Spain used to do before: So that our Trade to those Parts is extremely improv'd.

'Tis true, there may be some casual Abatements of our Exportation to some particular Parts of the World, and especially as Things stand at this Time, by the War, or by the unsettled Circumstances of the Nations, with respect to Continuance of Peace or War; yet nothing can be argued upon that Supposition, but what all Trades, and all trading Nations are subject to, and ever will be on the like Occasions.

LET US next view the Italian and Levant Trades, which are very great Articles, and which bear a considerable Part in the great Balance of our general Commerce; the Turkey Merchants have indeed complain'd, but what is the Complaint? If the just: Part be examin'd, it will appear to lye here, and here only; not that the Goods they carry Abroad want a Market, but that the Silk they have brought Home, has, from whatever Neglect we yet know not, abated in its usual Fineness and Goodness; and that to such a Degree, that the Manufacturers here, that is the Weavers, could no longer make use of it, at least not in such Works, and to such Purposes as they had formerly done; and so the Trade may have suffer'd, not from the Abatement of the Market Abroad or at Home, but from the Merchants not taking Care to import a good Commodity.

THIS can no more be call'd a Decay or Loss of the Turkey Trade, than it would be a Loss of the Trade now carried on by the South Sea Company to America; if the Returns for their Goods should be made in a false Coin, or in counterfeit Pieces of Eight in stead of the true; The Trade therefore is not sunk; for if the Weavers cannot use the Turkey Silk, because it is deficient in Quality, they must use other Sorts; that is to say, fine Italian and Piedmont thrown Silks, or Bengale raw Silk iri the Room of it, and 'tis certain they do so. And it is worth while to observe on this Occasion, how far this has been the Case, and how the Importation of those Silks has encreased, as the other has prov'd inferior; so that the Silk Trade has not been lessen'd at all.

(N. B. It was alledg'd in the late Dispute between the Throwsters and the Weavers before the House of Commons, that as the Turkey Silks were brought over worse than formerly; so the East India or Bengale Silks came better than ever, and accordingly were more in Demand: For it will for ever be true, that whatever Materials of Manufacture are furnish'd from Abroad, and decay in Goodness, they will decay in the Use, sink in Price, and at length sink out of Demand, or they will make the Manufacture they are employ'd in sink in its Value, which is still worse.)

WHERE then shall we look for a Decay of our Importations? if to the Navy, that is already answered in the Discourse of the Shipping: If the Number of Ships employ'd is not abated, as I believe our worst Enemies will not suggest, then our Commerce to the East Country cannot be abated; by our East Country Trade, is always understood our Trade in Hemp, Flax, Tar, Pitch, Iron, &c. That is to say in general. Naval Stores; Now, 'tis manifest by the Custom-house Books: (to which I refer) that these are not abated; but on the contrary, very much encreased, not with standing our great Importation of Tar, Oyl, Masts, &c. from our own Colonies.

IN what Part of the World then is our Trade decay'd, and in what Branch of our Business does it lye? for those People that insist upon the Decay of our Trade, and that make such loud Complaints about it, ought to let us know they do not raise groundless Complaints, that would be call'd Clamour and Disaffection, and would look like something particularly piquant, which I am loth to suggest.

I must therefore call upon them for their Explanations, and to let us see the Place where our Trade is decay'd, and what Goods they are, the Consumption of which is lessen'd and decay'd either at Home or Abroad; with such needful Descriptions of Trade in general, as may convince us there is no equivalent Encrease in other Branches to make it up, and to balance the Abatement.

THE immediate Reply to this, is what I have mention'd already, (viz.)Themimickingour Woollen Manufacture in several Parts of Germany, by which the Demand of those Manufactures from England is abated, and may in Time be laid aside in those particular Countries, such as our Bays, Flannels, Chamlets, Says, and several other kinds of Goods.

BUT what does this amount to in the general Article of our great Manufacture? let particular Cases be what they will, let Saxony, Swisserland, Piedmont, Austria, and Twenty more Places, if you could name them, interfere with, supplant or prohibit this, or that Manufacture, and make a visible Decrease of the Consumption here or there: If the Consumption is encreas'd in other Parts of the World, be it a Thousand Miles, or Ten thousand Miles from Germany, the thing is answered, the Manufacture is the same.

THE Question lies nearer Home, the Enquiry, like the searching for a Disease, is in the vital Part; the Search is at the Heart, if the Pulse of the Trade beats true and strong, the Body is sound, Wind and Limb; is in a State of Health, and flourishing in spight of all the little Casualties that may happen in other remote Parts.

THE Question in the Manufacture has no difficulty at all in it; and yet it seems that those Gentlemen who insist upon the Decay of the Manufacture do it upon the Presumption, that there is no coming at the Negative; but I shall put it upon a Certainty which perhaps they may not foresee. The Question is in few Words (as before) Is the Quantity of Wooll wrought up, or is it not? If all our Wooll is wrought up, nay if it is not sufficient for the Manufacture, then the Manufacture cannot be declined.

IT is within these Five and twenty Years, that we found the Wooll of England lye on Hand unsold, and the Farmers in the Sheep-feeding Countries, such as Northampton, Leicester, Lincoln, Warwick, Norfolk, and many other Places, had generally two or three Years Wooll upon their Hands unsold, and the Price low, and very little Demand for it.

BUT now, and especially since the several Acts prohibiting the East India Silks, Callicoes, Chints, and other Goods of that Kind, we find the English Wooll not only all used up at Home, but also the Irish and the Scots Wooll brought over in unusual Quantities to help; and yet the Price holds up, and there is no Glut of Wooll in the whole Island; how then can the Manufacture be declin'd? unless you will first make it appear, that the Quantity of Wooll is abated in England, which I believe will not be pretended, and if it were, would be hard to prove.

I might very profitably employ a whole Chapter here to prove to you, that the Quantity of Wooll in England is so far from being lessen'd and decreased, that it is greatly encreased for many Years past, and continues every Year to encrease: I could prove it by proving the Encrease of the Number of Sheep in England; and the Encrease of Sheep would be prov'd past Contradiction, by the Improvement of Culture, the enclosing vast Tracts of Land in almost all Parts of England which lay open before; and which being now improved either by the Plowman, or by the Grazier, still occasions greater flocks of Sheep, and those of the best and largest Kind, to be fed than were before.

I could add to it the vast Improvement made on the North-west and Eastern Coasts of England, as also on the Coasts of Wales, by saving and draining Lands from the Sea, and from the Rivers, by which multitudes of Sheep are fed, as they are in Rumney Marshes mention'd above: The almost incredible Improvement of Land in the Countries of Cumberland, Durham and Northumberland, by which the Number of Sheep are encreased on that Side the Country in a Manner, I say, hardly to be believed.

I might also speak of the improv'd Methods, even in the breeding and feeding of Sheep, by raising them upon the plow'd and fallow Lands, upon Salt Marshes, and other Grounds, such as were never known by our Ancestors to feed Sheep before. And, lastly, I might insist upon an Article little considered, but which is really of more Importance as to the Encrease of Wooll than all the rest, Namely, that the Nation is universally fallen into a way of breeding larger Sheep than they did before: So that not only the Numbers of Sheep are encreased by many Thousands of Acres being employ'd to feed and breed, which never fed a Sheep before; but even the Sheep themselves are of a different Kind, and two Sheep produce more Wooll than three Sheep, and in some Places, than four Sheep did before. To bring this into Evidence, we need do no more than appeal to the meanest of the Country People in Lincolnshire and Leicestershire; in the first you will see the feeding and breeding of large Sheep spread from the Country of Lincoln only, to which formerly it was confin'd, into all the level Grounds, Marshes and Fens of Norfolk, Suffolk, Cambridge and Huntington; from the County of Leicester the same Breed of Sheep is spread into the Counties of Warwick, Stafford and Northampton, and even the smaller Breeds of those Counties, which they now call Stubble Sheep, and which feed on the fallow and common Fields, are of a larger kind than ever before.

To look into the North, we see the Improvement in the Countries of Durham and Northumberland, running all into a large Breed of Sheep; and you may buy as large Mutton at the Markets in the City of Durham, as any you can buy at headenhall; l affirm it, and dare bring it to a Proof on any just Occasion; and we see large Northumberland Sheep brought up yearly for Sale in great Droves into all these Southern Parts of England, especially into Essex and Suffolk.

IF then there were no Encrease in the Numbers of our Sheep, the contrary of which is true to a Demonstration; yet if we run into a larger Breed, the Wooll may still be encreased as much as if the Numbers were encreased; but as it is apparent that both the Breed is altered, and the Generality of the Sheep-breeders run into another larger Kind, and the Numbers of Sheep by the Encrease of Culture and Enclosure is encreased also. How then can we pretend the Quantity of Wooll in England is declin'd? The Weight of this Part of the Argument may be sum'd up thus.

IF the Numbers of Sheep are not decreased, nor the Breed of the Sheep degenerated, then the Quantity of our Wooll cannot be decreased or abated.

IF the Quantity of Wooll is not abated, and yet it does not lye on hand, and want a Market, then the whole Growth of our Wooll is evidently used up and manufactured; for it would not be bought if it could not be used.

AGAIN, take it in the Reverse.

IF our whole Growth of Wooll is not only bought and used up, but that we buy great Quantities of Wooll and Woollen Yarn from Ireland, to such a Degree, as has been said, that it amounts to an hundred thousand Packs a Year: Then 'tis evident that the whole Growth of our Wooll is not equal to our Manufacture.

IF it is true, that our whole Growth of Wooll is not equal to our Manufacture; that is to say, that it is not sufficient for our Supply; but that greater Quantities than ever are brought in every Year from Ireland and Scotland, all of which (clandestine Trade excepted) is used up, and manufactured in this Part of Great Britain called England, as has been proved: Then the Manufacture of Wooll in England cannot be lessen'd or decay'd; but on the contrary, is evidently improv'd and encreas'd.

(N. B. As to the Exception for clandestine Trade; it is mentioned indeed to anticipate any Cavil which might be raised upon the Omission, as if we did not know there was such a Trade as owling or running of Wooll carried on among us; but the Quantity so carried off, tho' too much, with Respect to the Injury done our Trade, yet is small, and indeed not worth naming, in comparison of the Bulk of Wooll, which the Growth of the whole Kingdom produces, and of which we are now speaking.).

Chapter 2

An enquiry whether the exportation of our other goods, the growth or manufacture of England, or the home consumption of them is decreased or declined

I HAVE mentioned the Produce of our Colonies, and prov'd that they are evidently encreased, as well in their Exports to one another, as in the Consumption and Re-exportation of their Produce here in England.

I have mention'd the Encrease of our Woollen Manufacture, and prov'd it to a Demonstration by the Consumption of the Wooll.

IT seems only to remain, that we should enquire into some other Trades which are profitably carry'donamong us, and see whether they are not declin'd in Proportion, and to make way for the Encrease of the Woollen Manufacture; for if other Branches of Commerce are declin'd in Proportion, the Woollen Manufacture, however great, may be encreased, and yetour Trade in general be declin'd too, and at the same Time.

BUT I persuade my self, it will be hard to find any part of the Product of England which can be said to be declin'd and decreased, either in its Exportation to Countries Abroad, or in its Consumption at Home.

THE Product of England has been already at large describ'd, the Wooll is set in the Frontas the Chief, and it is so; but it is not the only Product, nor are the Woollen Manufactures the only things which employ the People of England, and set their Hands to Work; there are several Manufactures in England which employ a vast Number of Peopleinwhich the Wooll is no way concern'd, and upon Examination, we shall find, (1.) some of these are wholly now a mere modern Improvement, and on which no Hands were set to Work, no Stock employ'd before.

2. OTHERS, tho' known before, are yet exceedingly improv'd and encreas'd, and consequently employ many Hands which were unemploy'd before, which in short is the essential Part of all Improvement in Trade.

I shall give Examples of some of those Manufactures, which are more remarkable than others, and by which the most considerable Number of Poor are employ'd, and Materials consum'd; for the rest, it shall suffice only to name them.

1. THE Bone Lace Manufacture. It is true, that there was always, perhaps, for some Ages past, a Manufacture of Bone Lace carry'd on in England; but the Improvement and Encrease of it within about 20 to 30 Years past is such, and so visible, that he must be utterly ignorant of Trade that is not convinc'd of it. In former Times, the chief Place for this Manufacture was about Buckingham, Stony Stratford, and Newport Pagnaell, vulgarly Newport Pannel; you have it now spread, almost entirely over the Counties of Buckingham, Bedford and Ox-

ford, and far into the Counties of Berks, Northampton, Cambridge, Hertford and Surrey, especially where any or all those Counties border on the first: It is also erected in the West, and especially in the Counties of Dorset and Wiltshire, where particularly at Blandford they make Lace of an exceeding high Price, and not outdone, Brussels Lace excepted, by any out of Flanders, France, or even Venice it self. In a word, this Manufacture is so much encreased in England, that it employs many Thousands of our Peop e more than ever; and if I may credit the Report of the Country where 'tis chiefly made, where one was employ'd by it 30 Years ago, above 100 are employ'd by it now, and these of the most idle, useless and burthen some Part of our People (I mean such as were so before) are the principal Hands employ'd, viz. the younger Women, and female Children. These were a real Charge upon the diligent laborious Poor, such as the Husband-men, the Farmers, and the Handicrafts of other Trades; and are now made able to provide for themselves, and ease their Parents and Parishes of a dead Weight, which was in many Cases insupportable; but I cannot dwell upon the Particulars, which otherwise would be profitably enquired into. In short, 'tis believ'd there are above an Hundred Thousand Women :: and Children employ'd, and who get their Bread by this Manufacture, more than did formerly; for 'tis the Encrease of it that I am now discoursing of; and this Encrease has an Effect upon the general Commerce of this Kingdom, very much to the Advantage of England, for Example.

1. IN employing all this great Number of People in a Manufacture which employ'd, as may be reasonably suppos'd, the like Number of People in another Country, (viz.) in Flanders; so that it may be said to be taking the Bread out of the Poor of Flanders, and putting it into the Mouths of the Poor of our own Country.

2. It is a Turn in the Balance of Trade to the Advantage of England, in supplying us with the same Quantity of Goods by the Labour of our own Poor, which we, till now, bought abroad, and which buying abroad, was always attended with this as a Consequence, that either we paid for them in Money, or in our own Manufactures; whereas (if the first) that Money, is now kept at Home; and (if the last) those Manufactures must be paid for to us in Money, as they certainly are.

ANOTHER encreas'd Manufacture is that of wrought Iron and Brass: I need not refer to the Towns of Birmingham and Sheffield, and the People of Hallamshire, a District well known to the Nailers and hard Ware Men of Barns ley and Rotherham: But I appeal to the Iron Works of the late Sir Ambrose Crowley, and his Son Alderman Crowley, at Newcastle upon Tyne; and above all, to the same sort employ'd in London, where they certainly make the best Cutlery Ware at this Time in the World.

IT is not many Years since the best Scissars, the best Knives, and the best Razors were made in France, and the like of the fine Watches, Tweezars, and other small Ware; nothing is more1 evident in Trade at this Time, than that the best Knife Blades, Scissars, Surgeons Instruments, Watches, Clocks, Jacks and Locks that are in the World, and especially Toys and gay Things are made in England,

and in London in particular; and our Custom-house Books:, will make it appear, that we send daily great Quantities of wrought Iron and Brass into Holland, France, Italy, Venice, and to all Parts of Germany, Poland and Muscovy.

IN a Word, no particular Manufacture can be nam'd, which has encreased like this of the hard Ware, I mean, in Great Britain; and 'tis still an encreasing Manufacture: To make Calculations, and Comparisons, seems to be piquant in the Case, and particularly pointed at this or that Nation; but let it point where it will, the Fact is plain; 'tis the like in the grosser Part of the Trades, as our Toys, Scissars, Razors, Knife and Sword Blades outdo the French; so our common Bombs, Shells, Grenades, Caldrons, and all sorts of cast Iron, as much outdo the Germans, the Legois, or the Dutch.

IT is the like in wrought Brass; most of the Brass Locks of all the fine Palaces in France, if narrowly inspected, will be found to be English; the fine Gold Watches in the Pockets of the Grand Seignior, the Czar of Muscovy, and the Sophy of Persia, or the great Mogul, are generally English: We send our Toys to the Court of France, and the English Knives and Razors have quite outdone the French.

BY this Means it comes to pass, as I am well assur'd, that there are above 200000 People employ'd in the Manufacture of Iron and Brass in England, more than ever were before: Perhaps this may be of the most as to Numbers, nor will I take that Part upon my self, tho', if it be true, that the late Sir Ambrose Crowley did employ 30000 People in his own particular Part, the rest may be more than probable. But this, upon the whole, will (I doubt not) be allow'd, (viz.) that there is a visible Encrease of our Trade in Iron and Brass, as well as it is a Manufacture, as it is a Merchandice; for there is a manifest Encrease of the Exportation and Home Consumption, as well as an Encrease of Employment for the People.

(N. B. IN this Article should be included the Mines of Copper lately improv'd in England and Wales; as also the Battery and Brass Mills and Foundaries, which are in themselves very considerable; and if we may credit the Representations made to the Parliament a few Years since, do employ many Thousands of our People more than were ever employ'd in those things before.)

THESE are Improvements in Manufacture and Trade; and as they testify an Encrease of Trade, we can see no Room yet to suggest that the Trade of England in general is declin'd or decay'd.

3. THERE are some other Articles yet more considerable than these, and one of them is the broad Silk Manufacture; I cannot pass it over; it is an Encrease of this very Age. It is a Surprise to the World, as well in its Quantity as in its Value, and in the admirable Perfection which our People are arriv'd to in it, and the little Time they have had to raise it to the Degree which it is arriv'd to.

IT is but a very few Years ago, that the making of broad Silks began in England; the French and the Italians carried the World before them (as to Trade) in that particular Article; what Attempts had been made in England were chiefly at Canterbury by the Walloons and French Refugees, and they were so beaten out by the East India Silks, that if I am not misinform'd, there were not 20 Looms left at Work in the whole City of Canterbury, some say, not half so many.

WHEN the French Trade prevail'd, and before the Stop of Commerce between the Two Kingdoms began by the late War, the most moderate Calculations valued the broad Silks which were imported from France and Italy at 1200000 Pounds Sterling-per Annum; some say, we took off as much as that Value in the French Silks only, whereof one Half at least in Alamodes and Lustrings, the Manufacture of Lyons, and the Provinces upon the Rhosne.

BUT be it so or not; for we are not adjusting the Value of Things, in that or any other Part of that Country, but the general Tide or Current of the whole Trade; of which I might venture to say, it was known to the whole World, that is to the whole trading World, that it run to the Advantage of France, with a full Stream directly from England; I mean as to the Silk Manufacture, all which Trade is now sunk, I say, sunk and lost as to France and Italy, to the infinite Advantage of England; and this not that England may be said to leave off wearing Silk: No, far from it; as our Wealth is encreased, we do not pretend our Pride or Vanity is abated; our Ladies go as gay, and our Houses are furnish'd as rich as ever, and perhaps more so, and in the same Kinds and sorts of Silks, Lustrings, Mantuas, Velvets, Padua Soys, Garden Sattins, the best and richest Brocades, and the best and richest of all sorts of Silks; But the Difference lies here, that whereas we bought them before, now we make them at Home; we set the French Men of Tours, of Lyons, Avignon, and the Countries about them at Work before, and the Italians of Milan, Mantua, Genoa:, Florence and Naples, and paid them all at a vast Expence of English Money, a Profusion of Money, even a Million 200000 Sterling a Year; whereas now our own Poor gain all that Money; our own Merchants import the Materials, our own Manufacture purchases the Silk, the Drugs and Dye Stuffs; and the whole Manufacture of broad Silk is an Encrease upon our Commerce. But I shall say no more of this here, because I shall have Occasion to mention it again, when I come to speak of the English People improving upon the Manufacture and Inventions of other Nations.

4. I proceed therefore to another visible Encrease of Trade, which spreads daily among us, and affects not England only, but Scotland and Ireland also, tho' the Consumption depends wholly upon England; and this is printing or painting of Linen. The late Acts of prohibiting the Use and wearing of painted Callicoes, either in Cloths, Equipages or House Furniture, was without Question aim'd at improving the Consumption of our Woollen Manufacture, and in Part it had an Effect that way.

BUT the Humour of the People running another way, and being used to, and pleased with the light, easie and gay Dress of the Callicoes, the Callicoe Printers fell to Work to imitate those Callicoes, by making the same Stamps and Impressions, and with the same Beauty of Colours upon the Linen, and that this fell upon the two particular Branches of Linen, call'd Scots Cloth and Irish Linen: I need not take any Pains to prove this. The Consequence is also evident, (viz.) That the Linen Manufacture both in Scotland and in Ireland are considerably encreas'd upon that Occasion, and many hundred thousand Ells of Linen are yearly imported from Scotland and Ireland, and printed in England, more than ever were before; so that this is an Article wholly new in Trade, and indeed the Printing it self is wholly new; for it is but a few Years ago since no such thing as painting or printing of Linen or Callicoe was known in England; all being sup-ply'd so cheap, and perform'd so very fine from India,, that nothing but a Prohibi-tion of the foreign printed Callicoes could raise it up to a Manufacture at Home; whereas now it is so encreased, that the Parliament has thought it of Magnitude sufficient to lay a Tax upon it, and a considerable Revenue is raised by it.

IT may be enquired here concerning the great Numbers of People employ'd in these Improvements, what were they employ'd in before? and how do we call it an Improvement, if they are only taken from one Manufacture into another.

THIS might be fully answered, if we had Room here to enquire critically in the several Counties where those particular Improvements are made; we should there find, that in almost all the Improvements and Encrease of Business above mention'd, such as the Manufactures of Bone Lace, the Brass and Iron Manufac-tures, the Haberdashery; and in a Word, all the other improv'd Manufactures, except that of Broad Silk weaving, the People employ'd were not at all employ'd in the Woollen Manufactures before, but were, generally speaking, out of Busi-ness, idle and unemploy'd, there being no such thing as Woollen Manufactures settled in the Counties and Towns where those Improvements have been made, such as Buckinghamshire and Bedfordshire, Sheffield, Birmingham,, and New-castle upon Tyne.

THE broad Silk Trade indeed, being chiefly carried on in the Cities of London, might be said to employ some of the People formerly employ'd in the Woollen Manufacture in the same Place, (viz.) Spittle-Fields: But then it must be added, that even that Encroachment was only upon the Abatement of such Woollen Goods in that Place, which were imprudently launched out into before, upon the foolish Expectations of a great Encrease of the Woollen Trade, by the Prohibi-tions of East India Goods; so that even in this Part the Silk Trade has very little, if at all encroach'd upon the Woollen, tho', if it had, the Exchange had very little alter'd the Case.

UPON the Whole, after the narrowest Search, and with the utmost Impartiality, I cannot see that we have any Room to say our Trade is decreas'd, whether we speak of our Woollen or other Manufactures; whether of Goods imported or exported; whether of the Home Consumption, or the Consumption of our Growth Abroad. On the contrary, we have great Reason to insist, that our whole Trade is encreased to a very great Degree; it remains only in a summary Way, to account for the Encrease of our Commerce both Abroad and at Home.

PART III

Chapter 1

Of the improvement of the English in trade; upon the inventions of other nations, and the encrease of our commerce upon those improvements; in which we have beaten out the said inventors from their own trade; likewise of the several improvements of our own product, and of our own invention: by all which our trade is greatly encreased

It is a Kind of Proverb attending the Character of English Men, That they are better to improve than to invent, better to advance upon the Designs and Plans which other People have laid down, than to form Schemes and Designs of their own; and which is still more, the Thing seems to be really true in Fact, and the Observation very just,

WHETHER this Reproach upon them is raised upon the Suggestions of Foreign Observers, or whether it be our own upon our selves, is not worth while to examine; it seems we are very willing to grant the Fact.

UPON this Supposition then my Subject seems to be adapted to the national Temper; I offer here a Scene of Originals, for the improving Genius of our People to work upon a Stock of Invention for them to improve upon: May they take the Hint, try their Hands, and go to Work upon them with the usual Success.

HENCE most of our great Advances in Arts, in Trade, in Government, and in almost all the great Things, we are now Masters of, and in which we so much exceed all our Neighbouring Nations, are really founded upon the Inventions of others; whether those first Inventers were private Men, or Nations of Men, 'tis not material.

EVEN our Woollen Manufacture it self, With all the admirable Improvements made upon it by the English, since it came into their Hands, is but a building upon other Mens Foundations, and improving on the Inventions of the Flemings: The Wool indeed was English, but the Wit was all Flemish; we had the Materials, but no more understood the Virtue of them, than the World understood the Making Gun-powder, tho' they had always the Sulphur and Salts, which are now the proper Ingredients of that dreadful Composition.

WE had the Wool, but understood neither how to comb it or card it, spin it or weave it; nay, we cannot be said to know, that it was capable of those manual Operations, or what Spinning and Weaving was, any more than if we had not known what the Wool was: But when, as has been observed, by the Direction of King Henry VII. the English were put upon the general Notion of Improvement, inform'd of the Profit of manufacturing it, and but once directed how to go about it, by the Flemish Agents hir'd to instruct them: How soon did they outdo their Teachers, and to what a Pitch of Improvement did they rise in a few Years? Till now we see the World ambitious of imitating us in the same Manner, and to rival our Manufactures, are obliged to hire Instructers from hence, and to learn of those who were themselves but Learners before.

I might enter into almost all the Improvements of Art in which the English so much now excel the rest of the World: How in several Manufactures we have turn'd the Scale of Trade, and send our Goods to be sold in q those very Countries from whence we deriv'd the Knowledge and Art of making them.

THUS we were all said to learn the Art of building Ships from the Genoese and French, and at this Day so effectually outbuild them all, that the Genoese often buy Ships in England, and the late King of France, the great Lewis XIV. procured the Model of our Ships from England, by which to build his Capital Men of War; among which that glorious Ship burnt by English at La Hogue, called the Royal Sun, was said to be built by the Model of the Royal Sovereign, an English Man of War, built in the Time of King Charles the first, and rebuilt in King Charles the second's Time, and the Drafts of it were it seems transmitted to France.

FROM the Venetians and French we took the Art of Glass-Making, and of Cutlery, and several others; till now we outdo our Teachers, and export Glass Wares, Brass Locks, Fine Keys, Knives, Scissars, Razors, Surgeons Instruments, and Joyners Tools, to those very Places; and you may see the Doors of the Royal Apartments at Versailles, (as is said above) furnish'd with fine Brass Locks, and nice Hinges from England, because France cannot produce the like.

I might give Examples of the like Kind in many other Cases, wherein we excel in the Improvement those very People, who so much excell'd us in the Invention; of which the Silk Manufacture is now a surprising Example, in which we so much outdo the French themselves, who were our Teachers, and of whom we always bought the richest and finest broad Silks the whole World could produce, that we now sell broad Silks even into France it self.

To begin with probable Improvements in Colonies and Plantations; Columbus: a Genoese by Nation, discover'd the Coasts of America:, and his Successors the Adventurers upon those Discoveries, took Possession for the King of Spain: It is true, they spread themselves upon the Continent, reduc'd, or rather destroy'd the Nations who inhabited the several Countries, possess'd the immense Wealth of the Natives, and being led by the Hand to the Mines of Gold and Silver, and the other rich Product of the Place, they vouchsafed, as we may say, to stoop and take it up; but we can charge them with very little of Improvement: The Sin of Diligence cannot be lay'd at their Door, nor have they to this Day, after almost 200 Years peaceable Possession, brought the most fruitful and richest Provinces and Districts of America to be much more productive than they were before; not a Manufacture of any Value erected to employ and improve the People; not any Advantage considerable made of the Labour of the many Thousands of the Natives, who still remain among them, and are as willing as able to work for them for a Trifle; not any Culture carried on, no not in the most fruitful Provinces, to encrease the Product equal to the Strength of the Soil.

ON the contrary, the English tho' planting near 100 Years after them, and taking, as it might be called, the Fag-end of the Discovery, the northern, cold, and barren Parts, without Silver and Gold, without Mine or Mineral, without any apparent Product; yet how has the improving Genius of the English brought Gold out of their Dross.

I say Dross; for so it was with respect to the first Discoverers; and in their Esteem all our Colonies were but, as we may say, the Dregs of the Spaniards first Extraction, the Refuse Part of their Conquests, their meer Leavings, that Part of the Country which they did not think worth so much as looking into.

WHAT were all our Colonies upon the Continent, but a little narrow Slip of Land upon the Sea Coasts, in the cold, wild, unhospitable Climates of the North? And what our Island Colonies, but a few little despicable Islands not worth the Spaniards possessing, hardly worth their naming, in Comparison of their vast Possessions on the Continent; nay not worth naming in Comparison of the vast Islands of Cuba and Hispaniola, one of which is bigger than all our Islands put together; and yet Cuba and Hispaniola, tho' equally rich and productive, and infinitely full of natural Wealth, are left unplanted, as not worth their Pains to improve.

(N. B. Barbadoes is not above 70 Miles in Circumference, and Hispaniola is above 400 Leagues, Nevis not above 20 Miles, and Cuba above 690 Miles in Length.)

BUT let us turn our Eyes now and view the Effects of the improving English Genius, the Colonies of New-England and Virginia, despis'd by the Spaniards, as well before we discover'd them, as afterwards; for the same Columbus:, which discover'd New-Spain, discover'd all the Northern Coast, but left it again as not worth while to plant and possess it. I say, these barren, cold, poor and uncultivated Climates, the Leavings of the Spaniards, How have we improved upon them to infinite Advantages?

NOT discouraged by the Severity of the Cold, by the Surface over-grown with Briars and Thorns, by the early Opposition of the Natives, a Race of People fierce and false, untractable, treacherous, irreconcilable, bloody and merciless, even to the most horrible, and almost in expressible Cruelties, who would rarely make Peace, and more rarely keep their Agreements when made.

OFTEN massacred and butcher'd, and sometimes quite driven away by the Fury of the Savages, often starv'd out and famished, and either the whole Body of Planters wasted, and perishing with Cold and Want, and as often being reduc'd to Extremities, forc'd to abandon the Country in the utmost Distress, and return starving home.

BUT never to be discouraged, how have they by the meer Force of indefatigable Application, planted, inhabited, cultivated those inhospitable Climates, those suppos'd barren Countries, those trifling little Spots of Islands, not thought worth looking at by the Spaniards? How have they brought them to be the richest, the most improved, and the most flourishing Colonies in all that Part of the World? So populous, so fortify'd, the People so rich, the Product so great; and which is more than all, so adapted to Commerce, so universally embarked in Trade, that it is at this Time an unresolved Doubt, whether brings the greatest Wealth to Europe, take the Exportations and Consumptions of Manufacture there into the Account of the Return, the Sugars, Tobacco, and other rich Productions of the British and French Colonies; the Fish, the Corn, the Flesh, the Furrs, &c. I say. Which are the greatest in Value, these, or the Gold and Silver of Mexico and Peru?

BUT not to weigh the Particulars, and come to reckon by Ounces and Drams, this is certain, and will be granted, that the Product of our improved Colonies raises infinitely more Trade, employs more Hands, and I think, I may say by Consequence, brings in more Wealth to this one particular Nation or People, the English, than all the Mines of New Spain do to the Spaniards.

AND not to insist only upon the little Share Spain it self reaps from the Returns of Gold and Silver, made to and landed in their Country; most of which runs out again in the very same Species in particular Channels of Trade, to other Nations: I say, not to insist upon this, take the Opulence, the growing Greatness of the British Colonies, the Numbers of their People, and how prodigiously every Day encreasing; and above all, that the Encrease of Navigation, the Number of Ships employ'd, nay Ships built, and Seamen nurs'd up, the Wealth and Addition of Strength we reap from them, which is not easy to calculate. I say, add this to the Account, and, I doubt not, it will be granted, that the Return of Wealth from America: to this Nation, is equal to the Return of Gold and Silver from New to Old Spain.

LET any Man calculate the Value of our Returns in Sugar, Ginger, Indigo, Cotton, Cocoa, Drugs, Spice, and other Goods, from the Islands only, with the Furrs or Peltry; the Rice, Tobacco, Train and Turpentine Oil, Tar, Masts, and abundance of other things: Then let them add the Interchange of their other Product, between the several Colonies, one with another; such as the Supply of Corn, Pease, Rice, Meal, Beef, Pork, Beer, Horses, Leather, Fish, Lumber, &c. of all which, the Quantities are exceeding great; and in which Trade, several Hundreds, nay some say Thousands, of Ships and Sloops, are constantly employed.

In Return for which, a very great Quantity of Rum, Molasses, Cocoa, Ginger, Sugar, &c. is sent back to the Main-Land Colonies on the Continent; of which, all that they cannot Consume is sent to England for Returns.

IF these things are cast up together, including the Consumption of the Woollen Manufacture of Great Britain, and of all the Hard-ware Manufacture; also the Cordage, the Hats, Gloves, and other Leather Manufactures: In a word, the Consumption of all the other British Goods sent thither, the Comparison of Trade will be, out of Question, on the British Side; seeing almost all the Goods exported from Spain to their Colonies in America, are first bought from other Countries.

HAD the Spaniards been an industrious, improving Nation, like the English, the Islands of Cuba and Hispaniola alone, having been planted and improved, as our small Island of Barbadoes is improved, would have produc'd more Sugar,

Cotton, Indigo, Cocoa, Piemento, and other valuable things, than all Europe could have consumed; and they would have been able to have supply'd all their other Colonies with Flesh, such as Beef and Pork, and with Rice and other things, more than they could consume.

IN lieu of which, those fruitful Islands are now left to lye waste, untill'd, unplanted, and the great Discoverers have not made any one Step that deserves the Name of Improvement upon them, except only the fortifying the Port of the Havana; which Necessity almost drove them to for the Protection of their Commerce to their other Colonies, and forming the Rendezvouz of their Galleons in their passing and repassing between Europe and America.

WHEREAS, take our Colonies on the Leward Islands only into Consideration, (here indeed we have improv'd to the utmost) there is hardly an Inch of Ground lost in the Island of Barbadoes that can produce one Ounce of any thing more than it does; the like perhaps cannot be said of any one Spot of Ground in the World, which containing in the whole not above 70 Miles in Circumference, employs and maintains above 100000 People, in eluding the Negroe Slaves, : enriches the Planters to a surprising Degree, and fully employs above 200 Sail of Ships and Sloops, always running with Provisions of Fish, Flesh, Corn, and Cattle, from North America:, Wine from the Mad eras, and with Slaves (Negroes) from the Coast of Africa, and with Manufactory and Merchant Goods from Great Britain and Ireland.

THE same, in its Proportion, might be said of the Island of Jamaica, where the Spaniards were the Discoverers, that is, in the room of the Inventors, and made little or nothing of it, and we are the Improvers; and what that Improvement is, we all know: That Island for its Planting, and its other Advances of Trade, is at this Time the greatest Article in all our West India Commerce; and if some nice Calculators may be allowed to judge right, the Product of the Island of Jamaica, and the Consumption of Goods there from England, or which goes that Way, to New Spain, makes the Trade of the Island superior at this Time to the Trade of all our other Islands; that is to say, the Islands of Barbadoes, Nevis, Antegoa, Monntserat, and St. Christophers, put together, and this Trade every Day encreasing too.

NOR is the Improvement of Jamaica improperly call'd advancing upon the Invention of others; for the Spaniards did for themselves make several Experiments in Trade; they planted originally in Jamaica several things, which were then meer Inventions in Planting, which the English have since improved upon, and which are not to be produc'd in any of the other English Islands; such as the Cocoa, Piemento, Indigo, and several other things which the English have since brought to a great Perfection by their Improvement.

THEY likewise laid the Foundation of that secret Commerce with the Spanish Colonies, which the English have improv'd to such a Degree, as it is even threatning to the whole Trade of New Spain; for when the English conquer'd the Island from the Spaniards, those Spanish Families, which remain'd upon the Island, keeping up a Correspondence with their Friends and former Acquaintants in Cartagena, St. Martha, and the Coast of Caracas, and all the other Ports of that

Country, that Intimacy became the Foundation of an advantageous Correspondence, since carry'd on; and the improving English brought forth from it a Trade grown up by Time, and the particular Encouragements of succeeding Ages, to a prodigious Magnitude.

BUT these are things behind us, and may perhaps be call'd, looking back to what is past; whereas the Eyes of Mankind are rather fix'd upon things before them; and where we talk of Inventing and Improving, the Enquiry is, what Inventions are now upon the Anvil, for our improving Genius to work upon? What is there that at present offers for the Application of an ingenious People? And this brings me to the grand Head proposed in this Treatise, (viz.) Schemes of Improvement in Commerce, which are to be the Subject of this latter Part of the Work.

Chapter 2

Being a proposal for rooting out those nests of pyrates and rovers, the Turks or Moors of Tunis, Tripoli, Algier, and Sallee, who have for so many ages infested the mediterranean seas, and the coasts of Spain and Portugal, to the infinite loss and discouragement of all the trading nations of Europe. with a scheme for the improvement of trade, by restoring and establishing the ancient commerce on the north and north-west coast of Africa

In speaking of Africa, as it once was the Seat of Commerce for the whole World, we must look back as far as to the flourishing State of the Carthaginian Government; but it shall be as short as can be desired.

IT is true, as has been observed by a well informed Writer on this Subject, that the Romans (like the Turks in our Time) were no Friends to Trade; they carry'd on their War for Glory; like meer Soldiers they fought to conquer, and conquer'd to plunder, not to plant and people the World: So far were they from encouraging or improving the Commerce and Wealth of the Nations they subdued, that they overthrew and destroy'd the greatest Trading Cities in the World; such as Corinth, Syracuse, Carthage, and all the Cities of Egypt and Africa; Instead of encouraging Trade and Navigation, they murther'd the Merchants, burnt their Ships, and carry'd away the People, which are the Life and Support of Manufacture and Trade.

ON the other hand, the Carthaginians, as they had the richest Soil and a numerous People, (for Africa was then infinitely populous) they improved the first, and employ'd the last, to the utmost; their People were as rich as they were numerous; they carry'd on Trade to all the Parts of the World, planted Colonies, built Cities Abroad, and Ships at Home; and wherever they came, whether by Conquest, or by Consent, they planted the Country, not destroy'd it, carry'd People to it, not away from it; and, in a word, made them rich, not plunder'd and starv'd them.

Carthage and Corinth at that Time were the two great Emporiums of the World; this carry'd on all the Commerce of the West and that of the East: Corinth manag'd the Commerce of Asia, Persia, and India,, and brought the Wealth of the

East Indies, the Spices, the Silks, the Callicoes, the Gold, the Diamonds, and in a word, the whole Indian and Persian Trade in Caravans; Part from Ormus and the Gulph of Persia, to Bassora and Bagdat, by Water, and thence by Caravans to Aleppo and Scanderoon; and so by Sea to the Gulph of Cenchraea and Corinth, another Part to Trapezond in Armenia, and by the Euxine Sea thro' the Straits of Bosphorus and the Hellespont, and thro' the Archipelague to the same Gulph, and so to Corinth.

Carthage, on the other hand, planted Colonies, and extended their Possessions upon the Coast of Spain, as well within as without the Straits; built Cities from New Carthage, now call'd Carthagena in Spain, to the Groyn, as well in the Mediterranean as in the Ocean, and from Tangier, then a populous City of I00000 Inhabitants, to the Cape de Verde on the West Side of Africa, and from thence into America it self; which, there is no room to doubt, was discovered if not peopled from Africa, by the indefatigable Carthaginians; and had never been lost and forgotten to this Part of the World, if the Romans, those Destroyers and Enemies of all Improvement, Commerce, and Navigation, had not so utterly ruin'd Carthage, not the City only, but the very Nation, as not to leave them a Name under Heaven; and so of course caus'd all their remotest Settlements to be abandon'd; and in consequence, at last forgotten; but that by the way, it requires, and indeed deserves too long a Digression for this Place.

Now, when these two Cities of Corinth and Carthage fell, (for they were destroy'd by the Romans within a Year of one another) Trade receiv'd a mortal Wound; I may say the Trade of the whole World did so; and as those Cities never recovered, so the Trade, which was fixed among them, decay'd and dy'd, was divided and scatter'd, and, in effect, lost; for it never fully recover'd it self, no not to this Day.

THE Colonies, which the Carthaginians planted, sunk and dy'd away, and many of them lie in Ruins to this Day; especially on that Side of the Ocean from the Straits Mouth to Cape None; for as the Carthaginians planted Colonies for Trade, the Trade being lost by the Overthrow of the Merchants in the Mother City Carthage, the new planted Cities, and the Sea Ports, were ruined of course, and perished, as a Child starves when the Nurse is taken from it.

IT is true, the City of Carthage was rebuilt, and recover'd it self in some Degree, under the Government of the Western Emperors; and especially as those Emperors were Christians, and were Encouragers of the Industry and Application of their Subjects; then, I say, the trading Genius reviv'd very much, especially in Africa, and the Climate and Soil of that Country being particularly productive of many valuable things, and those things adapted to Trade, and encouraging to the Merchant, the African Merchants carry'd on a very considerable Business; Navigation also being very much their Peculiar, they traded by Sea to all the known Parts of the World, but nothing like what they did before.

THE principal Branches of their Commerce in those Times, as we gather from the Histories of the neighbouring Countries, consisted, 1st. in exporting the Growth of their Country, and the Manufacture of their People, just as it is with us in Britain: For the Nature of Commerce is ever and every where the same. And

2dly, in importing again the Product of other Countries, either for their own Consumption, or for Re-exportation to remoter Parts, which had not the same Product.

THEIR own Product consisted chiefly in Corn and Cattle, and among the last, chiefly Horses, of which they furnished great Numbers to mount the Roman Cavalry; for the Numidian Horse were then, as the Barbs and Jennets (which are the same) are now, fam'd for their Beauty, Swiftness, and fine Shapes, thro' all the Roman Empire.

But above all their Product, the most valuable were their Wax and Copper, in both which they still excel the whole World; also their Corn, Fruit, Druggs, and rich Gums, all which remain to them.

FOR Manufactures, we do not indeed read of their Woollen Manufactures, or at least, not much: But the Carthaginians, as well as the Egyptians (and both were Africans) are fam'd for the Product of fine Linen; and 'tis to be supposed the Soil produc'd a very fine kind of Flax, which, as the Fund of that Manufacture, they improved to great Advantage; but that Part is now lost.

AS to their Importations, we are assur'd they fetch'd Tin and Lead from Great Britain, Gold and Wine from Spain, for old Spain ever produc'd much Gold; Silks and fine East India Goods from Corinth and Alexandria; what Trade they had with Gaul (France) we do not find, but the other was very considerable, and is sufficient to our Purpose. Thus stood their Condition flourishing in Wealth and Commerce, when the Romans, as above, to the eternal Infamy, not Glory, of their very Name, destroy'd them all.

AS by that general Rule, I say, the Trade of the World receiv'd a mortal Wound; so when I say they reviv'd under the Roman and Grecian Emperors, it was apparent all their Recovery and Encrease was owing to their Commerce; that alone restor'd them, and enrich'd them; and they were in Justinian's Time the most valuable Branch of the Western Empire, with respect to the Taxes they paid, and the many Regiments, or rather Legions, they raised, for recruiting the Roman Armies under Belisarius and other Generals; and this continued long afterwards even in the most declining Times of the Western Empire.

BUT this rising Wealth of Africa was too rich a Bait for the Times; the Deluge of barbarous Nations, which overthrew the Roman Empire, broke in upon them also; and the Vandals, over-running Spain, spread themselves into Africa, wasted and over-run the fruitful Plains, and destroy'd and overturned the populous Cities; and in a word, Trade sunk a second Time, under the unsupportable Burden of War, the Vandals, over-running all, ruin'd and possess'd the Country.

AS the Vandals came in over the Bellies of the native Inhabitants, so some Ages after them the Saracens, Arabians, and Mahomitans, came in over the Heads of the Vandals.

WITH these, not the old Africans only were rooted out; not only Religion, but at last Trade too, sunk quite out of the Country; for, as the Followers of Mahomet are, wherever they come, like the Romans, the Destroyers both of Commerce and Cultivation, so it was here.

TRADE and Improvement being thus, I say, as it were rooted out in Africa, the Moors spread themselves, by a rapid and irresistible Torrent, over all Spain and Portugal, carrying all before them, and keeping Possession of it almost the Space of 800 Years; and as for Africa, they have by a strong Hand kept Possession there ever since:

To bring all this to the case in hand, These Mahometans, as I have said of the Turks, have very little Inclination to Trade, they have no Gust to it, no Taste of it, or of the Advantages of it; but dwelling on the Sea-coast, and being a rapacious, cruel, violent, and tyrannical People, void of all Industry or Application, neglecting all Culture and Improvement, it made them Thieves and Robbers, as naturally as Idleness makes Beggars: They disdain'd all Industry and Labour; but being bred up to Rapine and Spoil, when they were no longer able to ravage and plunder the fruitful Plains of Valentia, Granada and Andalusia, they fell to roving upon the Sea; they built Ships, or rather, took Ships from others, andravag'd the Coasts, landing in the Night, surprising and carrying away the poor Country People out of their Beds into Slavery:.

THIS was their first Trade, and this naturally made Pyrates of them; for, not being content with landing and plundering the Sea-coast of Spain, they by Degrees being grown powerful and rich, made bold and audacious by their Success, they arm'd their Ships, and began to attack first the Spaniards upon the high Seas, and then all the Christian Nations of Europe, wherever they could find them. And thus this wicked Trade of Roving and Robbing began.

WHAT Magnitude they are since that arriv'd to, what Mischiefs they have brought upon the trading Part of the World, how powerful they are grown, and how they are erected into States and Governments, nay into Kingdoms, and as they would be called, Empires (for the Kings of Fez and Morocco call themselves Emperors) and how they are, to the Disgrace even of all the Christian Powers treated with as such, is Matter of History, and I shall meddle no more with it here, than is absolutely necessary to my present purpose.

THE first Christian Prince that resenting the Indolence of these Barbarians, and disdaining to make Peace with them, resolved their Destruction, was the Emperor Char. V. He was mov'd with a generous Compassion, for the many Thousands of poor unfortunate Christians which were at that Time kept among them in miserable Slavery:; and from a noble Principle of setting the Christian World free from the Terror of such Barbarians, he undertook singly, and without the Assistance of any other Nation, to fall upon them with all his Power.

IN this War had he been join'd by the French and English, and the Hans Towns; (as for the Dutch, they were not then a Nation) he might have clear'd the Country, at least he might have clear'd the Sea Coasts of the whole Race, and have planted Colonies of Christians in all the Ports, for the Encouragement of Commerce, and for the Safety of all the European Nations.

BUT Francis the first King of France, his mortal and constant Enemy envy'd him the Glory of the greatest and best Enterprise that was ever undertaken in Europe; a Thousand Times beyond all the Cruisadoes and Expeditions to the

Holy-Land, which cost Europe a Million of Lives, and an immense Treasure, during one Hundred and twenty Years, to no Purpose.

AS it was, and tho' the Emperor was assisted by no one Prince in Christendom, the Pope excepted, (and his Artillery would not go far in battering Stone Walls) yet he took the Fortress of Goletta, and afterwards the City, and the whole Kingdom of Tunis; and had he kept the Possession, it might have been a happy Fore-Runner of farther Conquest; but miscarrying in his Attempt against Algier, by the meer Hand of Heaven, who we may hope reserved that Conquest for the Glory of Princes and Powers yet to come, and a terrible Storm falling upon his Fleet, the farther Attempt was laid aside, and the Kingdom of Tunis returned to its former Possessors, by which Means their Pyracies are still continued.

MY Proposal upon this Subject consists of two Parts.

First, THE Necessity there seems to be upon all the Powers of Europe, especially the Marine Powers, to free themselves from the Insolence of these Rovers, that so their Subjects may be protected in their Persons and Goods from the Hands of Rapine and Violence, their Coasts secured from Insults and Descents, and their Ships from Capture on the Sea.

Secondly, THAT this cannot be done effectually, but by rooting out those Nests of Robbers on the Coast of Africa, and at least driving them from the Possession of any of the Towns, Ports and Harbours, so as they may have no more Ships to appear upon the Seas.

Thirdly, THE Easiness of the Conquest, if the English, Dutch, French and Spaniards would but please to join their Forces, and Fleets, and fall upon them in separate Bodies, and in several Places at the same Time; the needr ful Quotas both of Ships and Troops might be also adjusted here.

Fourthly, THE Benefit of Commerce, which would immediately follow, by settling the Government of the Sea Coast Towns in the Hands and Possession of the several united Powers, so that every one should possess the least in Proportion to the Forces employed in the Conquests of it.

THE three first of these merit well to be spoken to, and that largely too, but I have not Room for it here, the last is particularly before me.

IT cannot be denied, that the Coast of Africa, some few Places excepted, is a fruitful rich Country; and tho' by its Latitude it must be exceeding hot, and that (especially on the Eastmost Parts of it) there are many Deserts and Waste Places given up to salt and Sand, and fit only for the Retreat of the wild Beasts, such as Lions, Leopards, Tygers, &c. the fiercest and most ravenous of those we call Beasts of Prey; yet even in that Part there are Valleys and Plains intersperst among the wildest Deserts, and which are fruitful, yield Corn in abundance, and Cattle, with several Fruits and other Productions, fitted not for the Use of the Inhabitants only, but for Merchandize, and in Quanties also sufficient for both.

THE general Product of the Country, and in which the chief Wealth consists, and upon which a Trade with them would be settled, if the Country was in the Hands of Christians, is as follows.

Corn Skins of Beasts Salt Drugs and Gums Wool Almonds Horses Pomegranates Wax Ostrich Feathers Honey Lions and Leopards Corall Provisions of sundry Copper Kinds

IF the Quantity of all these is so considerable as we find it to be, even now, under the Indolence and Sloth of the most barbarous People in the World, how may we suppose all those valuable Things to be encreas'd in their Quantity, by the Industry and Application of the diligent Europeans, especially the French or Dutch, or English; all which Nations joining in the Conquest, we might reasonably suppose should have their several and separate Allotments of Territory upon the Coast, and in the Country adjacent.

WE might also reasonably suppose, that the Moors being in the Consequence of such a Conquest, driven up farther into the Country (for I have not been proposing the rooting them out as a Nation, but only the supplanting or removing them from a Situation, which they have justly forfeited by their Depredations upon other Nations) and being obliged to seek their Subsistence by honest Labour and Application, I say we may reasonably suppose, that even these may be taught to apply to the Cultivation of the Earth by the meer Necessity of their Circumstances, and may be brought to encrease the Product by their Labour for all those Christian Nations.

AS the Product of the Country would thus be encreas'd, and Multitudes of People would be encouraged by the Advantages of the Place, to go over and settle upon it; the Manufactures and Merchandizes of Europe would by Consequence find a new Consumption, and the many new Ports and Harbours, where those Christian Nations would settle, would be so many new Markets for the Sale of those Manufactures, where they had Little or no Sale or Consumption before: And this indeed is the Sum of all Improvement in Trade, namely, the finding out some Market for the Sale or Vent of Merchandize, where there was no Sale or Vent for those Goods before; to find out some Nation, and introduce some Fashions or Customs among them for the Use of our Goods, where there was no Use of such Goods before, to vend our Goods at new or differing Ports, may be no Encrease of Commerce, or to send them to new and differing Places, because they may still be sent from thence to the same People, and to the same Nations as the last Consumers, who consumed them before.

THUS sending our English Manufactures to Jamaica, to be sold there by the Sloop-Trade; that is, by clandestine Commerce with the Spanish Smugglers, or to the Spaniards of Cartagena, and the Coast of Caracas, is no new Consumption, tho' it be a new Market; because it is only selling to the same People, who would otherwise call for the same Manufacture, and other Goods from Old Spain, and they from England; so that it is as Water issuing out of the same Fountain, and running into the same Gulph or Pond, only by new Channels.

THUS likewise the East India Company sending English Broad Cloth to the Gulph of Persia, to be sent from thence to Ispahan, to Georgia, and other Places in that Country, to be sold to the Persians, and others, as the last Consumers; is only supplying the same People, who were supplied before, with the same Goods from Alleppo and Scandaroon; so that it is only taking the Trade from the

Turkey Company, and transferring it to the East India Company, which is no Encrease of Commerce, the last Consumers being the same.

BRING this to the Case of the Barbary Trade; it is true we have some Trade there now, and some Places might on some Accounts be called the same Markets: But suppose the Barbarians to be removed as above from the populous Cities and Provinces of Algier, Tunis, Tripoli, &c. and driven up the Country, in order to suppress Pyracy and Robbers; and suppose those Cities, &c. peopled with a new Nation, or new Nations made rich by Commerce, and the Country adjacent cultivated and peopled after the Manner of Europe, and those People living, cloathing, furnishing their Houses and Equipages, and feeding after the Manner of Christians, and Christian Nations: Let it be answered, what Kind of Commerce would there be then? And would it be twenty Times what it is now, or would it not? besides delivering Europe from the Depredations of powerful Thieves, and their Commerce and Navigation from the Rapine of a merciless Crew, who are the Ruin of Thousands of Families, and in some Sense the Reproach of Christendom: I need say no more, the Proposal is great, but far from Impracticable, 'tis worthy being undertaken by the Princes and Powers of Europe; and what would bring more Glory to the Christian Name, than all their Intestine Wars, one against another, the Scandal of Europe; and the only Thing that at first let in the Turks, and other Barbarians among them.

Chapter 3

Being a proposal for the improvement and encrease of commerce upon the western coast of Africa, the coast of Guinea, from Sierra Leon, vulgarly called seraloon, to the coast and Gulph of Benin

THAT great Improvements might be made in Trade, on the north Coast of Africa, I have shewn I think past Contradiction; the only Objection, Which as the Case stands, I think is no Objection at all, is, that it must be made by CONQUEST, a Thing attended with Difficulty, Hazard, Expence, and a Possibility of Miscarriage.

HOWEVER easy it is to remove all the Objections of that Kind, it is not my Business here, nor have I Room for it; but I mention them here to illustrate and set off the happy Circumstance of another Proposal of Improvement on the same Continent; I mean this of Guinea.

HERE are no Conquests to be made, no Enemies to fight with, at least none worth naming; and yet here is a visible, an apparent, an undisputed Improvement to be made, of which this only is to be said. That 'tis rather wonderful, that it has never yet been attempted, and gone about with Vigour and Resolution, than doubtful whether it would succeed, if it were undertaken.

THE Climate on the West Coast of Africa, at least within the Bounds mention'd, is sufficiently known, being from the Latitude of about 13 Deg. to that of 5 Deg. North of the Line: The Soil is good in most Places, very fruitful, well water'd, notwithstanding the Heat of the Climate, with abundance of small Rivers, and in some Places with very great ones. THE Commerce to this Country is carried on, if a Kind of Stagnation of Business, or a going backward thro' innumerable Discouragements may be call'd a carrying it on, by the English having Possession of the Coast, and having made Settlements in proper Places, with Forts and Castles, and other Strengths for defending those Settlements, as well against their Christian Neighbours by Sea, as their Savage Neighbours on Land.

THE Trade carried on here, whether by the English, or other European Nations, consists in but three capital Articles, viz. Slaves:, Teeth, and Gold; a very gainful and advantageous Commerce, especially as it was once carried on, when these were all purchas'd at low Rates from the Savages; and even those low Rates paid in Trifles, and Toys, such as Knives and Sissars, Kettles and Clouts, Glass Beads, and Cowries, Things of the smallest Value, and as we may say next to nothing; but even this Part of the Trade is abated in its Goodness, since by the Strife and Envy among the Traders, we have had the Folly to instruct the Savages in the Value of their own Goods, and inform them of the Cheapness of our own;

endeavouring to supplant one another, by under selling and over bidding, by which we have taught the Negroes to supplant both, by holding up the Price of their own Productions, and running down the Rates of what we carry them for Sale.

THUS that gainful Commerce once superior to all the Trades in the World, which carried out the meanest of all Exportations, and brought home the richest, is sinking daily into a Kind of Rubbish as to Trade; and we are sometimes said to buy even the Gold too dear.

BUT all this while here is not the least Use made of the Land; the fruitful Soil lies waste, a vast extended Country, pleasant Vallies, the Banks of charming Rivers, spacious Plains, capable of Improvement and Cultivation, to infinite Advantage, lie waste and untouch'd, over-run with Shrubage and useless Trees; as a Forrest trod under Foot with wild Creatures; and the yet wilder Negroes, who just plant their Maize, and a few Roots and Herbs, like as we do for our Garden-stuff, and all the rest is left naked, and thrown up to the Wilderness.

Now, why is all this waste? What mean the English and the Hollanders, and other diligent Nations, to neglect such Advantages? Why do they not enclose, fence, and set apart such Lands for Cultivation, as by their Nature and Situation appear to be proper for the most advantageous Productions?

LET the same Climates be examin'd in other Parts of the World, and the Soil in those Climates be compared with the Soil in the same Latitudes on this Coast; and if it is the same, or so near the same, as no visible Difference is found in them, why should they not produce the same Harvest, the same Plants, Fruits, Druggs; or, whatever grows and is produced in one, why should it not be planted, grow, and produce the same in another?

LET us reduce this to Practice, and bring the Latitude of Places together, with the Productions proper to those Places: For Example,

1. THE Coffee-Berry is the natural Product of the Earth at Mocha, on the Eastern Bank of the Red Sea, and the South-west Point of the Arabia Faelix, in the Latitude of 13 to 14 Deg. there it grows, thrives, and produces, as it were wild, and with the least Help of Labour imaginable; what Assistance of Art is added to it, is after the Fruit is ripen'd and gather'd, viz. in the curing and drying the Berry, and preserving them for a Market; and that is to be done in the same Manner in any Part of the World as well as there.

The diligent Dutch seeing the Easiness of the managing and curing the Berry, and how that Part had no Dependence, either upon the Earth, the Air, the Water, or any thing else more there, than in another Place, took the Hint, and planted the Coffee Tree in the Island of Java, near their City of Batavia, there it thrives, bears, and ripens every jot as well as at Mocha; and now they begin to leave off the Red Sea, and bring 20 to 30 Tons of Coffee, at a time, from Batavia, in the Latitude of 5 Deg. S.

NOT content with this happy Improvement, others of the same Nation have made the like Experiment, in near the same Latitude, in another Quarter of the World, and with the like Success; and now they begin to bring large Quantities of Coffee from Surinam, on the North Coast of South America, Lat. 6 1/2Deg.

WE are told likewise, tho' this, however probable, I do not affirm, that the less industrious Portuguese are planting it on the Coast of Brasil, about the Rio de St. Francisco in the Latitude of 12 Deg.

AND besides these, we are assur'd the French have planted it with Success at their Colony of Port Dauphin on the Island Madagascar, in Lat. 2 3 1/2 Deg. S.

THE Dutch indeed planted it without Success at the Cape de Bon Esperanza: The Reason is plain, the Place was too cold, and it might as well be planted at our Colonies of Virginia and Carolina, the Cape lying, as we all know, in Latitude 34 Deg. 20 M. or thereabouts.

BUT if at Batavia and Surinam, in Latitude 5 or 6 Deg. if at Mocha, in Latitude 14 Deg. if at Port Dauphin, in Latitude 2 3 1/2 Deg. why not at Seraloon under Cape de Verd, in Latitude 13 to 15 Deg.? Why not at Cape Coast and at Accra, in Latitude 5 to 6 Deg.? And, in a word, Why not upon all the Grain Coast, Tooth Coast, Gold and Slave Coast, where we have a free Possession, Strength for Protection, and Soil for Production? But I proceed, I shall be shorter in the next Articles, because the Argument is the same.

2. THE Sugar Cane. Our Success with the Sugar Canes is well known, it is produced to an infinite Advantage in our Island Colonies of America. From St. Christophers in Latitude 17 1/2 Deg. and Jamaica, in Latitude 18 Deg. to Barbadoes, in Latitude 13 Deg. It is produc'd by the Portuguese in the Brasils, in the same Latitude, South of the Line from the Port of Phernambuquo, in the Latitude of 9 Deg. to the Bay de Todos los Santos, or Bay of All Saints, in the Latitude of 13 Deg. 20 M, and it is produced by the Spaniards on the Continent of North America:, in the Provinces of Guaxaca, Guatimala:, &c. in the Latitude of 14 Deg. And why not then by us on the Coast of Africa, where we have the Choice of the Country in the very same Latitude from the Gold Coast in the Latitude 6, to the Cape de Verd in the Latitude 15.

ADD to this the particular Advantages which offer themselves to the Planter, in such an Attempt as this, on the Coast of Africa, which he has not, nor can have, in any of those Parts where the Sugar is now planted, especially by the English. For Example,

1. THE easiness of procuring Negroe Slaves:, which would here cost from 30 s. to 50 s. or at most 3 l. per Head; whereas they are at this Time in Barbadoes and Jamaica, worth from 25 l. to 30 l. a Head; at the Brasils from 30 l. to 40 l. and to the Spaniards in the Provinces of Guaxaca, Guatimala, &c. 50 to 60 l. Sterling per Head.

(N. B. THE Difficulty of keeping the Negroes from running away, is not so great as some imagine, since as they are brought from distant Provinces, tho' it be upon the same Continent, they know nothing or their own Country; nor do they understand the Language of the next Negroes, any more than they do English; and if they should fly to these neighbouring Negroes, they would but make Slaves: of them again, and sell them to the Ships; so that the Slaves would not be apt to fly, and if they did, the Loss would not be near so great as in Jamaica, &c.)

2. THE Easiness of getting Provisions, which they would be so far from fetching from Ireland or New England, as our Colonies of Jamaica and Barbadoes do, and

at a very monstrous rate; that they would be always able to furnish themselves as they do now by the Produce of the Soil; as for Rice, Indian Corn, or Maize, with Roots, such as Potatoes, Parsneps, Carrots, Plantans, and innumerable other Sorts, they grow freely upon all the Coast.

3. THE Shortness of the Distance, and the safe Passage between England and these Colonies, is such, that the Voyage is often perform'd in 12 to 15 Days; whereas six to ten Weeks is counted no bad Voyage between Jamaica and London: The Expence as well as other Inconveniences of which are exceeding great, and the Difference would give the Sugars of Africa a great Advantage at Market.

4. I come next to the Planting of Tea. Every one that has been the length of Amoy or Chttsan on the Coast of China, knows that the Tea is produced chiefly in the Provinces of Xantung:, Nanquin: and Canton:, as also in the Islands of Japon: or Japan, most of it between the Latitudes of 30 Deg. and 24 Deg. North of the Line. With how much greater Advantage then of the Climate, might the same Plant be produced at Seraloon and on the Gold Coast of Africa, the Plants being fetch'd from China, as well as the Method of curing it; which, according to Mynheer Nieuhoft, is not difficult.

I need say very little to the Advantages of raising such a profitable Plant so near Home; the thing explains it self; and the Difficulty of making the Experiment, seems to me to be little or nothing. Nay, I am told, that in the Governor's Garden at Cape Coast Castle, there is, or at least was, in the Time of the Government of Sir Dalby Thomas, a large Plant of Tea planted, and that it grew and thrived to Admiration: I confess I cannot see why it should not.

I shall conclude this Head with one yet more considerable than all the rest; and that is, the great Article of the Spices, such as Nutmegs, Cloves, and Cinamon; the two last are found in the Islands of Ternate and others adjacent in the Latitude of 2 to 4 Deg. the Nutmegs indeed are found only at Banda and some small Islands adjoining and almost under the Line, and so it may be doubtful, except in the same Latitude, which is farther South than any of our Settlements in Africa go: But the Trial might be made of that too. But as to the Clove, it is found in the Island of Borneo: at Gilolo, and several other Islands, from the Latitudes of 2 to 7 Deg. which is exactly the Climate of our Gold Coast; likewise the Cinamon is found in Ceylon, in the Lat. of 6 to 7 Deg. and hits punctually with this Coast; and we can see no Reason why the same Climate on the shore of Africa may not by the Help of Art produce the same Fruit.

I sum up all with observing, That there is no reason to doubt, but all or most of the Productions, either of the East or West Indies, might be produced here; such as the Cotton, Ginger, Sugar, Cocoa, Piemento, Indigo, and several others known at Jamaica; as also the Cochineal, the Vinelloes, and even the Peruvian Bark also, if Industry and Application were set on work to plant them.

I cannot quit the Improvements which might be made on the Coast of Africa, without mentioning a great Correspondence carried on among the several Nations in the northern Part of that Country, which even as it is now causes a great Commerce over Land, taking Notice withal how wonderfully it might be improv'd: This Trade is said to be carried on by the Negroe Natives, upon the great

River Nigris or Niger; or as our Seamen call it corruptly, the River Gambia, in Conjunction with the Natives of several Nations, upon the same River, East from the Shore; and by all these together corresponding with the Moors on the north Coast of Africa, at Fez, at Morocco, at Mequiness, and other Cities, where they now carry on a Commerce, by vast Annual Caravans. They tell us, that it is already a very great Trade; but how would our Proposal not only encrease this Trade it self, but quite change and alter the very people themselves, while the North Part of the Country, (being Christians,) the Savage Part would be soon civiliz'd, and become so too, and the People learn to live to be cloth'd, and to be furnish'd with many Things from Europe, which they now want; and by Consequence would with their Manners change the very Nature of their Commerce, and fall in upon the Consumption of the European Manufactures.

IT would be needless to lay out Schemes of Commerce among the Inhabitants of the Nations within those southern Lands; Numbers of European People being but once settled on the Sea Coast, would soon spread the Commerce into the inland Nations, and employ and enrich the Inhabitants, by instructing them in the Arts of living, as well as of Trade; and this brings me to a View of one of the greatest Scenes of Improvement in the World, which is in short this, (viz.)

THAT there needs little more than to instruct and inure the barbarous Nations in all our Colonies, Factories, &c. in the Arts of Living; clothing with Decency, not shameless and naked; feeding with Humanity, and not in a Manner brutal; dwelling in Towns and Cities, with Oeconomy and civil Government, and not like Savages.

IT is the most unaccountable Mistake of its Kind that can be imagin'd, that one should suppose civilizing Nations do not encrease Commerce; the Contrary is evident in all our Colonies: Civilizing the American Savages, who inhabited the Countries on the Back of the European Colonies in North America:, as well our own, as those on the French Side at Quebeck and Canada; what has been the Consequence? Take it in the following Particulars, which tho' few and small in the several Articles, are yet considerable in the whole, and abundantly confirm the Proposition.

THE Indians or Natives, before the Europeans came among them, had neither Houses, Cattle, Clothes, Tools, Weapons, Ammunition, or Houshold Stuff; their Cattle were the Beasts of the Forrest, their Clothes were the Skins of Beasts, their Weapons Bows, wooden Swords, Clubs, Javelins and Darts, pointed with Teeth and Bones of Fishes, their Ammunition Arrows and Stones, their Houses meer Wigwams, Hovels and Huts, their Houshold-stuff Earthen Pans hardned in the Sun, their Beds Matts and Skins laid on the Ground; they could strike no Fire, but by rubbing two Sticks together; they had neither edg'd Tools or other Tools, for they had neither Iron, Steel, Brass or Lead; no Grind-stone or Millstone; their Meat was Flesh dried in the Sun, and their Drink no other than cold Water.

THE same Indians even those remaining wild and savage almost as before; yet being convinc'd by their Conveniencies, and prompted by Necessity, serve themselves of us with an infinite Number of Things, for the abundant Accommodation of Life; and those that are more civilized, do it more; and these altogether encrease our Trade; for Example, take their own Goods first, with which they purchase ours. They sell the Deer Skins, Bear Skins, FOX, Beaver, and other Furrs; all which together (as is said above) our Merchants call Peltry: These I say they sell to our People, and a very good Merchandize they are, and make a good and great Return.

WITH these they buy our Woollen Manufactures for their Clothing, such as Duffels, Blankets, Halfthicks, Kersies, and such course Goods; and others also of Leather, with which they dress and keep themselves warm, in the coldest Season; also they buy Caps, Stockings, Hats, Shoes, Gloves, for the same hard Weather.

IN order to provide Fuel and Food, they buy for the latt Fire-Arms and Ammunition, such as Powder and Shot, and for the first, Hatchets and Axes, Knives, Bills, as also Spades, Shovels, Pickaxes, and other Tools fitted for their Work: For the building and furnishing Houses to dwell in; they buy all Kinds of edg'd Tools, as also Nails, Spikes, Hammers, Saws, Chisels, wrought Iron for Hooks, Hinges, Locks, Bolts, and many other Things: For their Houshold Stuff likewise they sometimes buy Chairs, Stools, Benches, Beds, Bedsteads, and the like; also Pots, Casks, and other Vessels of Earth, Pewter, Brass and Wood, and in a Word every Thing they want, which either Art or Trade can supply them with.

ALL these make Trade, and as these Demands encrease, the Trade and Commerce of Europe must encrease; for Encrease of the Civiliz'd People is an Encrease of Commerce in the Main, let the Degree of their Demands be more or less.

WHAT then have the People of England more to do, but to encrease the Colonies of their own Nation in all the remote Parts, where it is proper and practicable, and to civilize and instruct the Savages and Natives of those Countries, wherever they plant, so as to bring them by the softest and gentlest Methods to fall into the Customs and Usage of their own Country, and incorporate among our People as one Nation.

I say nothing of christianizing the Savages, 'tis remote from my present Purpose; and I doubt much more remote from our practice, at least in most Places; but I speak of an Incorporation of Customs and Usages, as may in Time bring them to live like Christians, whether they may turn Christians or no.

To bring this Home to the Coast and Country of Africa, of which I was but just now speaking; let them calculate the Improvements proposed in Business, in Planting, Fishing, Shipping, and all the necessary Employments that would attend a publick improv'd Colony; and let them tell me, if the Consequence would not be a Consumption of Manufacture, among a People where there was none before, and in a Place where we had no Commerce to carry on before.

NOR let any weak-headed Christian suggest, that this would be to anticipate our West India Trade, supplant our other Colonies, and weaken us on one Hand, while it strengthens us on another; let those who talk so, consider, 1st, the great Improvements proposed, without meddling either with Sugar, Ginger, or any of our Island Productions, and how great the Improvement might be first made in these Things. And, 2dly, Let me add, that as it is evident all our Island Colonies are not at this Time sufficient to supply our Markets with Sugar, including the Quantity demanded for Exportation, the Quantity cannot easily be too great; nor indeed is there any Danger of it; so that those phlegmatick Objections are easily to be answered, and need take up no Room here: Let us see the Improvement begun, and let us see the Danger begun, of overcharging our Markets, and hurting the Trade of our Islands, and let us hear if the Islands complain; it is then Time enough to answer those Scruples, at present I must acknowledge they merit no Consideration.

ON the other Hand, there is a vast Ocean of Improvement in View upon the African Coast, (tho' the single planting of Sugar was omitted) and as there are as well on this Side of the Country, as on the Eastern Shores, of which I come next to speak, vastly populous Nations, nay Empires, where there are Millions of People yet to trade with, who were never traded with before the prevailing on these Nations to civilize and govern themselves, according as inform'd Nature would soon direct them, would necessarily introduce Trade, consume Manufacture, employ Shipping, employ Hands, and in Time establish such a Commerce, as would be more than equal to any one foreign Exportation we have yet to boast of.

Chapter 4

Being a proposal for an encrease and improvement of the British commerce on the east coast of Africa

HERE is but one considerable Country in the World that we have any Knowledge of upon the Surface of the Globe, to which the Inhabitants of Europe have no Commerce, or with whom they have no manner of Converse: And this is the great Empire or Class of Kingdoms call'd Ethiopia or the Abyssines.

THERE are but three Ways for us to come at any Part of this Country in a Course of Trade or Correspondence, and at present they are all made impracticable.

1. OVER Land from Tripoli and the Coast of Barcan; and were the Tripolins reduced, according to the Tenour of our first Proposal, for rooting out those Enemies of fair Trade, the Rovers of Barbary, this Trade would certainly be set on foot by Caravans, as is done in Asia, from Aleppo to Bagdat, to this Day.

2. UP the Nile from Grand Cairo into the Lake of Dombea: But tho' this is said to be in Use at some certain Times when the River is not swell'd beyond its Bounds and Banks; yet those that have examin'd it more nicely, tell us, that those People are mistaken, and that the Cataracts or Water-Falls, which are frequent in the River, from within 160 Miles of Grand Cairo South, out off all Possibility of a Navigation, or of any Commerce by Water farther that Way.

3. THE third Way is by the Coast of the Red Sea; and this also is cut off, by the Turks, who have seized upon all the Western Shores of the Gulphov Red Sea, and driving the Ethiopians from the Coast, have either shut all the Nations of the World out from the Ethiopians, or have shut up the Ethiopians from conversing with the rest of the World.

THE Commerce however is apparently practicable from the Coast of that Gulph, farther South than the Turks have yet possess'd it; and there are two particular Rivers on that Coast, viz. Zeila and the Houache, which I am assur'd, as well as I can be of things which we have so little Intelligence of, are navigable far in within the Country, and beyond the Coast, which the Turks are possess'd of; and that by these Rivers, a Commerce may be established into the very Centre of Ethiopia, which is indeed the richest and the most populous Part of it, and that the Mouths of those Rivers are open for any Nation to settle and fortify at; which Settlements would be easily defended, by having but two Ships of Force, from 40 to 50 Guns, always there, by whom also going and returning, the Trade would be carry'd on round the Cape.

IT may be suggested, that such a Trade would be within the Circle of the East India Company's Charter; to which it would be effectually answer'd, Why then does not the Company open the Trade, and make a Settlement themselves? If they do not, no exclusive Privilege of Commerce is granted to any Men, or Company of Men, to damn or destroy a Trade, but to improve and carry it on; and if they insist on their Charter to have the Right of Trading to Ethiopia, but; will not trade, their Right is so far void of course; otherwise they may as well tell us, they have a Charter granted them, to shut out the Kingdom of Great Britain from the Ethiopian Trade, which would be absurd, and contrary to the Nature of the Thing.

I need say no more to this Part, as to its being practicable; I shall at any Time mark out the Way, how to put it in Practice, and to open the Commerce, and prove that the Ethiopians have, on many Occasions, shewed themselves willing to embrace such a Proposal; it remains only, to shew a little Sketch of the Trade it self, and the Improvement which it might be to the Commerce of Great Britain in particular.

1. CONTRARY to the whole Tenor of our Correspondence in the Indies, this Trade would be exceeding much to the Advantage of Great Britain, because they would both receive our Growth and Produce, and make to us Returns in Specie; whereas, in all the Trade of India, and China, our Case is the reverse; for there we cannot sell our own Goods at all, and cannot buy theirs, but with ready Money. They will take off none or but few of our Manufactures, nor will they supply us with theirs, but for hard Silver; to the exhausting, not of England only, but even of all Europe, of their ready Money.

2. THE People, tho' the Country is hot, go all modestly and decently cloathed; and 'tis known by those who have travell'd among them, that they would buy our English fine Cloths in particular, such as are carry'd to Egypt and Persia, if they could come at them; and some Essays of that Kind have been made from Grand Cairo by Land, tho' not such as are considerable enough to be called a Trade.

UPON the whole, such a Trade would be infinitely advantageous; seeing, the Return for whatever of our Manufactures could be sold there, would be in Gold, in Ivory, Sulphur, Civet, Salt-Peter, Emralds, and such like valuable Goods: There are other Productions, which we have seen from thence also, as Deer Skins in exceeding great Quantities; Hides of black Cattle; Leopards. and Lions Skins, and others of those Kinds; also fine Copper, and some very rich Gums and Drugs, of which I cannot give the Names, except Frankincense, Gum-Arab. and Aloes Socotrina. I have been told of many others, but without Certainty enough to affirm it.

IN Exchange for these, we should without Fail introduce our broad Cloths, fine Scarlet Shalloons, Sayes, Serges, and such other thin Stuffs as are usually worn in hot Climates; besides a great Quantity of hard Ware Manufactures, wrought Iron and Brass, edged Tools, Weapons, Fire-Arms, Ammunition, Lead, Pewter, Tin, fine Linen, and perhaps Silks also; for we are well assured they have no more Trade with India or any other Parts of the World than they have with England.

THUS you have three great Articles for the Improvement of the British Commerce on the Coast of Africa only, all practicable, and all capable of raising an immense Consumption of our Woollen Manufactures, where there was little or no Consumption for them before: One of which Articles, viz. that of Guinea, is actually in our own Power, and so little to be said against the Experiment, that nothing of its Kind is more wonderful, than that it has never yet been propos'd to the World, and the Attempt not made.

Chapter 5

Being a proposal for turning the whole trade for naval stores, timber, deals,. from the east country, and from norway and sweden, to our own colonies, and yet without putting the government of England to the dead charge of bounty-money on that importation

A Fourth Improvement of Commerce lyes also within our own Reach, and some dull and weak, unperforming Steps have been made, which looked as if we knew the Advantage of it; but I say, in so phlegmatick a Manner, as if, like Solomon: s Sluggard, we would not pluck our Hands out of our Bosom to put them to our Mouths. This is the transferring our Demand of Naval Stores, Timber, Deals, Masts, &c. from Norway, Sweden, and the East Country, to our own Colonies in America; Countries, without Exception, as able effectually to supply us with Hemp, Flax, Tar, Turpentine, all Kinds of Fir, Timber, Deals, Pipe and Hogshead Staves, and perhaps, in Time, with Iron also, as all the Nations mention'd above, and with proper Encouragements, would soon produce them all as cheap.

SEVERAL Attempts have, as I have noted above, been made at this, as if we own'd the Prospect of Advantage, but knew not how to bring it to bear; all that has hitherto been offer'd for the Encouragement of this Commerce, and to make it practicable, has been that of a Bounty, to be paid in England, upon the Importation, so to encourage the Merchant: But, with Submission, this is not sufficient to make a Trade of it, and is but upon one Species of the Goods neither; whereas, the Encouragement must be universal, if you expect the Trade shall be so.

BEFORE I proceed upon this important Article, which seems to have great Difficulties in it; which Difficulties yet I profess to remove, I must lay down one Foundation; which nevertheless, tho' 'tis undoubted, yet we do take upon the Credit of the Inhabitants of New England, and the other Colonies on the North of America:; if they deceive us, they only therein deceive themselves, and we are where we were.

THE fundamental is this, viz. That they are able to furnish a sufficient Quantity of Hemp, Flax, Tar, Turpentine, Fir, Timber, Deal Boards, Masts, Yards, Pipes, and Hogshead-Staves, &c. fully to supply the whole Demand of Great Britain and Ireland, so as that we should suffer no Scarcity, or want of those Goods, tho' we should absolutely prohibit their Importation from any other Place.

BY being able to furnish, I am to be understood thus; for I must not speak more for them, than they speak for themselves; and it is meet we should be very exact in those Things we call first Principles: I say, I am to be understood not that they have Hands enough at present to fell and cut out the Quantities of Timber, &c. draw and extract the Tar and Turpentine, split out the Staves, &c. for that, I believe, at first, would be a Difficulty, tho' it would soon be master'd; but that the Country, and the Woods, have a sufficient Quantity of all these; that they are not to be planted, or waited for till grown; but that they have a boundless Extent of Woods, as well on the Hills as on the Plains, unexhausted, and indeed, unexhaustible; which are sufficient for all our Demands, and much more.

LIKEWISE, I do not say, or insist, that they do now produce or plant a sufficient Quantity of Hemp and Flax to supply our Demand; but that they have Land enough, sufficient in Strength of Soil, and sufficient in Quantity, and which by cutting down the Woods, would daily encrease: This I think is undoubted.

(N. B. THE Countries where this Supply of Timber and Naval-Stores would be produced, is, in a Word, the whole English Part of the Continent of North America, viz. New-England, New-York, East and West Jersey, Pensylvania, and all the Country, whether possess'd or no, upon the great River of Delaware, as far as that River is navigable, which may be for ought we know 100 Miles beyond Philadelphia.

ALL the Colonies of Virginia and Maryland, to the bottom of the Bay of Cheseapeake, all the Colonies of North and South Carolina, and all the Rivers thereof; in which last Colony alone, they tell us, there is as much Fir-Timber growing, as in all the Kingdom of Norway.)

LIKEWISE it is to be added, that mutatis mutandis, the Coin, and Value of Payment consider'd, they will be able to furnish all these Things as cheap as the East Country and Norway Trade does now furnish them.

THESE Things granted, the Proposal is brought into a narrow Compass; all the Difference then between England (the Market) and our Colonies, the Producers of these Goods, lies in the Price of the Freight, occasion'd by the Distance of Place, and Length of the Voyage; how to bring this to a Par, is the whole of the Enquiry: And this is to be done by the several Methods following.

(N. B. Bounties and Payments of dead Money to the Importer for Encouragement, I reject, as being a meer Charge upon the Nation, tho' not upon the particular Buyer of the Goods, and is not by any Means to be called a lessening the Disparity, only it removes the Burthen from private Hands to the Publick, which is not sufficient; and should it extend to all the Importations, would be a Burden too heavy to bear, even for the whole Nation.)

THE only Weight I would lay on the Publick, and even that but for a while, is to take off the Duties entirely from all those Species of Goods, (not to repeat 'em) and prohibit the Importation from other Places; and not this last Part neither, till the Colonies were fully entered into the Trade.

THEN for the Freight; we are to suppose, that the Freight of all these Articles, from the East and North Seas, stands now at a Medium of forty to fifty Shillings per Ton, call it more or less; and suppose the Freight of the same Goods from the Colonies should then stand at a Medium of six to eight lib. per Ton; so that the Freight would be three Times as much one way as the other; 'tis true, this is a very considerable Article; and especially considering them to be all bulky Goods also.

BUT two Articles will immediately contribute towards, if not be a full Equivalent to this Excess of Freight.

First, TAKING off the Duty upon Importation here, which being very high, suppose it, for Argument Sake, to be 20 per Cent. may fairly be calculated at one half of the difference, and must be found by the Importer in the Price of his Goods at Market.

Secondly, LAYING an Impost, suppose it to be about ten per Cent, upon all the Importations of English Goods into those Colonies, and this I insist will be equal to the other half: The Money so raised to be paid to the Commanders of the Ships, in such Proportions as shall be adjusted by the Publick, and upon so much Tonage only, as is Loaden upon them of such particular Goods.

THE Colonies will never complain of such a Duty, because 'tis in a manner paid to themselves, and is but taking the Money out of one Pocket, and putting it into the other; the Growth of their Country will be exported; (indeed the waste Growth, for they burnt it all before) their own People will be employ'd, and will be prodigiously encreased, and these two are of the last Importance to them; nay, they are of such Importance to them, that give them but an Assurance of these, they may give you Assurance, that in a few Years they will be the greatest, and most prosperous Colonies in the World.

I acknowledge, I despise (with the utmost Contempt of their Ignorance) the Suggestions of those Times, when this glorious Scheme of New-England's Prosperity was laid aside, (about two and forty Years ago) from a pretended Jealousy of those Colonies growing too powerful, and making themselves independent; insinuating, because they were independent in a religious Profession, they wanted to be so in Government; whereas first, the very Thought, besides a worse Principle it began in, viz. of Party Malice, was to the last Degree weak and foolish; since 'tis evident, the Prosperity, and indeed, the very Being and Subsistence of New-England in Matters of Trade, consists in, and depends wholly upon their Union with, and Subjection to Great Britain, as the Growth of their Country, which is the only Article that supports their Commerce, is taken off by the British Colonies only: Nor can any other Nation in Europe take it off but the English; and the same of the rest: For Example,

THE Dutch have no Islands at all, but one (remote and small) called Curacao, able to do nothing worth the naming. The French indeed have Martinico, a flourishing Island Colony; but the Island is large, and produces most of its own Provisions; and if it did not, they have a Colony upon the Main, viz. Canada, which supplies the French at all their Islands with Provision, such as Meal for Bread, Flesh, Fish, Peas, and all other Provision that they can want; and the French would never starve their own Colony of Canada, to feed New-England. But to make it unanswerable, if the French would do their utmost, they are not able to consume or take off, no not one twentieth Part of the Growth of our Colonies, who maintain, as some affirm, 1000 Sail of Ships and Sloops, constantly running with those Things from the Main of North America to the Islands, such as St.

Christophers, Antegoa, Nevis, Mountserrat, Barbadoes and Jamaica; the two last of which consume a prodigious Quantity.

THESE Provisions are the meer Growth of the Country, such as Flour or Meal in Barrels, Peas, Malt, Rice and Tobacco; Beef and Pork, pickled and barrelled; Sheep and Horses alive; Beer in Casks and in Bottles; white Fish salted and dry'd, and Salmon barrel'd; besides Lumber for building and repairing, as well Houses as Ships, and Ships and Sloops ready built and finish'd.

THESE all are the Product of the Country, and the Labour of the People in the Colonies of New England, New York, the two Jersies, Pensilvania, Virginia and Carolina; without this Export, those Colonies would perish. It is true, the Islands would starve for want of the Provisions too, at least at first: But on the Continent, if the Islands did not take off their Product, their Lands which they have been at a vast Expence to cure, and clear, and plant, would lie useless and uncultivated; the Swine which the Woods feed for them by thousands, would overrun them with their Multitude, and be worse to them in Time, than the Bears and the Wolves; their Plantations would produce more of every Thing than their Mouths could devour, or than they could find Markets to vend them at; their Timber would stand indeed where it was, for no Body would fell it to have it, and they might set their Woods on Fire as they did formerly, to clear the Land of them.

IN a Word, this being their Case, their Interest ties them to England, tho' their Duty should not, and to separate from England, would be to be undone.

THEN carry the same Argument on to the proposed Commerce, for Timber, Naval Stores, &c. this would still the faster, (if that were possible) bind them to their Dependence on England, for no Nation in Europe could give them the same Encouragement: I cannot enlarge upon this Article here, it is evident to all that understand Trade: If Courtiers and Statesmen are ignorant, let them enquire where they may be inform'd.

I return to the Proposal; having thus stated the Equivalent, by which the Government may be reimburst what they shall be out of Pocket for the Experiment; it remains only to give a brief Account of the Advantages of such a Commerce; take them in a few short Heads, for I cannot enlarge them as I ought, for want of Room.

I. INSTEAD of the Trade for Deals and Timber, Tar, Masts, &c. which we carry on now with Norway, almost all for ready Money, and which carries out more Silver in Specie, nay, in our very Coin, Crowns and half Crowns, than the East Indian Company it self, however little Notice has been taken of it: I say, instead of this disadvantageous Trade, we should then receive all the same Goods in Exchange for our own Manufactures, and they would be purchased of, and produc'd by the Labour of our own People, the industrious Planters, Subjects to the Government of his Majesty of Great Britain.

2. INSTEAD of having at least two Thirds of these Goods brought over in foreign Bottoms, Danes and Swedes, and the Ships navigated by foreign Seamen, to whom we pay dead Freight in the like ready Money, and which they carry away in Specie, as above; it would be wholly brought to us in our own Ships, New England built, and navigated wholly by our own Seamen.

3. INSTEAD of a very few English Ships which now use the Norway Trade, this new Commerce would at least employ a thousand Sail of Ships every Year, and all the Year, and most of them Ships of Burthen: So that besides the Benefit of building, repairing, and fitting out so many Ships, it would be a new Nursery of Seamen to us, having always 15 to 20000 Seamen employ'd in it.

4. THE Colonies would be encreased in People beyond expressing; and consequently, not only the Consumption of Provisions would be encreased there, which is, as before, the grand Fund of their Prosperity; but the Consumption of Manufactures, and all European Exportation to them, would be in Proportion encreased, which is the grand Subject of my Work. By the Calculations which I have seen, it is supposed, not less than 100, 000 Men would be employ'd in the Wpods, cutting and felling Timber, Deals, Masts, Yards, &c. in the managing and planting of Hemp and Flax; in the extracting and drawing off the Tar; and in preparing all the Articles mentioned, to be fetch'd from thence, on Account of this Trade; and this, besides Women and Children, who could not do much in that Part; and besides, the building Ships among them, an Article so considerable, as well deserves to be handled by it self.

5. IT would effectually furnish those Colonies with Returns for England, which they are now greatly distressed for, in order to pay the Ballance of their Trade with England; the Quantity of our Manufactures which they take off, infinitely exceeds what they have of their own Growth to send us in Return, whereas in Case of such a Trade for the Produce of their Country, they would be at about a PAR with us, and we should always be able to call for as much Goods from them, as would pay our selves.

6. BY this Means they would receive Silver in great Quantities from Jamaica, and the other Islands, for all that Trade would be clear Gain to them, and that Silver also would stay with them, which now it cannot do, all being snatch'd up for Returns to England in Specie, tho' it be at 12 s. to 14 s. per Ounce: So that in consequence of this Commerce, there would be a Circulation of current Money in the Colonies on the Continent, a Thing they have of late been Strangers to.

IT would take up a Volume by it self, to lay open all the glorious Schemes of Improvement in Trade, which would be the Consequence of such a Business, and particularly the Encrease of our Manufacture here, by the Demand of Goods from thence, when the Numbers of People in those Colonies should be thus encreas'd; let any one calculate (that is able to judge of these Things) by what it is already, what it must necessarily be on an Encrease of People: Let them cast up the Exportations to the five Colonies on the Continent; let them consider those Exportations to be as they really are, one entire Improvement, derived from meer nothing, or next to nothing in the last fourscore Years, for then it was all an Embrio, and some of them were not in Being as to Trade (viz.) New York and the Jersies conquered but in 1666 from the Dutch, Pensylvania not above 50 Years in Growth, Carolina less.

LET them tell us, or but guess at for us, what a glorious Trade to England it would be to have those Colonies encreased with a Million of People, to be cloth'd, furnish'd, and supply'd with all their needful Things, Food excepted, only from us; and ty'd down for ever to us by that immortal, indissoluble Bond of Trade, their Interest.

LET them consider, that all those People must fetch from Great Britain only, their Cloths, Woollen, Linnen, Cotton, and Silk; all their Haberdashery; all their Manufactures of hard Ware, wrought Iron, Brass, Chains, Edg'd Tools, Jack-work, Nails, Bolts, Screws, &c. all their heavy Ware, such as cast Iron and Brass, Guns, Mortars, Shot, Shells, Pots, Caldrons, Bells, Battery, &c. all their Clock-Work, Watch-Work, even so much as their Toys and Trinkets; all their House Furniture, Kitchen Furniture, Glass Ware, Upholstery Ware, Tin Ware; in a Word, every thing we produce, and every thing we make, and every thing we import: 'I would be endless to repeat it.

How preposterous must those Notions be, and how oddly must they think if they can be said to think at all, who suggest Mischief from the Encrease of our Colonies! Do any other Nations act thus? Do the Spaniards think their Empires of Mexico and Peru, Chili and St. Martha, too many and too great, tho' a hundred Times as large as those I am naming; and tho' they drain even Spain itself of People? Are the French jealous of the Number of their People in the vast Countries of Canada and Louisania? Do they not study, by all Means possible, to encrease them, and to extend their Plantations?

HAVE not we People enough to spare? Do we not encrease till we are ready to eat up one another, (I mean in Trade)? and can we not spare enough of the unprofitable Part of our People, those who are rather said to starve among us than to live? Who, if they were well settled there, would be Industrious, Thrive, and grow Rich; and 'tis by the Industrious that Trade is supported, and Wealth encreased.

LET us no more amuse ourselves, and raise the Vapours with our Phlegmatick Thoughts about every little German Encroachment on our Manufactures, and the Prohibitions of a few petty Princes in the North. Here we can raise a Consumption of our Manufactures, superior to all the Obstruction they can give us: Here our Manufactures will never be prohibited; here the Demand will be for ever encreasing with the People; 'tis like a Mill built by the Lord of the Manor, it grinds for all his Tenants, and is kept going by his own Stream; so that on one hand it can never want Work, and on the other hand can never want Water.

I have not Room to say more, tho' I scarce know when to leave it off. I conclude with telling you in a few Words, that here is the greatest Opening for an Improvement of our Trade, and the easiest to put in Practise, that ever was proposed, or perhaps can be proposed to this Nation; and till we go about it, we ought never to complain of the Decay of our Trade, or of the want of a Vent for our Manufactures.

THESE several Articles of the Improvement of our Commerce, have run out to such an unavoidable Length, that I shall not be able to add some others, which were in my Design, and which are equally advantageous in Proportion to their Circumstances; but I must touch lightly upon them, and refer them to farther Occasion.

AS the Encrease of Commerce and People in our Colonies, is, in Consequence of our Property in them, an Encrease and Improvement of our Trade in England, and in particular an Encrease of the Consumption of our Manufactures; so it is a natural Inference, and evident to Demonstration, that an Encrease of Colonies must have the same Effect.

I therefore lay it down as a Fundamental, that additional Colonies, where the People may plant and settle to their Advantage, is a visible Improvement to our Trade.

EMPLOYMENT of our People, or as we call them, our Poor, is the grand Support of our very being as a Nation; without it; the Poor would eat us up, the Parish Rates would in short devour not the Produce of our Land only, but the Land itself and the Church-Wardens would call upon you for 20 s. in the Pound for your Beggars.

THIS employing of the Poor is the Effect of our Manufactures; the Magnitude of which is, for that very Reason, already described; but as our Manufactures employ the Poor, so Trade carries off the Manufactures, or else they would soon over-run the Consumption, and come to a full Stop: The Manufactures support the Poor, Foreign Commerce supports the Manufactures, and planting Colonies supports the Commerce.

HERE you dispose of your encreasing Numbers of Poor; they go there poor, and come back rich; there they plant, trade, thrive, and encrease; even your transported Felons, sent to Virginia instead of Tyburn; Thousands of them, if we are not misinform'd, have, by turning their Hands to Industry and Improvement, and, which is best of all, to Honesty, become rich substantial Planters and Merchants, settled large Families, and been famous in the Country; nay, we have seen many of them made Magistrates, Officers of Militia, Captains of the good Ships, and Masters of good Estates.

THIS Way therefore, I say, we dispose of the growing Numbers of our Poor to an inexpressible Advantage, as well a publick as a private Advantage: It is a private Advantage, as 'tis really a Benefit to the Poor that go, (for pray take me, as I ought to be taken) When I say go, I am to be understood that I mean go freely and voluntarily. I am not moving you to transport the Poor, that would be sending them away because they are poor; but, those who being destitute of Employment here, are willing to seek it Abroad, would have a visible Advantage, and would soon give Encouragement to others to follow them, and Thousands of such Families would raise themselves there by their Industry, and grow rich; for where Wages: is high, and Provisions low, as is the Case there, the Labourer must be idle, or extravagant, or thriving, and grow rich; and the Consequence of the diligent labouring Man there, is always this, that from a meer Labourer he becomes a Planter, and settles his Family upon the Land he gains, and so grows rich of Course.

THE Advantage to the Publick I have spoken of, tho' but briefly. I only add here. That besides the Encrease of Commerce and People, it necessarily makes an Encrease of Seamen, a Point just now upon the Anvil of the State, and which they find hard enough for the hammering of all the political Smiths of the Nation; all this growing Commerce, to and from our Colonies, must be carry'd on by Sea; all the Commerce they can have there, one Colony with another, must be the same: The first by large Ships of Force, the last by Sloops, Ketches, and small Ships. The Encrease of the People encreases the Trade, the Encrease of the Trade encreases the Number of Ships, and the Encrease of Ships calls for an Encrease of Seamen: Thus your Strength, as well as Wealth, grows with your Colonies, the Climax is really pleasant to look upon.

MORE Colonies then is, without Question, extending the Commerce; it is enlarging the Field of Action; it calls in more Hands to assist in the Publick Prosperity; it employs profitably the unprofitable Numbers of your Poor, and lays a Foundation of an extended Trade, and thereby of a still larger Exportation from Home.

SUPPOSE I should propose a Place in the World, where, if the English could plant at this Time any Numbers of their People, even the poorest and meanest, supposing them only to be industrious, and willing to live; for I am not talking of Drones, and Solomon: s Sluggards, that will starve rather than work; or, as I have said above, will not pull their Hand out of their Bosom to put it to their Mouth. Such will starve every where, and may as well stay at Home as go Abroad: Such will not sow, and how should they reap? will not plant, and how should they eat? BUT suppose, I say, a Spot of Ground, where a Body of English People being planted, the Country, by its own native Production of Corn and Cattle, would immediately subsist them; and the being placed in a Situation to live and trade, they would want no other Support from hence, but their first carrying over, and the Subsistence of the first Year, till a Harvest supply'd them: Suppose them what Number you please, from one Thousand to an Hundred Thousand, or suppose them encreased from the one Number to the other: Grant me but that they wear Cloths, build, furnish Houses as they encrease, and that they gain enough to provide necessary Things for themselves; Is not the Supply of these, all Gain to us? Is not all they take an Encrease of the Consumption of our Manufactures and Produce? Is not every Ship employ'd between us and them, so far an Encrease of Navigation? and so of all the rest: An Encrease of Colonies encreases People, People encrease the Consumption of Manufactures, Manufactures Trade, Trade Navigation, Navigation Seamen, and altogether encrease the Wealth, Strength, and Prosperity of England.

BUT where in the World should we plant? what Country presents for new Colonies, at least that is not possess'd or claim'd by some other Nation? and where can we find a Place, where, with the Settlement of the People, a Trade will follow? and from whence they can, besides subsisting plentifully in that Place, find Returns to Europe, to purchase from us the Manufactures they want? My Answer is, that if I do not find out such Places, I have been saying nothing all this while: That there is Room enough still left on the Surface of the Globe, not taken up nor claim'd, or pretended to by Spaniards, Portuguese, Dutch, or French, Dane or Swede, Pope or Devil; Places where 100000 People may immediately plant and build, find Food, and subsist plentifully; the Soil fruitful, the Climate comfortable, the Air healthy, unmolested by Savages and Canibals, as in North America; unravaged by Lions and Tygers, Elephants and Monsters, as in Africa; fill'd with

Cattle useful and eatable, tame and tractable, abounding with Fish, Fowl, Flesh, wanting nothing but to be inhabited by Christians, and ally'd to the rest of the Christian World by Commerce and Navigation.

BUT I am too near the End of this Work to enter upon so large a Subject: It must be treated of by itself.

FINIS.

Index

www.ingramcontent.com/pod-product-compliance
Lightning Source LLC
Chambersburg PA
CBHW052334160426
42812CB00107BA/3220/J